Christian Peacemaking

From Heritage to Hope

Daniel L. Buttry

Judson Press ® Valley Forge

Christian Peacemaking: From Heritage to Hope
© 1994
Judson Press, Valley Forge, PA 19482-0851

Bible quotations in this volume are from the NEW REVISED STANDARD VERSION of the Bible, copyrighted 1989 by the Division of Christian Education of the National Council of the Churches of Christ in the United States of America, and are used by permission.

Library of Congress Cataloging-in-Publication Data
Buttry, Daniel.
    Christian peacemaking : from heritage to hope / by Daniel L. Buttry.
       p. cm.
    Includes bibliographical references and index.
    ISBN 0-8170-1213-3
    1. Peace—Religious aspects—Christianity. 2 Reconciliation—Religious aspects—Christianity. 3 Peace—Biblical teaching. 4. Nonviolence—Religious aspects—Christianity. 5. Conflict management—Religious aspects—Christianity. I. Title.
    BT738.B86 1994   261.8'73—dc2094-11998

Printed in the U.S.A.

94 95 96 97 98 99 00 01   8 7 6 5 4 3 2 1

To

Saboi Jum

"Blessed are the peacemakers
for they will be called children of God."

(Matthew 5:9)

Table of Contents

Foreword

Dan Buttry's *Christian Peacemaking* is an important book for the church at the end of the most violent century in human history. In his work as a denominational and an individual peacemaker, Dan Buttry has shown a remarkable understanding of the things that make for peace. He knows, and has shown here, that it often takes only one person's courage and determination to bring about phenomenal change. In this book he nourishes us with stories—lots of extraordinary but true stories—of peacemakers, both those who are our contemporaries and those among the cloud of witnesses who have gone before us.

Obviously, every author and theologian has his or her own special angle of vision. Although mine is not identical with Dan's, I believe he successfully covers a vast area of space and time in a skillful, illuminating fashion.

What makes this book unique is the way Dan has woven together the scriptural foundation for peacemaking with a focus on action—the transformation of real conflicts in the real world. He recounts powerful examples of faith expressed in action, often at great risk, that prove how peacemaking can flow out of the depths of Christian faith.

Dan clearly has a high view of Scripture and challenges others to get more involved in peacemaking efforts and to follow through on the Bible's teachings about peace and justice. I commend his challenge to us to make a dramatic, active, and positive contribution to shaping human life and society on this planet as we face the future.

Ronald J. Sider
President,
Evangelicals for Social Action

Acknowledgments

How long does it take to write a book? One answer regarding this book would be three months; another would be a lifetime. My own peacemaking has grown out of Christian convictions shaped as a child and nurtured through the influence of many people. From my parents who modeled and taught the gospel to me and gave me the strength to hold my convictions, to teachers whose questions stretched my mind and who opened to me the treasures of history and philosophy, to activists who taught me by example and story, my life has been filled with a rich heritage upon which I have drawn in writing this book. I give thanks to those upon whose shoulders I humbly stand.

I also give thanks to my companions along the way who have shared the peacemaking journey with me and often challenged me to fuller expression of my faith in action. First and foremost is my wife, Sharon, who has prayed, marched, dreamed, worried, cried, and rejoiced with me throughout this journey. She has always called me to my fullest humanity rooted in God. My children, Christopher, Jonathan, and Janelle, have also been my teachers. Sometimes they have shown the childlike faith of which Jesus spoke; at other times they have revealed my own growing edges in letting Christ's peace rule in my heart. Friends at the Dorchester Temple Baptist Church in Boston and in the Baptist Peace Fellowship of North America have been my community of nurture and faith as we have sought to enflesh the gospel in a variety of settings, and especially to build justice and peace.

More specifically in the production of this book, thanks must go to National Ministries of the American Baptist Churches for providing the time and funding for writing through granting me a professional development leave. Aidsand Wright-Riggins and Thelma Mitchell have been special sources of encouragement. My colleagues in the Division of Social Ministries have covered my responsibilities there as well as provided the intellectual and spiritual stimulation to refine my ideas. Marge Jones, my secretary, has been invaluable in her work, managing the office while I was on leave and overseeing the production of the text. Thanks also go to the staff of NM's Word

Management Center for their production assistance, particularly Dorothy Carew and Victoria Goff. The staff of Judson Press, most notably Kristy Pullen and Harold Rast, have provided direction and been midwives in the delivery of this baby.

In doing the research for many of the stories in this book I have depended on others with more direct access either to the events themselves or to the materials I needed. Alice Findlay, Fred Downs, Bob and Helen Delano told me the story of the Nagaland peace initiative. Beverly Carlson of the American Baptist Historical Society and Jim Stutzman and Carolyn Schrock-Shenk of the Mennonite Central Committee's Conciliation Service helped provide historical and academic material. Roger Dewey and Rich Thompson aided my memory about events in Dorchester, Massachusetts. Saboi Jum, Amparo de Palacios and John Paul Lederach all gave insight into their experiences in peacemaking and helped to correct some of my misperceptions. The United Nations Forces in Cyprus gave me an inside look at their work and challenges.

Collecting the photographs for this book has been a new challenge and an enjoyable experience. I thank all the people and organizations who allowed me to use their photographs in this book. Special thanks must go to Sherry Nelson for her efforts digging through the *Sojourners'* archives, to Sally Savage at the Fellowship of Reconciliation, to Fred Clark at the International Ministries Library for the American Baptist Churches, and to Paula Womack at the Baptist Peace Fellowship of North America. Their work in securing these photos has greatly enhanced the presentation of the stories told here.

Before the publisher received the manuscript a number of friends read the text and provided helpful critiques, from grammar to substantive ideas. I owe them all a great debt: my wife, Sharon Buttry, my mother, Harriet Buttry, Ken Sehested and Paul Dekar of the Baptist Peace Fellowship of North America, George Lakey, nonviolence activist and trainer, and Larry Pullen, my predecessor at the Peace Program Office. Whatever is in this book has been refined and improved by their input, though any shortcomings can only be laid at my door.

Finally, I wish to acknowledge the people of many countries who walked with me through this project, those who have suffered from war and have committed themselves to struggle for a just community. I have carried them in my heart in demonstrations, at peace conferences, and while writing at my computer. I have seen the face of Jesus in them, which has given me the perseverance to maintain the course in the peacemaking journey.

Introduction

A torrent of alien stimuli bombarded my senses as I stood, nervous and impatient outside the hotel on Nathan Road. Kowloon's bustle and ever-pressing human throng cascaded around me. I took in the double-decker buses with their gaudy advertisements, the splashes of color in the signs I could not comprehend, the lights of the alleys packed with merchants in their stalls and the constant cacophony of the traffic.

I had never been to Hong Kong before or even dreamed of it until a week earlier, when I was asked to come to meet with Brang Seng, the chairman of the Kachin Independence Organization and one of the leading figures in the ethnic insurgency in Burma.[1] The Kachins were fighting against the military dictatorship in a war almost three decades old which had often become a struggle for survival against genocidal policies. Many ethnic groups, such as the Karens, Shans, Mons, Arakans, and a host of others, had taken up arms since Burma achieved independence from the British in 1948. A year earlier I had begun working with Rev. Saboi Jum, a Kachin Baptist leader, in an effort to open negotiations between the military regime and the armed opposition. Months went by with no response; then, in January 1990 the first hopeful sign came from the government. After initial contacts with the insurgents, we were now waiting to meet with some of their leaders to discuss the prospects for negotiation and a response to the military's proposals.

My nervousness had not been eased by watching Gene Hackman in *The Package* on the flight across the Pacific. With my mind full of spy films and thriller novels, I waited for our secret rendezvous with "The Chairman." Suddenly a man armed with a cellular phone emerged from the crowd to greet us. He led us to a car that wound through the streets of the Kowloon District and brought us to a Chinese restaurant. When we were ushered in, we saw Brang Seng, a man of average build with a wide and gracious smile, who was waiting for us at a large round table. He played the host role with a gregarious charm, like the elder of a clan. And so began my baptism into a convoluted mediation process beyond my wildest imagination.

The process to bring about negotiations in Burma is no success story, at least not yet. It may never be. The deeper I got into the effort to bring peace to Burma, the more complex the solutions seemed to grow. The historical animosities and the political implications of any action or statement were tangled like a Gordian knot, leading many to despair and others to violence. Saboi Jum believed with an unflagging hope and passion that there was a way to bring peace, and that he as a church leader had a responsibility to labor for that peace. He had come to my office, where I direct the Peace Program for National Ministries of the American Baptist Churches, asking for assistance in the quest for peace. It seemed like an invitation to play Pancho to this Asian Don Quixote, but the more we talked, the more I knew we needed to do whatever we could. Even if we fell short we would achieve more than if we never tried. Saboi was my introduction to the world of courageous doers who put action to their words of peace, a far more populous world than I had known, of people both famous and unheralded.

The world in which peacemakers labor is going through a period of transition. The new centers of power are not yet clearly defined in the wake of the Cold War. Wars and social turmoil are being generated as old power centers collapse and new ones emerge. Though the nuclear standoff between the United States and the Soviet Union is over and treaties for substantial disarmament have been signed, the safety of nuclear arms cannot be take for granted. Nuclear proliferation is still a danger, as seen in the development of the Iraqi and North Korean nuclear programs. Pakistan and India may have nuclear weapons, and with their disputes over Kashmir the Indian subcontinent is one of the most dangerous flashpoints in the world.

A host of ethnic conflicts are exploding around the world during this period of transition, especially in the wake of the collapse of communism in the Soviet Union and Eastern Europe. Hatreds suppressed by Communist power are now wreaking havoc in former Yugoslavia and some former Soviet republics. Tribal rivalries in Africa are heightened by the artificial boundaries drawn by colonial powers, triggering long and grinding wars in already impoverished countries. The struggle of indigenous people in the Americas continues five hundred years after the arrival of Europeans, frequently flaring into insurgencies and military repression. Racism in North America and Europe is rampant, whether directed against the descendants of slaves from Africa or the immigrants from poorer countries coming to the industrialized nations for jobs. The gap between rich and poor is growing larger, accentuating the desperation of the dispossessed and the fear of those who cling to their dominant status. The new wars, then, are not so much conflicts over ideologies—with the background threat of nuclear holocaust—as they are conflicts over ethnic and economic issues. The fighting is close and face-to-face, rather than distant and technological. Civilians, especially the poor, women and children, are the main victims.

So what should Christians do to bear witness to the God of peace in this period of transition and turmoil? In this book we will examine two major forms of peacemaking: nonviolent action and conflict resolution. If we are to make effective use of these approaches to forging peace, we will need to understand their governing assumptions and dynamics. Before we can go forward, we need to look back. We need to learn about our heritage of nonviolent action and conflict resolution so we can use them effectively in the future. Western history is often presented in ways that give little attention to how peace is built, focusing instead on names of political leaders, battles and borders, technological breakthroughs, and cultural highlights. But peacemaking is often achieved through the work of lesser-known people who, with great courage and commitment, mobilize movements at the grassroots that shift the ground upon which political leaders stand. Mediators do their work behind the scenes and are seldom noted by any except the serious students of history. We need to recover and learn from the history of peacemaking so we can take a broader wealth of understanding and communal experience into our contemporary moments of challenge and decision.

This book undertakes that task by first examining biblical teaching on nonviolence and conflict resolution. Although Christians claim to draw their values from the Bible, they often have little understanding of the breadth of biblical teaching on peacemaking. A biblical grounding can help the Christian peacemaker draw upon the deep wells of spirituality that provide energy and guidance for facing contemporary challenges.

The history of the development of nonviolent action and conflict resolution will then be surveyed, with special attention given to the work of Christian people. These are stories not often told, so the lessons and inspiration of this part of history will be lost unless we intentionally recover and learn them. Often Christian peacemakers are isolated, not realizing that sisters and brothers in other contexts are grappling with similar concerns and conflicts. Gaining a sense of the global sweep of peacemaking can encourage us in our particular work for justice and peace; we sense we are part of a larger drama that gives our work greater significance.

Equipped with a biblical perspective and drawing upon the wisdom gained from the experiences of both distant and recent history, we can then face the questions of where to exert our energies in our own day. As we stand at the edge of a new century, can we give the gift of wise and hopeful action to the world? As the news bombards us with continually shifting crises, the temptation is to let our attention flit from one place to another, always reacting to immediate stimuli and never affecting more than the superficial layers of social experience. By gaining reference points that cover a wide span of time and space, we can move into the future with the strength that comes from having broad horizons. Armed with long-range vision, a large database of human and cultural experience, refined theoretical analysis and clarity about God's values for justice and peace, Christians can be shapers of a more humane and just way of being. The final chapter thus draws upon these resources to set forth an agenda for intentional Christian peacemaking that can take us into the next century.

Prior to plunging into the biblical and historical material, we need to be clear about the basic concepts of conflict, nonviolence, and conflict resolution covered in this book. Conflict is an integral part of human life and society. It is universally experienced as human beings or groups find their goals clashing with other people or groups. Though universal, conflict takes different forms in different cultures. Some forms of conflict are constructive, as people work through their differing needs and perspectives to create solutions that meet those needs. Other conflicts degenerate into destructive cycles of attack, defense, and retaliation which may ultimately be expressed in violence.

The variety of images used for conflict can reveal an individual's or a culture's attitude toward conflict. The word comes from the Latin *confligere* which literally means "to strike together." Images of sparks and heat are expressed in this more Western view of conflict. Many Eastern cultures have the understanding of conflict expressed in its Chinese symbol, which is made of the characters for danger and opportunity, thus focusing more on the challenge of conflict than on a collision of goals and interests.[2] Conflict itself is not evil, though many evils are born in conflict situations. Sometimes the absence of visible conflict can mask gross injustice and repression. Stimulating open conflict may be necessary to overcome such evils, as one lances a boil to drain its poison. The goal for Christians and other people of good will is to achieve a just peace whether between two individuals or between nations. How we approach conflict will determine to a great degree whether the goal of a just peace will be achieved.

One way people engage in conflict is through nonviolent action. "Nonviolence" is a negative and somewhat misleading term. It can suggest a passive refusal to engage in violent activity, but that is not what is in view in this book. Here nonviolence will be the term used to designate actions taken to engage in conflict and struggle without doing violence to persons or, in most cases, property. Gene Sharp defines nonviolent action as "a technique used to control, combat and destroy the opponent's power by nonviolent means of wielding power."[3] In Latin America the phrase *firmeza permanente*—"relentless persistence"— is used to overcome the passive connotation of "nonviolence."[4] It emphasizes keeping faith and holding on through the long struggle.

Some people engage in nonviolent action based upon a philosophy of nonviolence. That philosophy may emerge out of many different religious and ethical traditions, but philosophical nonviolence has at its core a value system that upholds the inviolability of the integrity of the human person. One must be willing to suffer violence rather than commit violence against another. That willingness to suffer can be a powerful tool against unjust, oppressive, and even violent expressions of power. This book is written from the basis of commitment to a philosophy of nonviolence, but it also tells the stories of people who may not have that same philosophy, yet who acted through nonviolent means. Nonviolent action can be a wise choice of tactics even for those who give an ethical place to violence.

Conflict resolution differs from nonviolence in its goal. Nonviolence is a means for engaging in conflict, whereas conflict resolution, as the very term implies, seeks to find a satisfactory end to the dispute. This resolution is not the destruction or domination of one side by the other. Defeating the opponent may end a phase of the conflict, but the bitterness and hatred are bound to resurface as circumstances change. History is replete with peoples and nations who experienced severe oppression and defeat only to become viciously oppressive when they came to power. Conflict resolution refers to a process, usually involving negotiation, whereby the parties to a conflict reach a mutually satisfying agreement that ends the dispute. The conflict is not displaced to another time or relationship, but is addressed at a point deep enough for all parties to accept the resolution. Conflict resolution is more than just managing the conflict to keep it within boundaries that can maintain creative tension, a popular concept in the business field. Rather, it seeks to bring a solution to the particular issue and restore the relationships, though probably in an altered form.

Nonviolence and conflict resolution have been practiced for centuries, but it is only in the twentieth century that they have become global movements for peaceful change with disciplined analysis and a broad exchange of ideas and experiences. This book will examine these two related and complementary movements, exploring their development and telling stories of the struggles, tragedies, and triumphs of the past few years. From this base of experience and analysis I will look ahead to the challenges that must be faced if we are to keep pressing on with hope toward peace in the twenty-first century.

I live and write as a Christian, particularly as a Baptist. Most of my experiences and stories come from within that framework. There will be an over-representation of Baptists appearing these pages, though not because we are more diligent in our peacemaking than other people of faith—to some, in fact, "Baptist peacemakers" is an oxymoron because of the many Baptists who have been shameless militarists. Rather, most of my companions on the peacemaking journey have been Baptists, and I know their stories best. The stories told here could also be told about Lutherans, Presbyterians, Anglicans, and Catholics. Likewise, many Jews, Muslims, Buddhists, and Hindus have been courageous peacemakers out of their religious traditions. There are even people with no religious faith but with a wealth of courage and creativity who have played key roles in struggles for justice, peace, and freedom. Though this book is primarily about Christian peacemaking, non-Christians have contributed richly to the heritage of nonviolence and conflict resolutions, and I will share some of their stories here as well. For me, however, my Christian faith is the primary motivation for involvement in peacemaking, so I will lay the biblical foundation for nonviolence and conflict resolution in the hope that this will strengthen my Christian sisters and brothers in their struggle for justice and peace alongside those of other faiths.

Chapter 1

The Biblical Roots of Nonviolence

"But what did Jesus say?" Christie persisted. She was sitting across from me in the college dining hall. We were arguing about the war in Vietnam. I was making the case, and making it quite well, that the Christian position is that of allowing just wars. Furthermore, Vietnam was a just war for the United States. I had argued that point on my high school debate team, so I was well armed with statistics, historical data, and brilliant quotes. Christie didn't have a chance, except for that one question: What did Jesus say? Having grown up in a military family, many of my dreams and ideals were shaped by the images of glory won on the battlefield or in dogfights in the skies. Christie's question threatened not only my debating points but the entire construct of values on which my political opinions were based.

What did Jesus say? I had recently made a decision to become a Christian, to follow Jesus as Lord. Christie was in the small Bible study group in which I was participating, and she kept bringing me back to that commitment. "If you really are serious about following Jesus," she said, "what does he say about our involvement in war?" Shaken, I went back to my dorm room and read the Gospels with new eyes and fresh questions. That night I had a second conversion experience, turning from values that glorified participation in war to following the path of this one called the Prince of Peace. I had no idea where that path might lead, but I had a guiding light in that simple question: What did Jesus say?

The answer is not as simple as the question. The Bible is full of violence, beginning with the story of Cain's murder of his brother, Abel. The story of Israel's conquest of the Promised Land drips with blood, most notably in the divinely sanctioned genocide of the Canaanite peoples. David, the hero-king, slays Goliath in single combat and brings Israel to its pinnacle of power through military conquests. Such stories have inspired Christian soldiers marching to war, whether under the banners of the Crusades or buttressed by the justifications of just war theory. I could have supported my debating position with many biblical passages of holy warfare. Amid all the violence in the Bible, how does one build or even find an ethic of nonviolence?

The starting point for Christian ethics is Jesus Christ, both in his person and his teaching. The book of Hebrews begins, "Long ago God spoke to our ancestors in many and various ways by the prophets, but in these last days he has spoken to us by a Son" (Hebrews 1:1-2). Jesus is the climax of biblical revelation, so rather than accepting the violence in the Old Testament as an ethical given and then trying to squeeze Jesus' teaching into that framework, we must begin with an understanding of what Jesus was saying and work our way into the rest of the Bible with a Christ-centered conceptual framework. The ancient Christian confession of faith was "Jesus is Lord" (1 Corinthians 12:3), but many theological and hermeneutical approaches have undercut the lordship of Christ by subsuming Jesus' ethical teaching under a framework which minimizes or limits the scope of its impact. The attempt is made, often with great theological sophistication, to sanitize Jesus, to make him "safe" so that the status quo will not be upset by his disturbing standards of righteousness and love. However, advocates of nonviolence and peacemaking, from the earliest days of the church to the present, find their own ethical core emerging from the core of Jesus' teaching. As a result, they have tended not to be wedded to those in power but have been voices of prophetic witness to their world and agents of social transformation.

The Sermon on the Mount is the key cluster of ethical teachings recorded in Matthew's Gospel, with parallels found throughout the other Gospels. For many people, however, the teachings in the Sermon on the Mount seem an impractical ideal at best and dangerously naïve at worst. Loving one's enemies doesn't make practical sense in a world of Adolf Hitlers, Joseph Stalins, Pol Pots, and Idi Amins. Turning the other cheek sounds to those who have been oppressed like another fetter for their bondage. Praying for your persecutors doesn't remove their guns, electric prods, or missiles. So is the centerpiece of Jesus' teaching fatally flawed with a trite passivity that is worthless in the world of power plays and law-of-the-jungle violence?

Jesus was a realist. He lived in an occupied country where the reality of violence was evident in the crosses that occasionally lined the roads to show Roman superiority. Acts of liberationist terror would flare up with regularity, and general criminality was known enough that you didn't travel in certain areas, such as the Jericho road, if you could avoid them. In the midst of a society well acquainted with the ways of violence, Jesus was familiar with the options available, and he explicitly taught an alternative to those options. He knew what he was doing and what he was calling others to do. But before we look at his alternative, what were the approaches to violence chosen by those around him?

Violence and Responses to Violence

The culture of violence begins with the violence of oppressive power. Someone or some group achieves dominance over others by force or the threat of force. A relationship is established and maintained by one side being able to coerce the other into complying with its demands. In Jesus' day that oppressive power was the Roman Empire. In 63 B.C.E. the legions of Pompey, the Roman commander in the eastern Mediterranean, conquered Jerusalem and incorporated the independent Jewish Hasmonean kingdom into the Roman Empire. Roman military might established the empire and enforced the *Pax Romana*, a peace on Roman terms and under Roman law. Those who resisted could be dealt with by means of crucifixion, carried out by the Roman legal system.

Roman might is no more, but new superpowers keep rising and falling, including the United States. When the U.S. imposes its will upon nations in the Caribbean, Central America, or the Middle East by the use or threat of military force, that force is often perceived by those on the other end of it as an oppressive exercise of power. And the violence of oppressive power can exist at every level of a social structure. In a family, the physical dominance of males can lead to patriarchal oppression and abuse of wives and children. Even when the threat of violence is never carried out physically, there remains the subtle but viciously oppressive violence of the threat, the sword of Damocles hanging over one's head not by a thread but by the will of the one in control. The ultimate expression of this violence of the threat of oppressive power is the doctrine of nuclear deterrence. Nuclear violence has not been unleashed since the end of World War II, but the threat of complete annihilation and even the extinction of humanity is both credible and the source of power for much political bullying in the global community.

A range of options is available in response to the violence of oppressive power. Counterviolence is a response using violent means, including self-defense, insurgency, revolution, and terror. The Zealots chose the option of counterviolence in Jesus' time. They saw themselves as the "freedom fighters" of the Palestinian Jews, though the Romans considered them terrorists—the labels given to acts of violence usually are colored by one's political position. The Zealots were political activists who engaged in acts of sporadic violence, including an uprising in Galilee during Jesus' childhood to which Rome responded by crucifying two thousand Galileans along the local roads. The Zealots were able to ignite a national insurrection which collapsed when Titus recaptured Jerusalem and destroyed its Temple in A.D. 70. Almost a thousand Zealots later committed suicide at Masada rather than surrender to the Romans.

Counterviolence is seen in nations today in insurgencies for liberation and freedom by whatever definition, by terrorist groups seeking political ends, and by defensive military actions by countries invaded by outside powers. On the domestic level, counterviolence can be seen in the battered woman who kills her sleeping husband or the abused children who kill their abusive parent, cases in which juries have often found the killer innocent because they appreciate the cause of the oppressive violence to which the killer was responding. This counterviolence is understandable to us and often called just.

Yet the response of counterviolence begins with violence and leads to more violence. Dom Helder Camara, the Archbishop of Recife and Olinda in Brazil, describes a "spiral of violence" that begins with what he calls "violence number one," the institutionalized violence in society that is willingly wielded by those in power. The violence number one breeds anger among the oppressed that can break out into the violence of despair, "violence number two." Then this violence becomes the excuse for those in power to commit "violence number three," the violence of repression in the name of "law and order." The spiral of violence seems inescapable as each side provokes the violence of the other.[1]

For the vast majority of people, the violence of oppressive power is used against them rather than by them, and they must find a way to adjust to the reality of life as defined by those in the dominant position. Accommodation is thus another option of response to oppressive violence, one usually hated by those who choose otherwise. Some within the oppressed group will choose to align themselves with the oppressive power, to make a deal to provide their services to the regime in order to maximize their own benefit. The Sadducees and the Herodian kings played out the accommodation option in Jesus' time. They were of the conquered Jewish people, but they worked within the Roman system to gain power. The Sadducees found their accommodating power niche in religious affairs, while Herod the Great and his sons joined the elites in the political arena. At the lower levels were the tax collectors, the main functionaries of Roman power who became symbols that focused the hatred of the conquered masses.

They became willing partners in the oppressive system and were both victims and victimizers. Perhaps their accommodation came from a drive to survive, but their survival was bought at the price of crushing others.

Dictators and wealthy elites in poor countries today also take the accommodation option. Rather than challenge the international structures that impoverish their countries, they serve as functionaries to those structures, adding to their own wealth and power in the process. The Somozas in Nicaragua, the Duvaliers in Haiti, Mobutu in Zaire, and a host of others have become fabulously wealthy while adding to the oppression of their own people. Accommodation is seen in a family in the dynamics of codependency, where other family members join in a protective conspiracy to avoid challenging the abusive power of the dominant family member. A mother may know her daughter is a victim of incest with her father, but the mother chooses to sacrifice her daughter to maintain her own marriage and hopes of security, thus becoming a party to the incest. Accommodation may feel like the best option for oneself since the oppressive system seems so impossible to change. It is a decision of social triage where I choose for myself at another's expense. Then the corruption of the choice tends to make the one who accommodates even more hated by the oppressed than the ultimate dominant power. Those who sell out their own people are deeply despised, and the names of tax collectors, Uncle Toms, and Quislings[2] are spat out when spoken.

Withdrawal is yet another choice many make in response to oppressive violence. As they look at the system that locks them into an inferior role, they choose to narrow their focus and shrink their world to a manageable scope. They may withdraw from society completely, either physically or psychologically. The Essenes were contemporaries of Jesus who chose to withdraw to the desert and live in isolated communities. They stayed clear of the struggle between Roman power and nationalist fervor. In the early church age, Greek mystery religions offered psychic escape from the physical world where politics and injustice were part of the evil their adherents fled.

Withdrawal or escape continues to be an attractive option today. In the face of possible nuclear holocaust many Americans followed the example of the ostrich. One mother I knew, when asked to support the nuclear freeze campaign, refused by saying it was too awful to think about. Drugs and alcohol became an epidemic problem among American youth as they struggled with their expectation of not living long because of inevitable nuclear war. If one is going to be incinerated in the holocaust, what is so bad about drugs? The multibillion dollar

entertainment industry shows the heavy value we place on withdrawal. Rather than talk politics, we talk sports, movies, and music.
These need not be bad expressions of human culture, but they can
become ways of avoiding life rather than reflecting creatively upon
it.

There is also a religious option among the responses to oppressive
violence, one closely related to withdrawal, that bears special attention. As we have seen, the Essenes and mystery cults responded by
withdrawing: the former withdrawing physically from the dominate
society, the latter withdrawing through philosophical disconnection.
The Pharisees, however, were contemporaries of Jesus who didn't
withdraw from the society. They were a lay movement in the synagogues that focused on careful and exact piety. The problem Jesus had
with them was that their elaborate religiosity didn't engage with the
suffering and struggles of those around them. They tithed in minute
detail but did not work for justice (Matthew 23:23), and they established theological contrivances to avoid caring for the elderly (Mark
7:9-13). The Pharisees practiced unengaged piety, a superspirituality
that had nothing to do with the pains of a world crushed under Rome's
oppressive power or the host of other human injustices and sorrows.
A few decades later the Pharisees were radicalized politically and
joined the Zealots in the insurrection at Jerusalem, but during Jesus'
ministry their disengagement exhibited another type of response to
oppression: withdrawal cloaked in an aura of self-righteous religiosity.

Pharisaism has had its Christian versions; movements of intense
personal spirituality with a disdain of social concerns have been a
repeated theme in church history. Much of American fundamentalism
and evangelicalism has had these tendencies, though the recent
politicizing of the Christian Right has shown a new fervor for political
engagement among these traditions. At the personal level, such
unengaged piety is seen in avid churchgoers whose spirituality masks
domestic violence, perhaps even buttressing such abuse with biblical
justification about wives submitting to husbands or statements like
"spare the rod, spoil the child." Rather than faith providing the
insight and inner strength to confront and overcome the violence in
one's life, that faith becomes a stumbling block to finding the way to
peace.

Jesus lived in a world of violence with all these options for response.
He knew the violence of oppressive power. He knew the choices many
made for counterviolence, accommodation, withdrawal, and unengaged piety. His band of disciples contained both former Zealots and

tax collectors. Perhaps he, and most certainly his cousin John the Baptist, had extensive contact with the Essenes. His temptations included accommodating to the devil's oppressive power (Matthew 4:8-9), and a revolt could have been ignited a number of times (John 6:15; Luke 19:37ff.; Luke 22:49ff.). But Jesus resisted all the calls to such options. He taught and lived out his own alternative, clear about the context in which he was calling his followers to make the same choice.

Glen Stassen, in his book *Just Peacemaking*,[3] calls Jesus' actions in response to violence "transforming initiatives," and this is the best label I have come across for Jesus' alternative. Jesus called for initiatives. In the context of violence all the initiative rests with the oppressive power, and others must simply choose how to respond to the violence. Jesus, however, calls upon his followers—who are perceived as powerless by the world's standards—to take the initiative themselves. They are not to respond to the oppressive situation by following a script acceptable and understandable to the dominant power. They are to act, to initiate a new set of events to which the dominant one must respond. The initiatives are transforming because the relationships and the context are jolted out of the expected patterns where victim and victimizer know their roles and act them out without much thought of what they are doing or why they are doing it. The transformed relationship and context open up new possibilities in which repentance, reconciliation, justice, and peace can take place.

With this understanding of the context in which Jesus taught and the alternative response to violence he offered, we can now turn to the Sermon on the Mount to see what exactly he did say and how it applied in practical terms.

Transforming Initiatives and the Sermon on the Mount

The key passage for Jesus' teaching on nonviolence is Matthew 5:38-41:

> You have heard that it was said, "An eye for an eye and a tooth for a tooth." But I say to you, Do not resist an evildoer. But if anyone strikes you on the right cheek, turn the other also; and if anyone wants to sue you and take your coat, give your cloak as well; and if anyone forces you to go one mile, go also the second mile.

Many people, pacifists and nonpacifists alike, have interpreted this passage as calling for nonretaliation and passivity in the face of violence or repression. Some see these teachings as posing an impossible ideal in order to bring the hearers to a dependence upon God's grace. At least one commentator holds that they are intentionally absurd and not be taken literally: they are just making the point that we are not to avenge ourselves for personal wrongs.[4] But others would argue that in the context of Jesus' culture these teachings made sense and presented creative alternatives to passive submission or violent resistance. Jesus *did* mean to be taken literally and seriously, not in a wooden legalistic way, but with the kind of creative thinking that can come up with transforming initiatives in any repressive situation.

In contrast to the *lex talionis* of "an eye for an eye and a tooth for a tooth" (Exodus 21:24; Leviticus 24:20; Deuteronomy 19:21), Jesus says, "Do not resist an evildoer." The Greek verb is *anthistemi*, which is usually taken to mean "to set oneself against, oppose, resist, or withstand." Walter Wink notes that the noun form of the root word of *anthistemi* is *stasis*, which means "violent rebellion, armed revolt, sharp dissension."[5] The more accurate translation would not signify a passivity in the face of evil, which went against so much of Jesus' teaching and life, but rather a refusal to respond in kind to evil actions. The *Good News Bible* translates the verse, "Do not take revenge on someone who wrongs you." The understanding is parallel to what Paul says in Romans 12:19-21: "Never avenge yourselves.... Do not be overcome by evil, but overcome evil with good." Wink suggests that the translators of the King James Version intentionally chose the passive terminology so that the teachings of Jesus would not be construed as encouraging action against the king and his authority. That passive construction of the text has dominated our thinking ever since.

Clarence Jordan, the Georgia Baptist farmer with a Ph.D. in New Testament Greek who founded the radical Christian community, Koinonia Farm, came to the same conclusion from a different grammatical point. The word for "evil" in the Greek is *ponero*, which is translated in the NRSV "an evildoer." The Greek form is identical for three cases—the locative, the dative, and the instrumental—and only the context can tell us which case in intended. The NRSV has chosen the dative case, but Jordan argues that Jesus surely resisted evil people and preached against what they did. The locative would mean, "Do not resist when you find yourself in the presence of evil." Yet such passivity clearly is absent in Jesus' life and teaching. The instrumental case, however, does reflect the full scope of Jesus' ministry and ethical challenge: "Do not resist *with* evil."[6] Here evil is not to be the instrument of one's resistance, which is precisely what Paul said in his parallel ethical teaching in Romans 12.

This interpretation of Matthew 5:39 is also consistent with its context in the Sermon on the Mount. Jesus is calling his followers not to respond in kind to the acts of injustice and dehumanization directed against them, but rather to respond with transforming initiatives. Wink describes this approach as Jesus' Third Way, one that stands in contrast to the "flight or fight" responses so deeply conditioned in human beings. Jesus then gives three specific examples that relate directly to the concrete experiences of his hearers. He addressed not those in power but those who were perceived, and who perhaps perceived themselves, as powerless.

"If anyone strikes you on the right cheek," Jesus begins. To strike on the right cheek requires that one use a backhand smack, assuming that the blow comes from the right hand. In ancient Jewish culture this was not so much an act of violence as an insult. It was an act done by a superior to an inferior—a Roman to a Jew, a master to a slave, a man to a woman—to "put them in their place." If the slap was done by a person of equal status, the offended person could sue in court and win severe damages (Mishnah, Baba Qamma 8:6). Wink compares the various fines listed in the Mishnah for blows: A four *zuz* fine for a blow to a peer with a fist, four hundred *zuz* for a backhand, but to an underling no penalty whatsoever.[7] Robert Guelich contends that Matthew is telling Christians to forego their right to legal action,[8] but the two following examples are of people with no legal leverage in the system, and for the person with inferior social status there was no legal recourse. Jesus' challenge to turn the other cheek is not advice to forego one's legal rights. Rather, he is calling on the powerless person to take an initiative that asserts one's own humanity and transforms the nature of the relationship.

When the humiliating backhand blow is struck on the right cheek and the struck person turns the other cheek, a number of messages are sent. First, the response says that the person is not cowed by the insult and has not assumed the inferior place the striker had in mind. The person refuses to be humiliated and claims his or her full humanity. Second, in turning the other cheek the person forces the striker to view him or herself as an equal. There is no possibility of another backhand blow; the striker would have to resort to some other form of violence, such as punching with a fist. But to commit such an assault would be to lose the assumed superior/inferior relationship. Thus the striker is forced to recognize the humanity of the one he or she has been oppressing. With the simple action of turning the cheek, the supposedly powerless person has redefined the relationship and forced the oppressor into a moral choice: Will the oppressor now escalate the violence and deepen the evil, or will the revelation of the humanity of the other call forth a response of repentance and even reconciliation?

Jesus' own experience of being beaten, while in a very different setting, shows the power of self-identity in the face of those who wish to humiliate. Though beaten, tortured, taunted, and then crucified, Jesus was so clearly aware of his own human dignity that those in power expressed frustration at his refusal to cower at their authority over him (Mark 15:4-5; John 19:10-11). Caiaphas and Herod raged and ridiculed ineffectively, Pilate shirked his responsibility, and the centurion confessed Jesus' innocence (Luke 23:47). Jesus, though seemingly in a position of powerlessness, took the initiative and forced all others to make moral choices in response to who he was.

The second example of Jesus' alternative response to oppression in the Sermon on the Mount involves a court scene: "If anyone wants to sue you and take your coat, give your cloak as well." The legal background to the passage is found in Exodus 22:26 and Deuteronomy 24:12, where a poor person is allowed to give his or her cloak as collateral for a loan, but it must be returned at night so that the person's suffering will not be aggravated by the evening chill. Amos condemned the system of exploitation of the poor whereby garments taken in pledge were piling up and being retained (Amos 2:7-8). In Jesus' day the Romans were taxing people to maintain their empire. The wealthy were investing in large estates worked by poor tenant farmers. The peasant landowners had been forced to give up their ancestral lands because of debt and were then kept tied to the land by the unjust debt system. Many of Jesus' parables and teachings reflect these practices (cf. Matthew 18:23-35; 21:33-41; Luke 7:41-42). The deep animosity toward this system was such that when the Zealot insurrection erupted in A.D. 66, their first act was to burn the Temple treasury where the debt records were kept.

In Jesus' example, the person who is being dragged into court is a poor debtor. He must face the power of a wealthy landowner who is supported by a legal system that will force the poor person to give up his garment as surety for his outstanding debt. This person seemingly has no power, but Jesus tells the debtor to give up not just his coat, but his cloak as well—perhaps even all his clothes. The debtor is to strip naked in court![9] This surprising action exposes not the nakedness of the debtor but the moral bankruptcy of the system that was oppressing the poor. The shame of nakedness in Jewish society rested not primarily in the naked person, but in the one who caused the nakedness and in those who witnessed it (thus the strange curse on

Ham in Genesis 9:20-27 for witnessing Noah's nakedness while he was in a drunken stupor). By stripping naked, the "powerless" debtor is holding up a moral mirror to the wealthy landowner and the court itself, indicting them over the systemic oppression that caused people to be deprived of their fundamental needs. Wink refers to the action as "clowning," a burlesque that unmasks the essential cruelty of the system and its pretensions to justice, law, and order.[10] The case is made not by assaulting anyone's humanity, but by symbolically stripping away the veil of legality and "business as usual," and thus presenting both the landowner and the judge with a moral choice. Will they break out of the system which they have now seen in its moral shamefulness, or will they harden their hearts and become morally culpable for profound intentional sin?

The third example from the Sermon on the Mount comes from the Roman law that civilians could be impressed to carry a soldier's baggage for one mile (literally *milion*, one thousand paces). The roads were marked at every mile, so it was an easy distance to judge. The law was intended to keep the armies mobile but not to create too much resentment among the populace. Resentment among the Jews was very deep, however, over this act of the occupier's domination.

Jesus turns the situation around from one where the Roman exercises his oppressive power to one of helping out someone in need: "If anyone forces you to go one mile, go also the second mile." As long as the soldier can force another to do his will, then he gets the expansive feeling of having power. But when the civilian offers to carry the pack another mile, the tables are turned. What was demanded is now freely offered, and the soldier is put into a delicate situation for which he has not been prepared. It is against the law to force someone to carry his pack two miles. Wink presents the kind of off-balance questions that would go through the soldier's mind: "What are you up to?...Is this a provocation? Are you insulting my strength? Being kind? Trying to get me disciplined for seeming to make you go farther than you should? Are you planning to file a complaint? Create trouble?"[11] The ego-gratification of oppressing another is taken away, and the soldier is put in a quandary.

In all three of these situations the "powerless" person has the power to act outside the accepted scripts of the oppressive relationships. By taking a transforming initiative, the person claims his or her own humanity, while at the same time not denying the humanity of the other. A moral mirror can be held up which exposes the evil of the system, or at least refuses to accept the definitions under which the oppressor operates. This response results in the oppressor being forced to make a moral choice, for the option is given for acting on the basis of the newly revealed truth, to move toward justice and reconciliation. Of course, the choice can be made to fight to maintain the dominant position and the system that supports it, but even so the lies defining superiority and inferiority are exposed along with the self-justification that oppressive systems require.

Jesus presented these three examples as concrete illustrations in his own cultural setting of taking transforming initiatives. They are not new laws to be woodenly applied in other cultural settings. Turning the other cheek is not a directive for a battered woman meekly to submit to further beatings; the context that gives the action of turning the other cheek its power doesn't exist there. Instead, the woman will need to think how she can assert her own humanity, perhaps with the help of a support system of other battered women. If I were to strip naked in court, I would probably be held thirty days for observation in a mental hospital. Imagine, however, a farm family at an auction of all their property, stripping naked before their community and adding their clothing to the sale. The power of that act would make it very difficult for a banker or sheriff to go through with the auction, knowing he or she had to continue to live and do business in that community. In Burma, where army soldiers forcibly compel civilians to carry their packs in the jungles with no rations until they drop, going the second mile is nonsensical. The context gives the power and meaning for the action. The challenge in application is not to reproduce the specific action in a different context, but within one's own context to take the transforming initiative that claims both one's own humanity and the other's, that exposes the evil of the situation, and that opens the door of possibility for constructive change, repentance, justice, and reconciliation.

Transforming Initiatives Throughout the Bible

Transforming initiatives are taught and illustrated in other parts of the Bible as well as in the Sermon on the Mount. In chapter 12 of Paul's letter to the Romans we find a strong echo of Jesus' ethical teachings. Verses 9-21 are a string of short, concise exhortations as to how to live a life that is "holy and acceptable to God" (Romans 12:1), many of which have to do with a life of peace. Verse 14, "Bless those who persecute you; bless and do not curse them," brings to mind Jesus' words, "Love your enemies and pray for those who persecute you" (Matthew 5:44). Jesus' saying, "Do not resist with evil" (Matthew 5:39), is picked up in verse 17: "Do not repay anyone evil for evil." "If it is possible, so far as it depends on you," Paul urges the Christians in Rome, "live peaceably with all" (Romans 12:18).

The climax of Romans 12 comes in a brief discussion of how to overcome evil:

> Beloved, never avenge yourselves, but leave room for the wrath of God; for it is written, "Vengeance is mine, I will repay, says the Lord." No, "if your enemies are hungry, feed them; if they are thirsty, give them something to drink; for by doing this you will heap burning coals on their heads." Do not be overcome by evil, but overcome evil with good (Romans 12:19-21).

Evil is to be resisted, even to be overcome, so passivity is not in view at all. But taking vengeance into human hands is expressly forbidden. Vengeance is the prerogative of the sovereign God alone. Instead, Paul sees Christians called to adopt a different approach than the "eye for an eye" vengeance cycle. He calls, as did Jesus, for transforming initiatives, illustrating his point by quoting from Proverbs 25:21-22. Feeding the hungry enemy and giving drink to the thirsty enemy certainly goes against the normal script of hostile relationships! When the enemy is expecting an attack, an offensive of love is launched, thus responding to the genuine needs of the enemy. The result is that "burning coals" will be heaped on their heads. For many years I assumed this was a "wimp's vision of vengeance": those unable to strike back could look ahead with gleeful anticipation to God's fiery wrath pouring down on their enemies. Such delayed, vengeful gratification was expressed frequently in the Psalms (for example, 54:4-5; 137:7-9). But the burning coals are not the fires of hell; rather, they indicate the burning of shame and remorse. The acts of love in the midst of the conflict break the cycle of retaliation and shatter the image and expectations about the one perceived as the enemy. Burning coals may also refer to the custom of many Middle Eastern cultures, including that of the Hebrews, of showing remorse by putting ashes on one's head. The enemy therefore repents, which is genuinely overcoming evil as it is transformed through loving action.

This very strategy was employed in a striking story from the life of the prophet Elisha in 2 Kings 6:8-23. The Arameans, also known as Syrians, were engaging in a series of raids against their southern neighbor, Israel. Elisha kept sending word to the Israelite king of the Aramean plans, thus foiling their raiding parties. When the Aramean king learned of Elisha's role, he sent an army to Dothan, where the Hebrew prophet lived. When Elisha's servant saw the army surrounding the city, he panicked. Elisha calmly prayed for God to open the servant's eyes. The man then saw that "the mountain was full of

horses and chariots of fire all around Elisha" (2 Kings 6:17). When
the Arameans began to attack, Elisha prayed for God to strike the
army with blindness, and they were suddenly blinded. The prophet
went out to meet the suddenly helpless army and led them to
Samaria, the capital city of Israel. What a sight that must have
been—long files of soldiers, each with his hand on the shoulder of the
man in front, following the prophet along the dusty roads of Israel!
When they were inside the fortified city of their enemy, the eyes of
the Arameans were opened. Now it was time for the massacre, and
the Israelite king was ready to strike. Elisha, however, had a different
plan. He said, "No! Did you capture with your sword and your bow
those whom you want to kill? Set food and water before them so that
they may eat and drink; and let them go to their master" (2 Kings
6:22). So a great feast was prepared for the enemy army, and after
they had eaten and drunk their fill they returned to Aram. The
concluding verse says, "And the Arameans no longer came raiding
into the land of Israel" (2 Kings 6:23). Feeding the enemy, with the
help of divine intervention, proved to be a more effective and less
bloody defense policy than a retaliation-provoking slaughter would
have been. As a postscript, the next story begins with King Benhadad
of Aram mustering his army for an attack on Samaria, so obviously
the political situation later deteriorated. The sequence of these stories, however, must not be allowed to overshadow the successful
conclusion of Elisha's transforming initiative, which must have affected the two countries for a significant amount of time.

The most profound example of a transforming initiative lies at the
very heart of the Christian gospel. In response to human sin, God took
flesh in Jesus of Nazareth. Instead of divine judgment, as portrayed
in the story of Noah and the flood, Jesus reflects the promise of mercy
seen in the rainbow. Jesus did no evil, yet was crucified under the
judgment of the religious and political authorities. Many of the Old
Testament Scriptures reflected the desire for vengeance; Jesus' mock-
ers at the cross threw the dream of divine retribution in his face. Even
as he was arrested Jesus said, "Do you think that I cannot appeal to
my Father, and he will at once send me more than twelve legions of
angels?" (Matthew 26:53). Vengeance was an option that was expressed in the helpless bitter cursing of one of the thieves crucified
alongside him and that could have been expressed in miraculous
intervention. But Jesus was following a different script to which he
had submitted in the Garden of Gethsemane when he prayed, "Yet
not what I want but what you want" (Matthew 26:39).

In the crucifixion and the resurrection of Jesus, God engaged in a transforming initiative whereby human violence and evil was turned into God's life-redeeming action and loving invitation. Whereas Jesus' death on the cross was an expression of the human tendency to victimize others, looking for the easy way out in the face of moral challenges and protecting one's power base at the cost of ethical integrity, as well as our propensity toward violence as a solution to our conflicts, God turned the cross into an expression of self-giving love, a sign of bearing the wrongs of others and a witness to the power of nonviolence and self-sacrifice in the face of human evil. The Resurrection resoundingly announced the breaking of the grip of death upon humanity, a hold broken not by forceful assault but by willing and determined submission and endurance.

In announcing God's transforming initiative in his sermon on Pentecost, the apostle Peter contrasted the two scripts—humanity's brutal tragedy and God's divine, liberating comedy whereby God laughed at the plans of the nations:

> This man, handed over to you according to the definite plan and foreknowledge of God, you crucified and killed by the hands of those outside the law. But God raised him up, having freed him from death, because it was impossible for him to be held in its power (Acts 2:23-24).

As God's loving initiative prompted remorse and repentance in those who had placed themselves as enemies to God, the gifts of God's grace could then be received. Peter concluded his sermon with the invitation to join in the bounty of mercy: "Repent, and be baptized every one of you in the name of Jesus Christ so that your sins may be forgiven; and you will receive the gift of the Holy Spirit" (Acts 2:38). In Jesus Christ we have the ultimate example of evil being overcome by good.

Other Forms of Nonviolence in the Bible

Besides the kinds of transforming initiatives about which Jesus, Paul, and Peter taught, there are examples in the Bible of other forms of nonviolent action used to address people in power in conflict situations. Sometimes the nonviolent action was used to create an open conflict in a context where injustice was being masked by repressive power.

The Hebrew prophets often employed nonviolent actions in presenting their messages to kings, the religious hierarchy, and the public. The spoken word was the most common form of nonviolent action. Amos, the farmer driven by divine inspiration, stormed into the sanctuary of the two golden calves in Bethel, the religious center for the Northern Kingdom of Israel. He roundly denounced the nation for its injustices and idolatries, much to the consternation of the priest, Amaziah, who tried to throw him out (Amos 7:7-17). When King Ahab arranged the execution of the farmer Naboth in order to seize his vineyard, Elijah went directly to the king to denounce the injustice and pronounce God's judgment upon his dynasty because of his evil actions (1 Kings 21:1-24). Shortly afterward, the prophet Micaiah taunted the prophetic "yes men" who blessed Ahab's war plans, called them all liars and predicted disaster while standing in the king's throne room. His boldness and minority opinion, though it proved to be correct, earned him a trip to the dungeon (1 Kings 22:13-28). For these and many other prophets, speaking boldly against those in power or against their policies has been one of the major components of their nonviolent action.

Often prophets added symbolic actions to their words of protest or judgment. Hosea gave names to his children illustrating God's rejection and later gracious forgiveness of Israel (Hosea 1:2-8; 2:21-23). Isaiah walked throughout Jerusalem naked for three years to protest Judah's policy of pursuing military alliance with Egypt and Ethiopia (Isaiah 20:1-6). Ezekiel was famous for dramatizing his messages. He once made a model city to act out the consequences he foresaw for Judah's policies (Ezekiel 4). Another time he used a pre-punk bizarre haircut to foretell disaster, using a sword to cut his hair and beard into three sections (Ezekiel 5:1-4). When his wife died, Ezekiel turned the occasion into a public protest calling people to mourn their unfaithful actions rather than their personal losses, which were about to increase dramatically (Ezekiel 24:15-27). Jeremiah engaged in a struggle over symbols with Hananiah. Jeremiah wore a yoke for oxen to symbolize the yoke coming upon Judah through the rising Babylonian empire. Jeremiah particularly criticized the prophets, priests, and counselors who urged King Zedekiah to follow a strategy of militant resistance. Hananiah attacked the symbol, breaking the yoke bars from around Jeremiah's neck, reaffirming the policies of Zedekiah and predicting the rapid demise of Babylon. Jeremiah responded that the wooden yoke would be replaced by a yoke of iron (Jeremiah 27–28).

In the book of Esther two pivotal nonviolent actions were taken. The Jewish exile Mordecai refused to bow in obeisance to Haman, the arrogant, self-serving counselor to King Ahasuerus of Persia (Esther 3:1-6). This civil disobedience enraged Haman, who then began a plot which eventually led to his own downfall. When Haman began to plan to exterminate Jews in retaliation for Mordecai's civil disobedience,

Mordecai convinced Esther to engage in civil disobedience herself. As a queen in the harem of Ahasuerus, Esther had access to the king, but she would have to break the law by going unannounced into his presence. The punishment was death, unless the king chose to show mercy. Esther took the risk, and through her courage was able to change the king's policy (Esther 4:11; 5:1-2).[12]

In another exile community civil disobedience was used to protest an issue of religious liberty. Shadrach, Meshach, and Abednego refused to bow before the idolatrous image of King Nebuchadnezzar of Babylon. The penalty for refusing to honor the king as a god was to be put into a fiery furnace. When they were dragged before the king with a last chance for mercy, the three Jewish young men continued their calm defiance, asserting:

> O Nebuchadnezzar, we have no need to present a defense to you in this matter. If our God whom we serve is able to deliver us from the furnace of blazing fire and out of your hand, O king, let him deliver us. But if not, be it known to you, O king, that we will not serve your gods and we will not worship the golden statue that you have set up (Daniel 3:16-18).

A similar stand was taken by the apostles Peter and John following their arrest for preaching about Jesus on the Temple grounds. They were brought before the Sanhedrin, the ruling council, and given a gag order. They refused to be bound by it, committing civil disobedience in obedience to a higher authority: "Whether it is right in God's sight to listen to you rather than to God, you must judge; for we cannot keep from speaking about what we have seen and heard" (Acts 4:19-20). When they were released from prison, they went back to their illegal activities of proclaiming the gospel. Again they were arrested and told to cease and desist. They responded quite bluntly, "We must obey God rather than any human authority" (Acts 5:29). Then the famous rabbi Gamaliel, who sat on the Sanhedrin, urged that they be released. If they were just a passing movement it would be better to let them wither away on their own, he counseled, but if these followers of Jesus were a movement born of God, no repression would stop them (Acts 5:35-39). Gamaliel's wisdom has seldom been followed in history, as repression is all too frequently viewed as the best means to retain power.

The most controversial nonviolent actions were taken by Jesus himself in the last week of his life. The first was the triumphal entry (Mark 11:1-10; Matthew 21:1-9; Luke 19:28-38; John 12:12-19). Jesus entered Jerusalem at a time when messianic fervor was high. Earlier there had been an attempt to ignite a popular revolt with Jesus as the leader, but Jesus had turned his back on the eager crowd (John 6:15). As pilgrims were streaming into the Holy City for the celebration of the Passover, Jesus planned and carried out a provocative symbolic action that hooked into the messianic expectations. He rode into Jerusalem on the first day of Passover week on a young donkey, deliberately fulfilling the messianic prophecy of Zechariah: "Rejoice greatly, O daughter Zion! Shout aloud, O daughter Jerusalem! Lo, your king comes to you; triumphant and victorious is he, humble and riding on a donkey, on a colt, the foal of a donkey" (Zechariah 9:9). Jesus' action triggered a spontaneous demonstration that carried into the Temple itself, with people laying palm fronds and cloaks in front of him and shouting praises, to the consternation of the authorities.

The second action took place the next day when Jesus "cleansed" and occupied the Temple (Mark 11:15-19; Matthew 21:10-17; Luke 19:45-48; John 2:13-22). The Court of the Gentiles was the outer courtyard, the only area in which Gentiles were allowed to enter. Two Temple businesses operated in the Court of the Gentiles: one sold animals for sacrifice, the other exchanged currency. Only a special Temple currency could be used to purchase the sacrificial animals, so all the other currencies brought by pilgrims from various lands had to be exchanged into the Temple coinage, usually at a tidy profit for the concession. Jesus entered the Court of the Gentiles and without warning began turning over the moneychangers' tables, scattering coins everywhere. He loosed the animals and drove them out. John 2:15 says Jesus made a whip to help clear the Temple.[13] His presence was so commanding that nobody could stop him. The Temple merchants scrambled out the Temple gates for safety. Jesus roared, "It is written 'My house shall be called a house of prayer'; but you are making it a den of robbers" (Matthew 21:13).

The one place where Gentiles were allowed to worship had been turned into a marketplace, so Jesus reclaimed it for its holy purpose. He occupied the area with his followers and all those who came to be healed. He blocked off all access through the area for trade, and instead made it his special place for teaching (Mark 11:16). The occupation continued in the following days while the chief priests and other allies debated and strategized about how to get rid of this one who had so blatantly challenged their authority and thrown their commercial enterprises into disarray.

Some may question whether this action was nonviolent. Force was definitely used—force of character and force in overturning the tables and driving out the animals. No violence was directed at people, but the exploitative structures were directly assaulted. The Temple cleansing was a nonviolent action as a definite exercise of power, and the response which came a few days later was with the full force of legally sanctioned government violence.

To argue more fully the issue of whether violence can ever be used by a Christian is beyond the scope of this study. It is clear that Jesus' life and ethical teaching were nonviolent, while directly challenging human sin and evil at its very core. The transforming initiatives which he taught and exemplified provide the guiding light for Christian action to bring justice and peace out of the conflicts that rage in our contemporary world.

Chapter 2

The Bible
and Conflict Resolution

I could see the explosion beginning to erupt and felt as helpless as if I had been at ground zero when the bomb went off. We were in the church basement, all seated around tables. The church executive board had earlier denied the request of the youth group to hold a sleep-over in the church on Good Friday night. The youth had been upset, not knowing why their request, which seemed reasonable to them, had been denied. Each side kept talking to the other through me, and I had finally gotten tired of being the one in the middle. So I called a special meeting for the board and the youth group to get together and discuss the issue face-to-face. It sounded like a simple enough idea.

A complicating factor, and probably a major contributing factor to many of the participants, was the racial composition of the conflicting groups. The board was composed of older members, all of whom were white except one black man who mostly socialized with older white people. The youth group was entirely black, led by a dynamic and sometimes fiery mother of one of the teens in the group. The church was located in a racially mixed neighborhood that had experienced population shifts a few years earlier, but was now fairly stable. Most of the younger whites had moved to the suburbs, leaving their parents back in the old neighborhood, still serving as pillars in their local church. Now, however, most of the kids who came to the church, sometimes with their parents, were black. An earlier, white youth group in the church had held a sleep-over in the church that turned out to be a disaster: a girl was sexually assaulted in the back of the church. Though the incident was not directly connected to the church activity, it had been forever linked to the sleep-over in the minds of the older white members. As they now looked at the black youths whom they did not know and to whom they were not related, the white members were not about to assume that these black teens would behave better than the teens of white families. The result was that the already difficult generation gap was compounded by a racial gap of suspicion and fear which could barely be masked by Christian good will.

I had planned the meeting very carefully so that our communication process would be fair and so we could resolve the dispute in a rational manner. I intended to help each group hear the concerns of the other, to build some trust through direct communication, and to develop a plan that would satisfy everyone's concerns and desires. I began by trying to set out the ground rules for the discussion, but before completing one sentence, an older women on the board began to lecture the youth in a very hostile tone. She was so domineering that I, as a young and timid pastor, was at a loss as to what I should do. The longer she spoke out of feelings that were coming from somewhere beyond this particular issue, the more emotional damage she inflicted. The youths and their leader were incensed and responded with angry accusations about the lack of caring by the older members. A loud argument ensued, and only concluded when the board's moderator excused the teens. The board voted again on the youth group's request, and again turned it down, 4 to 3.

From this attempt to resolve a small disagreement by the biblical admonition to "be reconciled to your brother or sister" (Matthew 5:24), the church was torn by a deep generational and racial schism. The congregation was divided by deeper hostility and suspicion. As a recent seminary graduate in my first year of pastoring, I was devastated. The church eventually experienced renewal and became a vibrant multicultural congregation, but that is another story.[1] As I surveyed the relational ruins in our congregation at the time, I knew there must be a better way to handle conflict than what we had just experienced.

A Biblical Perspective on Conflict Resolution

As a record of human life, the Bible is full of conflict. The story of Adam and Eve begins with a conflict about who was responsible for eating the forbidden fruit. Adam began the war between the sexes by blaming Eve rather than taking responsibility for his own actions. He also blamed God for providing the woman as a companion. Eve did no better, shifting the blame to the serpent. Neither owned their own feelings or actions, and so the distorted ways of handling conflict were born.

The next recorded conflict is between Cain and Abel. Rather than dealing with his own issues Cain projected his wrong onto Abel, then killed this enemy created out of his misdirected rage. God warned Cain to look inside himself, but the heat of his anger swept him into alienation and murder. His inner conflict became relational and then social and environmental, as divisions erupted between himself and other humans and between himself and the land itself.

Most of the conflicts in the Bible end as tragically as Cain's. Unresolved or poorly resolved conflicts fill the biblical pages from Lamech, the father of all escalations—"If Cain is avenged sevenfold, truly Lamech seventy-sevenfold" (Genesis 4:24)—to the early church's missionary team of Paul and Barnabas, split over a dispute concerning John Mark (Acts 15:36-41). Trade wars, ethnic cleansings, divorce rates, and arms sales show that humanity is still living out these old stories. As with nonviolence, a Christian examination of conflict resolution needs to begin with Jesus Christ. At his birth the heavenly announcement of peace on earth was made (Luke 2:14). That peace began to take shape as people who had been excluded from the community of God's people were drawn into the community of Christ's followers. Outcasts such as women, children, Samaritans, laborers, tax collectors, lepers, the mentally ill, and "sinners" were invited into the new community, the kingdom of God, the reign of God. Jesus told parables of such ones being reconciled with great joy (Luke 14:15-24; 15). He worked the reconciliation of people like Zaccheus with God, whom he then guided to the practical reconciliation of making restitution with those whom Zaccheus had abused and defrauded (Luke 19:1-10).

As the early church reflected on the life, death, and resurrection of Jesus, reconciliation was at the center of its reflections. The apostle Paul wrote that "in Christ God was reconciling the world to himself" (2 Corinthians 5:19). Human sin had created alienation between us and God, but "while we were enemies, we were reconciled to God through the death of his Son" (Romans 5:10). By Christ's death the barriers between humanity and God are overcome, and the kind of reconciling grace exhibited in Jesus' relationships with the outcasts is forever extended to all who wish to receive it.

The reconciliation between humanity and God has an immediate and intimate horizontal impact. Humans who were alienated to each other are now reconciled in Christ, at least theologically. Ephesians 2 describes the reconciliation between humans and God in the first ten verses, then immediately moves into the reconciliation between alienated groups of people in the following section. Christ is called "our peace," and "in his flesh he has made both groups into one and has broken down the dividing wall, that is, the hostility between us" (v. 14). This intra-human reconciliation is forged by the cross:

He has abolished the law with its commandments and ordinances,

that he might create in himself one new humanity in place of the
two, thus making peace, and might reconcile both groups to God in
one body through the cross, thus putting to death that hostility
through it (Ephesians 2:15-16).

Because we are reconciled to God through the cross, all of us from whatever human identity group are brought into a new oneness. "There is no longer Jew nor Greek, there is no longer slave nor free, there is no longer male nor female; for all of you are one in Christ Jesus" (Galatians 3:28). "There is no longer Greek and Jew, circumcised and uncircumcised, barbarian, Scythian, slave and free; but Christ is all, and in all!" (Colossians 3:11).

The challenge to the early church was how to live out that theological reality of reconciliation and oneness amidst the personal and social baggage of the old order. Paul faced a conflict over who can eat with whom in Antioch and attacked the divisions at dinner by an analysis of what it means to die with Christ (Galatians 2:11-21). After speaking eloquently of the self-giving love of Christ and the unity he brings, Paul asks for two women leaders in the church at Philippi, Euodia and Syntyche, to resolve their disputes, even asking for church members to assist in mediation (Philippians 4:2-3). Theological reconciliation must be worked out at the real places of division among us. The teachings of the early church in the New Testament were always related to the pragmatic concerns of living as a reconciled people.

Jesus said, "Be at peace with one another" (Mark 9:50). One of the basic transforming initiatives he presented in the Sermon on the Mount was to go and be reconciled (Matthew 5:24). When a relationship is broken, our own anger can lead to words and actions that deepen the division. Or we can simply resign ourselves to the alienated state of affairs, which leaves the unresolved conflict as the defining element of the relationship. Jesus calls for his followers simply to break out of the communication deadlock and go and talk to the other person (Matthew 18:15-17). Without communication there can be no conflict resolution. It doesn't matter who is at fault, which is usually a complex matter anyway. In Matthew 5 the one who is to go is the offender; in Matthew 18 the offender is the other person. In both cases it is the hearer of Jesus who is given the responsibility to act. Conflict resolution begins with me; it is my responsibility, just as Paul told the Christians in Rome: "If it is possible, so far as it depends on you, live peaceably with all" (Romans 12:18). Taking responsibility to initiate the communication is the starting point.

We also have to deal with our feelings. Cain could not examine his feelings as they raged out of control, in spite of God's warning that sin was "lurking at the door" (Genesis 4:7). God told Cain that he must master his anger if he was to avoid disaster. Jesus also warned of the self-destruction which comes from anger as the prelude to his challenge to go and talk to the other party in the dispute. Ephesians presents a helpful distinction: "Be angry but do not sin; do not let the sun go down on your anger, and do not make room for the devil" (Ephesians 4:26-27). One's feelings are neither good nor bad; anger is not evil in and of itself, for both Jesus and God are portrayed as being angry at times (Mark 3:5; Isaiah 5:25). The issue is what we do with our anger. Ephesians warns us not to sin or give an opportunity to the devil. Instead, we are to deal quickly with the matter that stirs up the anger, before the sun goes down. Anger recognizes that there is something wrong, that conflict exists, but through communication and conflict resolution a way can be found to resolution and reconciliation.

Paul gave specific instruction about trying to understand the other person's position and needs. In the context of talking about unity he exhorted, "Let each of you look not to your own interests, but to the interests of others" (Philippians 2:4). In his discussion of not being a stumbling block to others he urged, "Each of us must please our neighbor for the good purpose of building up the neighbor" (Romans 15:2). Glen Stassen also speaks of the need to affirm the enemy's valid interests as he develops the paradigm of transforming initiatives in *Just Peacemaking.*[2] Jesus calls his disciples to love their enemies (Matthew 5:44); affirming their valid interests is a concrete way to do so no matter how much emotion is generated by the conflict. Affirming those interests and acknowledging the needs of others is fundamental to a comprehensive and satisfying resolution of conflict.

But is it accurate to say that Jesus sought to resolve all conflicts? It seems he aggravated a number of situations, engaging in provocative actions such as the triumphal entry and the cleansing of the Temple. He also said, "Do not think that I have come to bring peace to the earth; I have not come to bring peace, but a sword. For I have come to set a man against his father, and a daughter against her mother, and a daughter-in-law against her mother-in-law" (Matthew 10:34-35). This sounds hardly like conflict resolution but rather like conflict escalation!

Sometimes conflict resolution must begin by heightening the conflict. Often one of the parties, usually the one who benefits from an unfair advantage, doesn't see any problem. The conflict is there, but the pain is disproportionately felt by one side. Before reconciliation can take place there must be an exposure of the problem, which can be experienced as an increase in conflict. Martin Luther King, Jr., in his *Letter from Birmingham Jail*, responded to his white clergy critics by showing the healing necessity of bringing conflict into the open:

> Actually, we who engage in nonviolent direct action are not the creators of tension. We merely bring to the surface the hidden tension that is already alive. We bring it out in the open, where it can be seen and dealt with. Like a boil that can never be cured so long as it is covered up but must be opened with all its ugliness to the natural medicines of air and light, injustice must be exposed, with all the tension its exposure creates, to the light of human conscience and the air of national opinion before it can be cured.[3]

To be genuine, conflict resolution has to be built upon a foundation of truth. A resolution to the conflict that buries one party's experience of injustice or pain is merely a continuation of the oppressive system, perhaps under a new guise. The conflict is postponed rather than resolved; it will simmer on until a time comes for it to emerge again, probably with increased intensity and destructiveness. The prophet Zechariah challenged the people to "love truth and peace" (Zechariah 8:19). There is no peace unless truth is a part of its fabric. The exposure of falsehood and injustice is a necessary part of the resolution process, even if for a while it seems that the conflict is getting worse.

This is where nonviolent action and conflict resolution complement each other. Nonviolence exposes the injustices at the root of a conflict, but in a way that opens the possibility for resolution and restoration of the relationship. Conflict resolution needs to have the issues brought to the surface and acknowledged by both sides if there is to be a genuine reconciliation process. Jesus taught and lived out both aspects of the quest for peace.

Mediation in the Bible

Mediation is given a central place in the Bible in the person of Jesus Christ. First Timothy 2:5-6 speaks of the identity of Christ as the mediator between humanity and God: "For there is one God; there is also one mediator between God and humankind, Christ Jesus, himself human, who gave himself a ransom for all." In the conflict between human beings and God, human sinfulness had created a severely polarized situation. The prophet Isaiah expressed God's perspective of the divine/human separation in this way: "When you stretch out your hands, I will hide my eyes from you; even though you make many prayers, I will not listen; your hands are full of blood"

(Isaiah 1:15). Yet in this context of alienation, God takes the initiative in the incarnation of Jesus Christ. Driven by divine love, Jesus becomes the one in the middle. Christ is God's Word become flesh and addressed in mercy to humankind. Christ stands in humanity's place as the righteous atoning sacrifice.

The mediator also presents a peace accord, known in the Scriptures as the "new covenant." This covenant is presented extensively in the letter to the Hebrews, contrasting the new covenant through Christ with the old covenant mediated through Moses. The first covenant resulted in death, because none could keep its requirements. The Christ-mediated covenant brings forgiveness and thus life: "For this reason he is the mediator of a new covenant, so that those who are called may receive the promised eternal inheritance, because a death has occurred that redeems them from the transgressions under the first covenant" (Hebrews 9:15). The price of the new peace accord is the sacrifice of the mediator, and so those who now wish to enter into this new relationship with God must come "to Jesus, the mediator of a new covenant, and to the sprinkled blood that speaks a better word than the blood of Abel" (Hebrews 12:24). Christ's work becomes the ultimate example of mediation as well as a model of mediation for those who seek to carry out God's work in the world. Paul speaks of this work in 2 Corinthians 5:19-20:

> In Christ God was reconciling the world to himself, not counting their trespasses against them, and entrusting the message of reconciliation to us. So we are ambassadors for Christ, since God is making his appeal through us; we entreat you on behalf of Christ, be reconciled to God.

Mediation of human conflicts is frequently seen in the Old Testament as well. This mediation follows the patterns of traditional mediation in which the mediator is part of the community, usually a trusted and respected leader, rather than the outside professional we are accustomed to seeing in Western cultures today.[4] The most famous example is the case brought to Solomon involving two women arguing over a child (1 Kings 3:16-28). The two women and their babies lived in the same house, and one of their babies died during the night. Each claimed the surviving child, so the case was brought to Solomon to decide. He asked for a sword to divide the child in two so each mother could have one part. The true mother surrendered her claim rather than risk the life of the child, so Solomon awarded the child to her.

Moses had served as the communal mediator during the early days of the Exodus, but had been rapidly worn down by the caseload. Guided by the wise advice of his father-in-law, Jethro, Moses had the community select judges who were "able men among all the people, men who fear God, are trustworthy, and hate dishonest gain" (Exodus 18:21). These judges acted less as interpreters of law and more as mediators and arbitrators. This traditional mediating role was carried on in the earlier stages of Israel's political development by the judges, charismatic figures who both led in battle and settled disputes among the people. Samuel rode a circuit, visiting regional centers on a regular basis to judge the people (1 Samuel 7:15-17). Deborah had a site under a palm tree to hear the disputes people would bring (Judges 4:4-5).

The judges had a mixed record of performance, for some became corrupt and abusive. They were generally chosen by a communal recognition of divine call and giftedness. When individuals tried to seize the leading role out of their own lust for power, the community suffered. Instead of mediating justice, these judges enriched themselves and created conflicts which were often horrifying in their brutality.[5] The court system developed from these roots of judges called from within the community, and the process for obtaining justice eventually became formalized, as in the code in Deuteronomy 16:18-20 and 17:8-13.

During the New Testament era, the Roman legal system was highly developed, but the apostle Paul urged members of the Christian community not to use the courts to settle their own disputes. Within the society of the church, he said, mediation built on relationships and the wisdom of trusted leaders should be the norm. Paul called upon Christians, who one day "will judge the world," to bring their disputes to be handled by people within the church; if they don't receive satisfaction, it is better to suffer wrong than to go to law in a Roman court against another Christian. He asked the Corinthians, "Can it be that there is no one among you wise enough to decide between one believer and another, but a believer goes to court against a believer—and before unbelievers at that?" (1 Corinthians 6:5-6). Clearly, mediation within the context of the Christian community was viewed as the preferred manner of handling disputes if the parties could not reconcile on their own.

Biblical Case Studies

There are a number of positive examples of conflict resolution in the biblical text. One of the earliest is found in Joshua 22:10-34. Following the conquest of Canaan, the Hebrew tribes were divided geographically. Two and a half of the tribes had chosen to settle on the eastern side of the Jordan River. The other tribes settled in

Canaan proper. When the easterners built an altar, the westerners mobilized for war. Before fighting, however, they decided to talk; a delegation was sent, led by the priest Phinehas, to negotiate the issue of the altar. It was a good thing the sides talked first, for this was a classic case of each side projecting their own fears onto the other.

The westerners approached the situation with the history of the wilderness wanderings, the forty years of purifying the people of God from their idolatrous ways. A whole generation had died short of the Promised Land because they gave in to the influences of paganism. As the westerners saw the altar being constructed, they envisioned yet another deviation from the faith given to them through such struggle and anguish. To keep God's judgment from falling on the entire community, they had to purge the offenders. So they set forth their case. The rhetoric was inflammatory, laced with accusatory language such as "treachery" and "rebellion." But they did state their case clearly, including the framework for their understanding, referring to the early incident with Achan where God's judgment affected the whole community until the one offender was eliminated (Joshua 7). They also made an invitation and space for a change of mind. It was not a great start for a conflict resolution process, but the westerners did communicate their concerns and open themselves to listen to the other side.

The easterners were stunned by how far off the westerners' perception of their actions was. They protested that turning from God was not their intention. Far from an interest in breaking from the covenant community of God's people, their concern was that because of the geographical separation caused by the river, their descendants would be victims of an exclusionary prejudice from their western compatriots. The altar for them was a sign of inclusion and union, not rebellion; it was a sign of their faithfulness to God. The easterners were clear in stating their own fears, motives, and concerns so that the other side could make their own judgments with all the facts at hand.

The westerners, to their credit, were open-minded and had come to listen as well as speak. Phinehas accepted the easterners' line of reasoning and even applauded their clarity of communication in saving the people of Israel from a disastrous civil war. The conflict was resolved, and the altar was named "Witness" to stand as a witness to all the people that "Yahweh is God."

In this case study of conflict we can see some key elements to successful conflict resolution. Each side needs to state its own perspective, hopes, needs, and fears clearly enough to be understood by the other. It is best to use "I" or "we" statements, so that the other side can get an accurate understanding of where your concerns lie and what your experience is in the matter. Though the westerners in our case study were harsh and accusatory in their rhetoric, the "we" statements of the easterners helped tone down the intensity of the conflict so that a reasonable resolution could be achieved. The less threatening response allowed the two sides to become joint problem-solvers of a misunderstanding, rather than remain as adversaries. Both sides, in spite of the deep feelings generated by the conflict, were willing to listen. Their conversation was not a mere exchange of ultimatums prior to war so each side could justify itself later. Rather, there was sincere and honest effort to communicate before the blood-letting would begin. The relief and joy that resulted from achieving a successful resolution was evidence of the good faith both sides brought to the conflict.

The early church had a number of conflicts at pivotal stages of its development. Acts 6:1-7 tells of the institution of the office of deacon. The diaconate was a solution to a conflict. In the confusion of the earliest days of the Christian community, thousands of people were being incorporated into their network. Many of the people were Greek-speaking Jews who had traveled to Jerusalem for the religious festival of Pentecost. These Jews were called Hellenists, for they had settled in various parts of the Roman Empire as a result of political upheavals in past centuries. They maintained their Jewish faith, but they had adopted some Greek habits and culture which alienated them from the more traditional Hebrew Jews living in Palestine. It was an ethnic difference which then led to a racist situation. The poorest Greek-speaking widows were being neglected in the daily food distribution set up on an *ad hoc* basis to take care of the needy. The dominant Hebrews may not have intentionally discriminated, but their ethnic bias was harming the most vulnerable in the community. The Hellenists complained, and the conflict began to grow.

The twelve apostles were at that time acting as the leadership group for the church. They took a proactive approach once the issue came to their attention, calling a gathering of the Christian community to face the issue directly. They established a division of labor, instituting a new leadership team to handle the feeding of the poor. The key to their solution, however, was the selection of the new deacons. The decision was given to the community as a whole, and they chose seven people, all from the discriminated group, the Hellenists. The solution was ratified by a time of prayer and laying on hands. The result of their successful resolution of this conflict was that the community grew as "the word of God continued to spread."

In selecting seven Hellenists to be the ones responsible for the food distribution, the church chose to give power to those who had been powerless. Injustice was dealt with by establishing a more just system. The brief account Luke gives us of this conflict does not reflect any negotiation. How was the complaint raised to the apostles? Did the apostles come out with their own solution and hand it down from on high, or was there a process of discussion and negotiation to shape the proposal? How did the community arrive at the decision about who should be deacons? None of these questions can be answered from the text, so we cannot see the process as clearly as we might like. But the deliberate choice to tackle the issue in a forthright manner stands out, as does the dramatic justice of empowering the dispossessed members of the community. The conclusion to the passage also shows that conflict resolution is a means of growth. Any group of people will experience conflict. If conflict is resolved through careful and sincere efforts, all parties will grow as persons and will find mutually beneficial ways to live and work together.

New conflicts emerged in the early church as it continued to expand, again with ethnic overtones. As Gentiles became Christians, a theological and cultural conflict erupted over what their inclusion meant and how it was to be carried out. The conflict fills many pages of the New Testament, as questions of the nature of salvation, the identity of Israel and the church, the practicalities of love, and a host of other issues were hammered out.

Acts 15 tells of the Jerusalem Council, which was one of the key milestones in the debate over how to include Gentiles in the church. The conflict had come to a head in Antioch, where the first genuinely multicultural congregation had been established. Paul and Barnabas were leading figures there and had entered into "no small dissension and debate" with some Jewish Christian teachers who had come up from Judea asserting that circumcision was necessary for salvation. A delegation had been formed, led by Paul and Barnabas, to take the conflict to the highest levels of church leadership. Acts 15 tells of the council called to debate the issue from the grounds of theology, experience, and Scripture. Eventually James made a proposal, which was accepted (though a case could also be made that James made an authoritative decision on the basis of the debate). I believe that more of a consensus process took place, as indicated by the "decided unanimously" description in Acts 15:25, with James gathering the basis of the consensus and concretizing it into a plan of action. In any case, agreement was reached on a position and a plan of action. A letter was sent to Antioch informing the Christians there that circumcision was not necessary for Christian faith, but calling for them to maintain some of the dietary laws, to abstain from idolatry, violence, and unchastity, and according to Paul's version in Galatians 2:10, to remember the poor. The process seems to have been a good and orderly one that allowed all the viewpoints to be expressed, thoroughly examined, and critiqued. A consensus was achieved, at least to some degree. Space was given in the discussion for people such as Peter and Paul to relate their own experiences, which evidently had a significant impact on the direction of the council.

At some point, when consensus is beginning to emerge, someone needs to crystallize the forming resolution into a proposal that can then be refined. It is interesting to note that one of the major concerns left in the final agreement was abstaining from eating strangled meat;[6] this concern seems to have quietly faded from view as incorporation of Gentiles into the church gathered momentum. Even agreements produced out of intense conflict and hard negotiations may have some fluidity to them as the parties then live out the terms of the agreement in their own settings. Dietary laws were recognized as a cultural concern as the church refined what it meant to be Christian, while the moral concerns of abstaining from violence and unchastity and caring for the poor proved to be basic ethical issues transcending cultural particularities. Idolatry also remained central, but how that related to eating meat that had been butchered on temple premises still was a debatable issue (see Romans 14–15 and 1 Corinthians 8-10). Major issues of personal, communal, or international life have to be resolved many times as they evolve and take new shapes amidst the twists and turns of our histories. A resolution of a conflict does not mean the parties will never have to visit the issue again at the negotiating table.

Chapter 3

The Development of Nonviolence

Our family sat around the dinner table with five unlit candles in the center. We were about to begin our family tradition of celebrating All Saints' Day in a uniquely Buttry Baptist style. Each member of the family tells of one person who taught us about God or how to live for God. Some of the people we name are family members who have died. Others are people in history whose stories have shaped our values and commitments. After naming our saint and telling why we chose that individual to remember, we light a candle. Through this tradition we seek to make our history as people of faith a resource for ourselves and our children as we face the challenges before our own generations.

One year among our list of saints were two teachers of nonviolence. We lit a candle for Martin Luther King, Jr., and recalled his *Letter from Birmingham Jail*. Our family was planning to attend a Baptist Peace Fellowship conference the next summer in Birmingham to observe the thirtieth anniversary of the pivotal year of the Birmingham movement. Remembering Dr. King was a part of our journey of preparation for that event. We also lit a candle for Mary Dyer, whose statue stands on the Boston Common, where our children once played. She was a Quaker woman who was hanged in Puritan New England for her nonviolent witness to religious liberty and the freedom of conviction. She was offered clemency if she would recant, but responded, "What is life compared to the witness for Truth?"[1] The clarity of her words and the courage of her death inspired the abolition of the death penalty in Massachusetts as a means to control the Quakers. Her witness began as a child when she walked out of church following the banning of a Quaker from her congregation. After lighting the candles for our saints, we composed a poem together in their honor that would hang on the kitchen until the next All Saints' Day:

Dr. King made the law more fair;
He went to jail and wrote his famous letter there.
His letter was about justice and peace;
His dream for right will never cease.

Mary Dyer was very brave;
She kept her faith right to the grave.
Mary Dyer walked out of church.
Then she sat down under the birch.
She thought til she could think no more;
She stood up for what was right 24 years more.
There is a statue of Mary Dyer,
She fought and spoke for her heart's desire.

The stories of the "saints" of nonviolence and the development of thinking and action in this area is part of a rich heritage of peacemaking that has seldom been told.[2] The war-makers are well known to us, but those who have waged peace are often unsung heroes, even if their witness and work led to significant social change. Great figures like Mahatma Gandhi and Martin Luther King, Jr., have rightly become beacons of truth and courage for people around the world, but there are many other stories to be told as well of people and movements that have helped to shape the understanding and practice of nonviolence that has emerged with such revolutionary power in the later years of the twentieth century.

Early Roots

In the Americas and Europe, nonviolence has its roots in the pacifism of the early Quakers, Anabaptists, and other religious nonconformists. Quakers such as Mary Dyer, Robert Barclay, William Penn, and John Woolman bore witness to the call of Christ to peace and refused to defend themselves other than by speaking the truth as they understood it. Their peacemaking efforts consisted primarily of their verbal witness and an effort to be consistent with their principles as regards their actions. During the French and Indian War, John Woolman led a number of Quakers to resist paying taxes that paid for the war, writing, "We therefore think that as we cannot be concerned in wars and fighting, so neither ought we to contribute thereto by paying the tax directed by the said Act, though suffering be the consequence of our refusal, which we hope to be enabled to bear with patience."[3] For the most part, these religious pacifists did not try to change society through political means but faithfully proclaimed and modeled a life of nonviolence and sought individual conversion to their convictions.

Nonviolent actions were also widely used in the resistance against British colonial domination, and played a key part in the American— and later in the Indian—independence struggles. In colonial America these actions were taken not so much out of a political or religious philosophy as from a pragmatic basis of how best to resist British policies. Nonviolent resistance was so effective that by 1776 nine out of the thirteen colonies had already achieved *de facto* independence.[4] The greatest period of unity during the independence struggle was during the nonviolent resistance to the Stamp Act, a unity that was seriously strained when the conflict became a military one.[5]

In the late 1700s and early 1800s, peace societies were formed to advance pacifist philosophies, often from a humanist perspective. Henry David Thoreau's essay "On Civil Disobedience" had a major impact internationally. The essay grew out of his experience in tax resistance. When he refused to pay the poll tax from 1842–1846 in protest of the government's support of slavery, he was arrested and jailed briefly until a relative paid the tax. Thoreau was angered over this thwarting of his attempt to force a test case in the courts, so he turned to writing and lecturing in order to present his position. He asserted that conscience was a higher authority than governmental law, and when the law was immoral the individual had a duty to engage in civil disobedience. Through such action and the resulting punishment, the moral cause of the legal martyr would arouse the citizenry to bring about change. Thoreau's ideas would have a profound influence on Gandhi, resisters to the Nazis, and others who employed civil disobedience on the basis of conscience in the twentieth century.

The nineteenth-century abolitionist movement marked the first organized effort to change national policy in the United States through nonviolent means. Adin Ballou and William Lloyd Garrison formed the New England Non-Resistance Society which organized bold direct actions to free slaves and fight racial segregation of the railways. Boycotts of slave-made products and walk-alongs, in which a black person and white person would walk in the streets arm-in-arm, were common tactics in their struggle. Black abolitionist organizations developed to support the freedom movement. The oratory of Frederick Douglass stirred anger at the injustice of slavery, while the Underground Railroad, an extensive network of thousands of blacks and whites opposed to slavery, provided a way to freedom for tens of thousands of slaves, in direct violation of federal law. Many of those who went into the South to assist the escaped slaves were captured and imprisoned, and even killed.

Harriet Tubman was one of the bravest and most creative of the "conductors" on the Underground Railroad. Though suffering physically from abuse received as a slave, she made nineteen trips to "Pharaoh's Land" to bring out at least three hundred slaves, earning the name "Moses" on the wanted posters because nobody believed a woman could accomplish the feats she did. Though slave owners offered rewards of $40,000 for her capture and pledged torture and death for her, Tubman's profound trust in God enabled her to return again and again into the heart of danger. She spoke of Saint John having seen four gates in Paradise, on facing South: "I recon if they kill me down there, I'll get into one of them gates, don't you?"[6] Harriet Tubman was also known for her great capacity to forgive, and expressed hope that even Confederate President Jefferson Davis would find peace after the Civil War.

Though the abolitionist movement confronted the evil of slavery and to some degree that of racism, sexism was a serious beam in the movement's eye. Women abolitionists worked on two fronts and had to form their own abolitionist societies because they were excluded from the societies by men who thought women should never speak in public to men or to mixed groups. Through the efforts of women such as Sojourner Truth, Angelina and Sarah Grimke, and Lucretia Mott, emancipation of both blacks and women was brought into national consciousness. The Philadelphia Female Antislavery Society was the first national, politically active organization for women; it wove nonviolence and feminism into the abolitionist cause. During the Women's Rights Convention held in New York City in 1853, Lucretia Mott nonviolently transformed a hostile confrontation. The Rynder gang, a group of politicized thugs, had decided to break up the meeting, but Mott refused to call for police protection. She persuaded all the women to leave the hall with an escort. When asked who would escort her, she took Captain Rynder's arm and said "This man will see me through." The stunned thug courteously complied.[7] In the ongoing struggle for women's suffrage, nonviolent actions such as lobbying, silent vigils, mass demonstrations, and hunger strikes were effectively employed.

Early Movements for Peace

On the eve of World War I, religious leaders gathered in Germany for the first "World Conference of Churches for Peace." Germany had already declared war on Russia, and the conference had to be suspended and the conference participants evacuated through the German and French lines as the European powers plunged into the war that would devastate their continent. Earlier, on a train platform, the British Quaker Dr. Henry Hodgkin and the German pastor Friedrich Siegmund-Schultze had pledged, "Whatever happens, nothing is changed between us. We are one in Christ and can never be at war."[8] Their commitment to peace was the beginning of the International Fellowship of Reconciliation (IFOR).

Peace organizations grew in various European countries and the United States, witnessing to Christian pacifism and engaging in relief efforts among war victims. Dr. Henrietta Thomas undertook a reconciliation visit to Germany in 1915, where she visited peace groups and provided words of encouragement. Siegmund-Schultze was arrested and sentenced to death by a military court, but direct intervention from the Kaiser led to his release. Over six hundred Fellowship of Reconciliation members were imprisoned in England for their conscientious objection. Following the war, fifty men and women from ten countries met in Holland to establish formally the IFOR from all their national fellowships. What began as an ecumenical Christian anti-war organization has since become an interfaith network with affiliates on every continent advocating nonviolent direct action for justice and peace.

Another Fellowship of Reconciliation member, Muriel Lester, was raised in a wealthy family but was moved by her faith to take a vow of voluntary poverty and to give her life working among the poor for justice and peace. She became a social worker and founded Kingsley Hall in the Bow section of London's East End. Her deep spirituality and daily discipline of prayer provided the roots to withstand the stress of the struggles in which she was engaged. She was invited to spend time in India with Mahatma Gandhi, which led to a life-long friendship; when Gandhi came to England in 1931, he stayed at Kingsley Hall with Lester. She traveled around the world protesting war and serving as IFOR's traveling secretary. Following the Japanese invasion of China, she picked up a piece of shrapnel beside a dead Chinese boy. When she was next in the United States, she placed it on the desk of a scrap metal dealer in Seattle to confront him with the evil his business partnership with the Japanese war machine was producing.

During World War II in the United States, Clarence Jordan led a group of pacifists in starting Koinonia Farm in southern Georgia as a witness for what Jordan called the "God Movement." From the beginning it was an interracial undertaking to model justice and reconciliation, but it became a target for violence from the racist white community. The farm, in response to a boycott by neighbors, began a mail order business to stay afloat. When they were firebombed and shot at, they responded with a nonviolent witness. Ora Browne courageously took the night watch, standing unarmed under the light on the road. Jordan always presented Jesus Christ as the center of his witness and challenged the conservative religious Southerners to take their Lord seriously, using a gentle but blunt earthy wit. When one proud woman said, "I want you to know that my grandfather fought in the Civil War, and I'll never believe a word you say," he responded, "Ma'am, your choice seems quite clear. It is whether you will follow your granddaddy or Jesus Christ."[9] Jordan's "Cotton Patch" translations of the New Testament brought the teachings of Jesus regarding justice and peace into the racial conflicts of the South with ringing clarity.

Nonviolence and the Labor Movement

In addition to the religious pacifists and advocates of nonviolence, the labor movement provided another stream of nonviolent action in the early twentieth century. Strikes, picketing, and boycotts were used extensively in worker struggles. The Industrial Workers of the World (IWW or "Wobblies") was the most radical of the labor movements, seeking to organize workers without division by race, sex, or skills. Though they were branded as violent by the press, they used mainly nonviolent means of struggle, except when attacked by police. The Wobblies campaigned for free speech in many western states in the early 1900s, challenging the ordinances that were enacted to curtail union organizing. Thousands would march, defying gag orders by local courts. The arrested Wobblies filled the jails, but continued to make speeches and sing songs from behind bars. In Fresno, California, in 1911, the fire department turned their fire hoses point-blank on the singing prisoners in their jail cells. They were silenced only when the icy water was knee-high in the prison, but then thousands more IWW supporters joined in the Fresno demonstrations, forcing the city officials to lift their ban on street speaking.[10]

Usually there was not much involvement of the churches in the labor struggles, though occasionally people spanned both the religious and the workers' movements. During the 1919 textile strike in Lawrence, Massachusetts, for example, A. J. Muste joined the strike's Boston Defense Committee. Even though he was pastoring a Quaker church, because of his charismatic leadership he became executive secretary of the strike committee itself. Facing provocations to violence and police brutality, the strike succeeded, the first victory by a coalition of nonviolent workers aided by members of the religious community and the radical Left. Muste later left the pastorate and became a full-time labor leader. For a while he adopted revolutionary Marxist-Leninist thought and became a follower of Leon Trotsky, but just prior to World War II Muste returned to his Christian roots. After conferring with the Russian revolutionary, Muste rejected Bolshevism and embraced "revolutionary nonviolence." He called for an activist form of pacifism that would make common cause with the oppressed in their struggles for justice, whether industrial workers, sharecroppers, or American blacks. Following World War II, as executive secretary of the Fellowship of Reconciliation, A. J. Muste would become a key link between the earlier labor and anti-war struggles and the emerging civil rights and anti-war movements during the Vietnam era.

In the Vietnam era the labor and religious movements came together again under the leadership of a young Mexican American named Cesar Chavez. Chavez organized the migrant workers in California, founding the National Farm Workers Association in 1962. Because of their nomadic life and often illegal status in the U.S., migrants were especially vulnerable to exploitation. Chavez and the UFW organized national consumer boycotts of lettuce, grapes, and wines. He campaigned for better working conditions and against the use of pesticides that endangered the health of the field workers. Chavez was deeply committed to nonviolence, coming out of an intense Catholic spirituality. He frequently said, "to be human is to suffer for others,"[11] and Chavez used fasting as a spiritual method for nonviolent struggle, including a thirty-six-day fast at the age of sixty-one to protest hazardous pesticide use. One long fast in 1968 ended when he was joined by Senator Robert Kennedy in taking Holy Communion. His own spirituality, as well as the justice of *la causa*, the struggle, drew many Christians and other people of faith into solidarity with the farm workers.

Before turning to other nonviolence movements of the 1960s in the United States, we must first consider the nonviolent struggle for independence from colonial rule of another country, India. It was there that the roots of the philosophy of nonviolence were developed in the early twentieth century in a way that would later influence the civil rights movement in America through its leader, Martin Luther King, Jr.

Gandhi and the Movement for India's Independence

Mahatma Gandhi deepened the conceptualization of the philosophy of nonviolence and refined its practice in what he called "experiments with truth" in the struggles for justice in South Africa and independence in India in the late nineteenth and early twentieth centuries. He began his career as a lawyer in South Africa, leading resistance in the Indian community against the rising repressiveness of the white power structure. In the context of this struggle he developed a method of resistance he called *satyagraha*, which he translated "soul-force" or "truth-force." *Satyagraha* was a method of civil disobedience in which the *satyagrahi*, the resister, would disobey unjust laws with willing self-sacrifice to the forces of repression. The power of truth and conscience and self-discipline thus revealed would be greater than the power of violence and injustice.

Gandhi's first major campaign was against the Asiatic Registration Act of 1907, which required every Indian in South Africa to register with the Registrar of Asiatics and to take out a certificate that had to be produced any time a police officer demanded it. The campaigners refused to take out certificates and picketed all registration offices. The police began to arrest the campaign leaders, including Gandhi, but the resistance spread. Some two thousand certificates that had been taken out were voluntarily offered to be burned at a public demonstration. The repression escalated until at one point, of the thirteen thousand Indians in the Transvaal, twenty-five hundred were in jail!

For years the struggle twisted and turned, with Gandhi always counseling and modeling a gracious but firm attitude toward those in power. Finally, in 1914 the Indians Relief Bill was passed, overturning the key repressive legislation. When Gandhi departed for India, he gave a gift to General Jan Christian Smuts, his main protagonist in the struggle: sandals he had made while in prison. As a testimony to the force of truth and love that was the foundation for Gandhi's resistance, Smuts later remarked, "I have worn these sandals for many a summer...even though I may feel that I am not worthy to stand in the shoes of so great a man. It was my fate to be the antagonist of a man for whom even then I had the highest respect."[12]

On his return to India, Gandhi became a leader in the effort to expel the British colonial government and attain independence. His first political act was to call for a nationwide strike in 1918. Distressed over the violence that erupted following his arrest, he called off the strike, but in Amritsar nonviolent public meetings continued until General Dyer sealed off the walled park where the meetings were held and ordered his troops to open fire. Over fifteen hundred casualties, including 379 dead, resulted from the firing of 1,650 rounds of ammunition, a later inquiry into the massacre learned. Britain had showed itself willing to employ severe violence to maintain its colonial system. But the nonviolence movement for independence in India had just begun.

A campaign for economic independence began as Gandhi encouraged Indians to boycott British textiles and produce their own homespun clothing. He worked daily at the spinning wheel, and encouraged all Indians to do the same. Then Gandhi challenged the British monopoly on salt production. Salt was a necessity for every Indian in the tropical climate, and the British salt tax was the second leading source of income from India for the empire. Resistance to the salt tax struck a blow at colonial tyranny in such a way that any Indian could participate and that was immediately understandable to all. Gandhi led a march to the sea where he dried his own salt, igniting a nationwide illegal industry of salt-making. Over one hundred thousand arrests of the protesters, including Gandhi and other *satyagraha* leaders, were made as the British tried in vain to stop the movement.

In the North-West Frontier Province along the border with Afghanistan, an astounding nonviolence movement developed among the Pathan people. The Pathans were noted for their violence, engaging in endless rounds of blood feuds and upholding a code of honor that valued killing for revenge and dying in battle. British military expeditions into the frontier had often suffered high casualties and responded with brutalities unparalleled in the British Empire. But Badshah Khan transformed Pathan society through the teachings of Islam and Gandhi.[13] He began as an educator, establishing schools in spite of British opposition and the resistance of the conservative mullahs. He taught the Islamic values of *amal, yakeen*, and *muhabat*—selfless service, faith, and love. In the struggle for independence from colonial rule he raised a volunteer army of Pathans committed to nonviolence. They combined service to humanity and love with the courage and fearlessness of their warrior culture. Thousands of Pathans joined the Khudai Khidmatgar, "Servants of God," as the army was called. The Khudai Khidmatgar wore red tunics, practiced military drills, had officers and a drum and bagpipe corp, but they also swore an oath—a life and death matter for a Pathan—to refrain from violence and taking revenge, and to live a simple life of service.[14]

When Gandhi ignited the salt protests, the Pathans rapidly picked up the action. Badshah Khan spoke to mass meetings, encouraging his followers to join the resistance. The British promptly arrested him, but thousands of Pathans demonstrated around his jail, and in the city of Peshawar a general strike was called. The British sealed off the entire province and began a massive campaign of repression. Troops were sent to Peshawar to confront nonviolent demonstrators at the Kissa Khani Bazaar.[15] Arrests were made, with demonstrators peacefully being hauled off to jail. Then two armored cars drove into the crowd, killing a number of people. The crowd maintained the nonviolent discipline Badshah Khan had taught them and quietly collected the dead and wounded, but refused to disperse unless the soldiers and armored cars also left. The troops were then ordered to fire on the demonstrators. When those in front fell, more Pathans stepped forward, sometimes with chests bared, and the demonstrators stood their ground without panicking. From 11 o'clock until 5 o'clock, demonstrators peacefully yet defiantly presented themselves before the firing British soldiers. When the corpses filled the streets, the government ambulances hauled them away to be burned. Two to three hundred people were killed that day, with thousands wounded. One crack regiment, the 2/18th Royal Garhwal Rifles, refused to fire on the unarmed civilians. Their courage in disobeying orders moved all of India, but they were sentenced to long prison terms for their disobedience.[16] The British then abandoned the city for ten days until reinforcements could arrive.

The British soldiers began a reign of terror throughout the province, burning villages, beating "Red Shirts" of the Khudai Khidmatgar, killing livestock, destroying harvests, and jailing thousands. But no matter what provocation the British tried, the Pathans maintained their courageous nonviolent discipline. In one town when all the Red Shirts had been beaten unconscious, the British officer yelled, "Any more Red Shirts?" An old villager, Abbas Khan, covered a shirt with red fluid and presented himself smartly before the officer. Badshah Kahn later wrote, "The British feared a nonviolent Pathan more than a violent one."[17]

In addition to the struggle for freedom from British rule, Gandhi also turned *satyagraha* upon two internal issues of the Indian people: Hindu/Muslim strife and untouchability. He employed fasting as a means to raise the seriousness and immediacy of these issues, though he refused to use fasting against the British because he believed it was a tactic to be used only against one's nearest and dearest. During his fast against untouchability, Indian society was shaken from top to bottom by his moral courage and demands. Though that three-thousand-year-old system of segregation did not end, Gandhi had destroyed the public belief in untouchability. What had once had religious sanction was now viewed as morally illegitimate.

By 1946, a war-weakened Britain realized it could not stand against the power of the nonviolent movement for Indian independence, and the British colonial government withdrew. India's birth as an independent nation immediately became tragic, as violence erupted between Hindus and Muslims. Hundreds of thousands were killed in the social earthquake as India split into two nations, which brought profound grief to Gandhi, who had given so much of his efforts to the cause of peace and unity. And the strife between Hindu and Muslim would cost Gandhi his life: a Hindu radical who viewed Gandhi as too accommodating to Muslims assassinated the apostle of nonviolence after receiving Gandhi's blessing. Likewise, his close Muslim associate, Badshah Khan, was jailed in the newly formed Pakistan by his own Muslim leaders because he sought unity with Indian Hindus. Thus, the two great heroes of Indian independence both suffered from the violent and bloody schism between the Hindu and Islamic people of India following independence.

The drama of the struggle for India's independence and the scope of Gandhi's writings had a global impact. His definition of *satyagraha*, "truth-force" or "soul-force," broke the conceptual bonds of negativity of terms like "passive resistance." Nonviolence was more clearly understood as a force that could dramatically affect the course of human affairs, not just a quaint philosophy for a few social radicals on the fringe. Gandhi had led a movement that set free the world's largest colony from the most powerful colonizing empire, and people around the world took notice.

Gandhi's teachings about nonviolence emphasized the religious core of nonviolence as a life philosophy. God's truth expressed in love was the foundation. Love could not be particularized, but must be expressed to all people, including one's adversaries. The practical manifestation of this love was a respectful yet firm statement of one's position, seeking to connect to the moral roots of the adversary. Gandhi wrote, "Our motto must ever be conversion by gentle persuasion and a constant appeal to the head and heart. We must therefore be ever courteous and patient with those who do not see eye to eye with us."[18]

The relationship between means and ends is essential for understanding the philosophy of nonviolence. The end one pursues can only be attained by means consistent with the desired end. Gandhi saw the failures of violence in light of this understanding: "Experience convinces me that permanent good can never be the outcome of untruth and violence....I object to violence because, when it appears to do good, the good is only temporary, the evil it does is permanent."[19]

To achieve a unified India with the inner strength for independence and self-government, Gandhi focused on the nonviolent method of action, which builds inner strength and interdependence among all the people engaged in the struggle and even among their adversaries. He argued, "They say 'means are after all just means.' I would say 'means are after all everything.' As the means so the end.... If we take care of the means we are bound to reach the end sooner or later."[20] The means were something that Gandhi and his followers could control, whereas the end was to a significant degree beyond their control. If, however, they gave in to the lure of violence, they would lose control over both the means and their ability to shape the end.

Satyagraha requires more courage than participating in violence, for the advocate of nonviolence cannot hide behind a weapon but must first stand before the truth and master the oppressions and evils within. "Non-violence cannot be taught to a person who fears to die and has no power of resistance."[21] Self-purification, therefore, is viewed as the beginning point for nonviolent action. Violence of heart, thought, and word has to be truthfully confronted and mastered before engaging in acts of struggle. Gandhi rejoiced in his times in jail (of which he spent 2,089 days in India and 249 in South Africa) as a time to face his inner issues. He wrote: "Self-purification is the main consideration in seeking the prison. Embarrassment of the Government is a secondary consideration."[22] Through the process of growth in nonviolence, truth, and love, sacrifice was transfigured by joy: "No sacrifice is worth the name unless it is a joy."[23]

Gandhi's major contribution to the political underpinnings of nonviolence was an understanding of the role of the consent of the oppressed in their oppression. Every government depends for its power upon the consent of the governed, whether that assent is willingly given by agreement to a constitutional system or coerced by violence and terror, since "all exploitation is based on the cooperation, willing or forced, of the exploited."[24] Gandhi believed that even the most despotic government could not stand except by the consent of those whom they govern, even though that consent was often obtained through force. Yet when "the subject ceases to fear the despotic force, the power is gone."[25] Gene Sharp makes this understanding of power and consent the foundation of his analysis of nonviolence:

> A ruler's power is dependent upon the availability of its several sources. This availability is determined by the degree of obedience and cooperation given by the subjects. Such obedience and cooperation are, however, not inevitable, and despite inducements, pressures, and even sanctions, obedience remains essentially voluntary. Therefore, all government is based upon consent.[26]

Centuries earlier, the French philosopher Etienne de la Boetie exposed the vulnerability of tyrants to the withdrawal of consent:

But if not one thing is yielded to them, if without any violence they are simply not obeyed, they become naked and undone and as nothing, just as, when the root receives no nourishment, the branch withers and dies.... Resolve to serve no more, and you are at once freed. I do not ask that you place hands upon the tyrant to topple him over, but simply that you support him no longer; then you will behold him, like a great Colossus whose pedestal has been pulled away, fall of his own weight and break into pieces.[27]

Though this concept is difficult for oppressed people crushed by the suffering inflicted upon them to bear, Gandhi made it the foundation for his application of nonviolence. A nonviolence movement has a potent tool in the withdrawal of the consent of the governed. Gandhi blamed Indian cooperation more than British guns for their subjugation, then turned to self-improvement and self-reliance as pivotal fronts on which to wage the struggle:

The outward freedom... that we shall attain, will be only in exact proportion to the inward freedom to which we may have grown at a given moment.... The responsibility is more ours than that of the English for the present state of things. The English will be powerless to do evil if we will but be good. Hence my incessant emphasis on reform from within.[28]

Those who are viewed as powerless have the critical power to say yes or no, and a willingness to suffer while refusing to give assent to repression arms the proponent of nonviolence with a weapon more powerful than guns, tanks, court injunctions, or prisons. A government or tyrant unable to gain consent will of necessity collapse.

Through his numerous campaigns of civil disobedience, Gandhi also developed a pragmatic wisdom with deep roots in the nonviolent philosophy. Trust was essential to the success of a mass movement. Leaders could not expect to have people follow unless they had earned the people's trust over a period of time through their continuous and consistent efforts. The preparation of the people for the days of intense struggle depended upon the leaders being known and trusted, so Gandhi was careful in judging the timing of his efforts and the building of the community of trust. He also advocated trust toward the adversaries, requiring openness about the plans for the movement:

> *The best and the quickest way of getting rid of the corroding and de-*
> *grading Secret Service is for us to make a final effort to think every-*
> *thing aloud, have no privileged conversation with any soul on earth*
> *and cease to fear the spy. We must ignore his presence and treat eve-*
> *ryone as a friend entitled to know all our thoughts and plans. I know*
> *I have achieved most satisfactory results from evolving the boldest*
> *of my plans in broad daylight....Many have apologized for having*
> *to shadow me.*[29]

At times Gandhi would even write the leading authority involved about his plans, using his courteous manner with disarming forth-rightness.

Gandhi also encouraged each campaign to have a particular focus, thus maintaining the energy for the campaign and giving a clear sense of accomplishment when the goal was achieved. Each campaign was a particular step along the longer road to justice, independence, or unity. He wrote, "Civil Disobedience can never be directed for a general cause, such as for Independence. The issue must be definite and capable of being clearly understood and within the power of the opponent to yield."[30] When the South African government gave in on the laws the Indians were protesting, some wanted Gandhi to press for more demands, but he refused on the ground that to do so would not be true to what they had stated in their campaign.

Gandhi viewed the nonviolence movement in India as his country's gift to the world. As he talked with American blacks about their own oppressive situation, he saw them as carrying a similar hope. After his death, with the growth of the civil rights movement and the rise of a similar leader in the person of Martin Luther King, Jr., Gandhi's prediction came true. These two leaders and the movements which they helped direct and shape became the great beacons of inspiration for those seeking justice and freedom in nations all across the globe.

Martin Luther King and the Civil Rights Movement

The nonviolence movement in the struggle for civil rights in the 1950s and 1960s had deep roots in the earlier black American strug-gles for justice and freedom. Abolitionists such as Frederick Douglass, Harriet Tubman, and Sojourner Truth provided models from the earlier freedom struggles, and leaders such as Marcus Garvey had stirred black pride, especially in the growing urban centers. The flowering of black literature in the 1920s and 1930s and the intellec-tual stature and fire of W. E. B. DuBois gave sharp expression to the passion for justice. When black soldiers returned to the entrenched racism of the segregated South after fighting in a war to make the world "safe for democracy," the social climate was ripe for upheaval.

At the same time, the organizational infrastructure that would support the civil rights movement was growing in the early 1900s. The black churches were the major base, for they were independent from white institutions and thus provided a sphere for black leadership to flourish as well as a deep wellspring of spirituality to energize and provide expression for the struggle. The National Association for the Advancement of Colored People (NAACP), formed in 1909, had mainly pursued justice through the court system. In addition to their legal victories, the NAACP laid a foundation for the civil rights movement through its extensive development of regional chapters and local leadership. As the mass movements began to organize across the South, NAACP chapters and youth councils furnished key portions of the leadership for the emerging local organizations.

The Highlander Folk School, founded by Miles Horton in Knoxville, Tennessee, played an important role in leadership development in the formative stages of the civil rights struggle. Working on the assumptions that education through experience can be a powerful force for social change and that the oppressed can find the solutions to their problems through their own experiences, Highlander sought out potential leaders in black communities as well as from poor white communities and labor groups. They developed education programs to equip students for action in their communities upon return. Furthermore, in the midst of a brutally segregated society, the Highlander School provided a successful model of an integrated community. The list of people attending Highlander workshops reads like a "Who's Who" of the civil rights movement.[31]

In the early 1940s some small nonviolent actions and education events were undertaken by the Fellowship of Reconciliation. James Farmer, FOR's Race Relations Secretary, provided leadership for the events, along with A. J. Muste, George Houser, Bayard Rustin, and John Swomley. They held "Race Relations Institutes" in several northern cities, which involved discussions between blacks and whites followed by actions to integrate segregated public facilities through the use of "sit-ins" before that term was coined. In 1947, white and black pacifists took a bus trip throughout the South called the "Journey of Reconciliation" in the first attempt to desegregate interstate buses. Many of the riders were severely beaten, and the bus was burned by a white mob. Three riders spent thirty days sentenced to prison chain gangs, separated from each other in the segregated system.[32] The Congress of Racial Equality, a civil rights organization eventually headed by Farmer, also utilized the tactics of sit-ins and freedom rides in nonviolent campaigns throughout the South.

The first mass movement occurred in Baton Rouge, Louisiana, in 1953. After months of trying to integrate the buses through a change in city ordinances and facing a strike by white bus drivers when a mild ordinance was passed, the black community initiated a boycott. For ten days in June no blacks rode the buses, causing the transportation companies to lose $1,600 a day. A free "car lift" was organized to provide service to blacks going to work or shopping, following the bus routes but charging no fares. The expenses were paid by the United Defense Leagues set up by the churches to direct the boycott, drawing upon funds donated by individuals and churches at mass meetings held each night. A compromise agreement with the white power structure gave a partial victory to the black community and brought an end to the boycott. Though segregation of the buses was not completely overturned, the Baton Rouge boycott stirred the southern black churches as word spread through the ministers' networks that direct action against white power structures could work through massive mobilization of the black community, especially with the churches as the organizational base.

When Rosa Parks sparked the Montgomery bus boycott of 1955–1956 by her refusal to give up her seat, it was not a spontaneous act inspired by fatigue but rather a protest by a courageous woman who had prepared herself for struggle. Four months prior to her famous action she had attended a training session at the Highlander Folk School.[33] Mrs. Parks was the branch secretary for the Montgomery chapter of the NAACP and had several times refused to comply with segregationist laws on the buses. She said, "My resistance to being mistreated on the buses and anywhere else was just a regular thing with me and not just that day."[34] In a meeting held the night after Rosa Parks was arrested, Jo Ann Robinson, president of the Montgomery (Black) Women's Political Council, suggested a bus boycott. She and other women stayed up all night mimeographing flyers to inform the black community of the boycott. The Brotherhood of Sleeping Car Porters, under the leadership of E. D. Nixon, planned the strategy for the boycott, and in looking for an articulate leader prompted Dr. Martin Luther King, Jr., the new pastor of the Dexter Avenue Baptist Church, to become the movement's spokesperson.

King had been refining his thinking on a Christian philosophy of nonviolence growing out of the social gospel teachings of Walter Rauschenbusch and the Christian realism of Reinhold Niebuhr. When King learned of Gandhi in seminary, he discovered the tactical vehicle for Christian love to bring about transformation on a social scale. The bus boycott in Montgomery provided King his first opportunity to put his ideas into action. After a year of blacks boycotting the buses, walking or using their own taxi system for shopping or getting to work, the public transit system was integrated. Terror tactics of racist whites, including the bombing of King's home, were countered with a consistent and persistent witness of love toward those filled with hate. King proclaimed from his pulpit:

> We shall match your capacity to inflict suffering by our capacity to endure suffering. We shall meet your physical force with soul force. Do to us what you will, and we will continue to love you. We cannot in all good conscience obey your unjust laws, because non-co-operation with evil is as much a moral obligation as is co-operation with good. Throw us in jail, and we shall still love you. Send your hooded perpetrators of violence into our community at the midnight hour and beat us and leave us half dead, and we shall still love you. But be ye assured that we will wear you down by our capacity to suffer. One day we shall win freedom, but not only for ourselves. We shall so appeal to your heart and conscience that we shall win you in the process, and our victory will be a double victory.[35]

Following the Montgomery boycott, Dr. King and other black leaders organized the Southern Christian Leadership Conference. The SCLC was an "organization of organizations," serving as a decentralized political arm for the churches.[36] The civil rights movement was not a centrally controlled uprising, but one of dozens and later hundreds of local organizations that took on particular aspects of the injustice oppressing African Americans. The SCLC provided a connection between these various groups to encourage and strengthen them through the knowledge that they were a part of a larger movement. The SCLC also helped strengthen the internal workings of the local organizations by providing guidance and counsel and the unifying vision of outside figures who had won stature through successful struggle. Perhaps the most significant contribution of the SCLC was the shaping of the mindset necessary for nonviolent struggle. The SCLC trained local people in the politics of agitation, drawing upon black religion by refocusing it from inner piety to outward action for freedom. The importance of the role of preachers like King, Ralph Abernathy, Fred Shuttlesworth, and James Lawson in shaping the driving power of the black church cannot be underestimated.

In 1963, the freedom movement's efforts came to a creative climax. The black community in Birmingham, Alabama, led by Rev. Fred

Shuttlesworth, invited SCLC and Dr. King to come to Birmingham to help with a campaign against the downtown businesses and their segregationist policies. Careful protest actions were planned, beginning on a small scale and building each day. Daily demonstrations and sit-ins were met by arrests by the police, followed each night by rallies at local churches to instruct people on the philosophy and practice of nonviolence and to call for more volunteers for the nonviolent army. When a court injunction was issued against the demonstrators, King and his close associate Ralph Abernathy led the next march and were arrested. While he was incarcerated, King wrote his *Letter from Birmingham Jail,* in which he articulated his basic philosophy and provided an answer to the critique from white church leaders who chided him for being "unwise and untimely." Later in the campaign a decision was made to let the children join in the march, since their freedom was also at stake. The children and local college students faced the fire hoses and the dogs, filling up the jails until there was no space. One young child, no more than eight years old, who marched with her mother was confronted by a policeman who mocked her with the question, "What do you want?" With a fearless bluntness and the courage born of moral clarity and conviction, the girl answered simply, "Freedom."

A key breakthrough in Birmingham occurred during a march led by Rev. Charles Billups. As the marchers approached the police line, Bull Connor, the Commissioner of Public Safety, ordered them to turn back. When they refused, Connor ordered his men to turn the fire hoses on. Many of the marchers were on their knees, prayerfully awaiting the powerful blasts that might injure them. They stared unafraid at the police and firemen, who did not move. Slowly the marchers stood up and began to advance. Connor's men fell back with their limp fire hoses, and several hundred marchers continued on as planned. The days that followed saw more violence against the nonviolent demonstrators, but the business leaders of Birmingham began to negotiate on the issues presented by the black community. When it became apparent that the movement would not go away, that the jails were full and the number of marchers was still growing, and that the nation was filled with revulsion over the police violence against praying and singing people, the business community gave in and opened their lunch counters and employment opportunities to blacks.

Birmingham was the national focal point of the black revolution of nonviolence that summer, but a hundred other communities were engaged in similar struggles. Religious people—black and white,

Protestant, Catholic, and Jewish—joined in the struggle that arose from the depths of the black communities across the country. Many people were killed by racist violence, from Medgar Evers, who was shot in front of his home by a sniper, to four girls killed in their Sunday school class by a bomb attack of the Sixteenth Street Baptist Church in Birmingham. Martin Luther King was the most visible and articulate spokesperson of the movement and stood at the organizational hub of the SCLC network, but he did not control the movement. The civil rights movement was broad-based, with leaders arising from every community and from many different sectors of society. The spirit of nonviolent suffering came out of centuries of oppression and resistance refined by a faith that kept hope alive in the harshest days. It was this faith that provided the love ethic empowering the movement. As Fannie Lou Hamer, who led the Mississippi Freedom Democratic Party in their bid to unseat the fraudulently elected all-white delegation to the Democratic National Convention, said, "Ain't no such thing as I can hate anybody and hope to see God's face."[37]

There were many types of nonviolent actions undertaken throughout the fifties and sixties: freedom rides on buses throughout the South, sit-ins at lunch counters, economic boycotts, voter registration drives, and countless marches, including the 1963 March on Washington for Jobs and Freedom which drew over two hundred thousand people, making it the largest demonstration at the nation's capital at that time. Eventually the national preoccupation with the war in Vietnam, the explosion of riots in northern cities, the "benign neglect" of the Nixon administration, and, in a more positive way, the growing involvement of blacks in local politics resulting from civil rights gains changed the nature of the ongoing struggle for racial justice in the United States. Dr. King's assassination deprived black America and the world of a valiant leader, but from this struggle a generation of leaders was developed in both black and white communities who had refined both the practical understanding of nonviolent action and the philosophy behind it. They would provide the basis for the ongoing justice and anti-war organization in American cities and in rural communities, and Dr. King's writings and actions would instruct and inspire activists in the nonviolence movements that emerged in every continent in the 1980s. Though the prophet is dead, he continues to speak.

One of King's greatest gifts was that of vision: he was a dreamer who opened up the imaginations of many to envision a new way of living together. He dreamed of the "beloved community," in which "sons of former slaves and the sons of former slave owners will be able to sit down together at the table of brotherhood." King had a dream "that my four little children will one day live in a nation where they will not be judged by the color of their skin, but by the content of their character."[38] Nonviolence was not just a tactic to achieve political, civil, or economic goals; it was a means in line with the explicit end of a human community marked by friendship, understanding, and justice. But King was also a dreamer rooted in the pains and injustices suffered by the black community. King refused simply to endure the tension, but rather through nonviolent means brought the tension into the open and created a crisis in order to address the root issues of society's fracturing of the beloved community. As he wrote from the jail in Birmingham:

> Nonviolent direct action seeks to create such a crisis and foster such a tension that a community which has constantly refused to negotiate is forced to confront the issue. It seeks so to dramatize the issue that it can no longer be ignored....I have earnestly opposed violent tension, but there is a type of constructive, nonviolent tension which is necessary for growth. Just as Socrates felt that it was necessary to create a tension in the mind so that individuals could rise from the bondage of myths and half-truths to the unfettered realm of creative analysis and objective appraisal, so must we see the need for nonviolent gadflies to create the kind of tension in society that will help men rise from the dark depths of prejudice and racism to the majestic heights of understanding and brotherhood.[39]

Through the combination of direct nonviolent action and spirituality forged together in the churches and the nightly rallies during the campaigns, King made love and struggle one:

> With every ounce of our energy we must continue to rid this nation of the incubus of segregation. But we shall not in the process relinquish our privilege and our obligation to love. While abhorring segregation, we shall love the segregationist. This is the only way to create the beloved community.[40]

Martin Luther King, Jr., also spoke of the broad interrelationship between the oppressions of racism, poverty, and war. When critics tried to undercut his standing to speak out against the war in Vietnam, he refused to have his moral concern segregated. "Justice is indivisible," he stated. In the war he saw not simply funds for anti-poverty programs being drained away for the military build-up, blacks and whites fighting and dying together who could not sit together in schools back home, poor Americans of all colors fighting against poor Asians, but rather a "far deeper malady within the American spirit."[41] He spoke against "the giant triplets of racism, materialism, and militarism" that left victims across America and across the globe.[42] For King, nonviolence as a Christian required that he act with and on behalf of the victims of these structural injustices in a comprehensive way. He proclaimed he was "increasingly compelled to see the war [in Vietnam] as an enemy of the poor and to attack it as such."[43] There could be no split between peace and justice or between civil rights and disarmament.

King provided some clear guidelines for nonviolence campaigns as he and the SCLC staff worked in struggles in over a hundred cities in the United States. In his *Letter from Birmingham Jail* he listed four basic steps for a campaign: "Collection of the facts to determine whether injustices exist; negotiation; self-purification; and direct action."[44] It was important to select a particular focus, since segregation was such a vast issue. Actions to integrate the bus system in Montgomery or the downtown businesses in Birmingham provided clear, realizable goals that could be articulated to both the oppressive powers and the community of resistance. Negotiation was the preferred approach; it was offered before direct action, and then picked up again later in the struggle to help work out a just resolution.

Key to the transforming power of nonviolence in the oppressed community was the breadth of involvement by people in the struggle. Unlike war, where only a limited segment of the community can directly engage in action, in the nonviolent struggle everyone can be involved, as illustrated by the children of Birmingham. King summed up the qualifications for participation clearly when he wrote:

> In the nonviolent army, there is room for everyone who wants to join up. There is no color distinction. There is no examination, no pledge, except that, as a soldier in the armies of violence is expected to inspect his carbine and keep it clean, nonviolent soldiers are called upon to examine and burnish their greatest weapons— their heart, their conscience, their courage and their sense of justice.[45]

However, King did require training in nonviolence for those who would be engaging in direct action. After the training, usually held at one of the local churches, the volunteer would be required to sign a "Commitment Card" that included a pledge to practice nonviolence through the spiritual disciplines of prayer and meditation, courtesy, and self-sacrifice; to refrain from violence of fist, tongue, or heart; and to follow the directions of the captain of the demonstration. With the careful planning that went into campaign strategy and the training of the volunteer demonstrators, the civil rights movement presented a model of discipline and organization which was able to maximize the movement's impact.

Vietnam and the Anti-War Movement

As the Vietnam war slowly grew in scope for the American government in the 1960s, an anti-war movement also grew, eventually playing a major role in the ending of U.S. military involvement in Vietnam. The movement started with small protests—a few hundred people marching in Washington in 1965, black students distributing leaflets to their classmates about not going to fight in Vietnam when blacks were not yet freed in Mississippi, and a few hundred men refusing to be inducted by the draft. Within a few years, the protests were staggering in scope—two million people demonstrating across the country on October 15, 1969, almost thirty-four thousand men refusing induction, and over 60 percent of the country in favor of U.S. withdrawal.[46] In 1971, twenty thousand people blocked traffic around the Pentagon and throughout Washington, and over fourteen thousand were arrested in the largest mass arrest in U.S. history.[47] Some of the soldiers in Vietnam refused to carry out orders or wore black armbands in protest. Vietnam Veterans Against the War was formed by many soldiers when they returned, and in one demonstration more than a thousand veterans threw their medals over the White House fence and, one by one, made statements against the war.[48]

Students played leading roles in the anti-war movement. Nationwide student strikes briefly shut down many campuses, underground papers proliferated, and graduations turned into protest events. When Henry Kissinger spoke at Brown University's 1969 commencement, two-thirds of the graduating class turned their backs to him. Following the invasion of Cambodia ordered by President Nixon in 1970, protests erupted on a number of campuses. Unarmed demonstrators were killed by National Guardsmen at Jackson State and Kent State Universities. Draft card burning was a vivid symbol of defiance. Many draft-age men went to prison, some for as long as four years, while others fled to sanctuary in Canada. When one eighteen-year old deserter sought sanctuary at Boston University Chapel, a thousand students stood vigil for five days and nights to protect him until, on a Sunday morning, federal agents stormed the chapel, smashing doors and charging through students to take the young man away.

Civil rights leaders made direct connections between the war in Vietnam and the poverty and racism at home. In 1966, six leaders of the Student Nonviolent Coordinating Committee were sentenced to several years in prison after nonviolently invading an induction center in Atlanta. Martin Luther King, Jr., proclaimed from the pulpit at Riverside Church in New York: "I speak as a child of God and brother to the suffering poor of Vietnam and the poor of America who are paying the double price of smashed hopes at home and death and corruption in Vietnam....The great initiative in this war is ours. The initiative to stop it must be ours."[49]

Within the churches, grassroots activists participated in the anti-war movement, while, for the most part, the hierarchies either supported the war or were silent. Radical Catholic priests and nuns whose consciences had been awakened by the civil rights movement or by experiences with the poor in Latin America were often on the leading edge of the protests. Father Philip Berrigan and three friends went into a draft board office in Baltimore and drenched the records with blood. While out on bail, Berrigan, his brother Daniel, who was also a priest, and seven other people removed the records from the Catonsville, Maryland, draft office and burned them in an adjacent parking lot. For four months Daniel Berrigan evaded the FBI, popping up to speak at churches or rallies and then disappearing again, until an informer let the FBI know where he was hiding.

New religious peace organizations sprang up to join long-standing organizations such as the Fellowship of Reconciliation and the American Friends Service Committee. Clergy and Laity Concerned (CALC),[50] a broad-based ecumenical movement, was one of the first groups intentionally to move beyond being merely anti-war to working to establish justice as the basis of peace. CALC dealt with their own institutional dynamics that hampered racial inclusiveness, and worked to be as just internally as they were in their prophetic proclamations. The Sojourners Community grew from the desire of several Chicago-area seminary students to live a radical witness for justice and nonviolence. Their magazine, first called *The Post-American* and then changed to *Sojourners,* became the major communication link between widely disparate parts of Christian tradition that had found common ground in their search for justice and peace. Many denominational peace fellowships were established, some with direct ties to church structures and others initiated from the grassroots.

When the Vietnam war ended, the massive demonstrations faded away, protest music evolved into pop, and the nation turned toward self-indulgence to drown out political shame and military defeat. But there remained a generation of people in the churches who had been socially awakened. In Christian traditions—from evangelical to liberal, from Catholic to black—there were people with roots from the witness of an earlier generation who had experience from the front

lines of the civil rights and anti-war struggles. These people supported organizations that had gone through the various traumas of
development as well as journals and magazines that expressed and
refined their thinking and gave focus to their actions. These Christians were ready to play an increasingly central role in the struggle
for justice and peace within the United States. They had also developed a global awareness that would lead them into solidarity with
the struggles which were about to erupt in the 1980s and 1990s to a
degree unprecedented in world history.

Chapter 4

The People Power Explosion

In August of 1988 I was in Riga, Latvia, in what was then the Soviet Union with a group from the Baptist Peace Fellowship of North America. The new policies of *perestroika*[1] tolerated the expression of Latvian independence sentiment: the colors of the free Latvian flag could be displayed, and a few weeks earlier the first demonstration for independence had taken place peacefully. As we headed from our hotel to a church service, we noticed about thirty or forty Latvians with the red and black flags in front of the statue of Lenin. After a brief ceremony, the group began to march down the avenue toward the Freedom Monument erected to commemorate Lenin's act to grant the Baltics independence. Lenin had said they would be "free forever," a promise Stalin soon broke. As the small band continued toward the Freedom Monument, I saw crowds coming down all the side streets, swelling the demonstration by the hundreds.

We had to go on to the church service, but there we met some of the Baptist young adults who later took us to the demonstration. The formal rally had ended, but thousands were still milling around, talking excitedly and waving flags. We had some pamphlets of the writings of Martin Luther King, Jr., which we shared with the Latvian Baptist demonstrators, and we talked into the night about nonviolence and their hunger for independence. Having stood with those friends at the demonstration for freedom that night, I felt a special joy when I watched the people of Latvia celebrate their independence at the Freedom Monument a few years later, an independence won in a nonviolent struggle against one of the greatest empires in history.

The 1980s and early 1990s witnessed a transformation of the way people engage in struggles for freedom, justice, peace, and human rights. Wars, insurgencies, ethnic violence, and acts of terrorism still occur with horrifying frequency and tragic consequences, but for the first time in human history a global phenomenon of nonviolent movements shook up political powers, redrew national boundaries, and brought hope to millions of people ground down by oppression and poverty. The struggle in the Philippines to overcome the Marcos dictatorship took a name that is also appropriate for the global movement: People Power. Through nonviolent action, ordinary people who had often been locked out of political decision-making processes became agents shaping their own destinies.

As part of this global movement, the teachings and works of Gandhi and Martin Luther King, Jr., spread around the world. Chinese students in Tiananmen Square quoted King. The movie *Gandhi* played in Lithuania in 1987 just as the Sajudis independence movement was beginning. People from all around the world began linking together formally and informally to exchange ideas and practical information about nonviolence, even as the Baptist Peace Fellowship group had done with the Latvian Baptists. The International Fellowship of Reconciliation provided nonviolence training in Brazil, the Philippines, South Africa, Burma, Korea, and a host of other countries. Hildegard and Jean Goss-Mayr of the International Fellowship of Reconciliation were nominated for the Nobel Peace Prize for their efforts to disseminate nonviolence through their workshops. Adolfo Pérez Esquivel from Argentina received the Nobel Prize in 1980 for his work in linking together nonviolent movements as diverse as the Mothers of the Plaza in Argentina protesting the disappearance of their relatives, cement workers in Brazil striking for better working conditions, and Indians in Ecuador struggling for land reform. Pérez Esquivel founded Service for Peace and Justice in Latin America (SERPAJ), a Christian human rights organization with branches in most Latin American countries, to share strategies and information and to provide solidarity among the various groups engaged in their protracted struggles. The theory and history of nonviolence has received more intellectual attention by people such as Gene Sharp, whose three-volume work, *The Politics of Nonviolent Action,* has become a classic in the field. These connections have helped to break down the walls of isolation that have aided repression and have provided new insights, creative examples, and moral solidarity for people in a wide range of contexts as they struggle to better their lives and shape their destiny.

This chapter will provide a survey of the global eruption of people power movements. Obviously, much will be missed in such a short span. The religious movements or movements with Christians playing key roles will be highlighted, not because Christians are better at the life of nonviolence than others but because these stories relate more intimately to this effort to refine and expand an understanding of the history and theology of Christian peacemaking.

Latin America

The nonviolence movements in Latin America can be traced to the Medellin conference of Latin American Catholic bishops in 1968, where they called the church to take the "preferential option for the poor." The Roman Catholic Church, clearly one of the institutions of power and wealth in Latin America, began to get involved in efforts to organize people in poor communities and to address the issues of poverty which they faced. The Medellin Declaration stated:

> It is necessary that small basic communities be developed in order to establish a balance with minority groups, which are the groups in power.... The Church—the People of God—will lend its support to the downtrodden of every social class so that they might come to know their rights and how to make use of them.

The bishops committed the church to active pursuit of organizing in poor communities for the sake of building justice:

> Justice, and therefore peace, conquer by means of a dynamic action of awakening (conscientization) and organization of the popular sectors, which are capable of pressing public officials who are often impotent in their social projects without popular support.[2]

In a follow-up conference held in Puebla, Mexico, in 1979, in spite of rising conservative reaction to liberation theology the bishops reaffirmed their historical break with the traditional Latin American power structures to work alongside the poor:

> Because we believe that a re-examination of the religious and moral behavior of men and women ought to be reflected in the political and economic processes of our countries, we invite all, without distinction of class, to accept and take up the cause of the poor, as if they were accepting and taking up their own cause, the very cause of Jesus Christ.[3]

Liberation theology began to spread in Protestant churches as well as Catholic, describing God's saving work in terms of the historical experiences of oppression, often by following the paradigm of the Exodus of the Hebrew people from Egypt. Christ was envisioned among the suffering poor, or, as Adolfo Pérez Esquivel portrayed him, "Christ in a poncho." Base communities were organized where people studied the Bible and applied its teachings to their own contexts, developing profound grassroots theological-political analysis. Eighty to one hundred thousand base communities were developed in Brazil alone, sparked by the prophetic leadership of Cardinal Paulo Evaristo Arns and Archbishop Dom Helder Camera. These groups became communities of action seeking justice on specific issues of concern to them, including wages, control of land, sanitation, and police repression.

El Salvador

Those in positions of power in Latin America and their backers in the United States responded to these actions with repression, often targeting church leaders and the base communities. One of the early prophetic voices in El Salvador was Father Rutillo Grande. This priest organized Christian peasants to examine their living conditions in the light of the Bible and then to organize unions in order to press for more just living conditions. While leading a peasant march in 1977 he said, "Remember that we are not here because of hatred. We did not come with machetes. We even love those Cains, for the Christian does not have enemies. What we have is a moral force, the Word of God...which unites us and brings us together even if they beat us with sticks."[4] A month later, Rutillo Grande was assassinated. Over one hundred thousand Salvadorans defied the government's state of siege to attend his funeral at the San Salvador cathedral.

In El Salvador more church people were assassinated in the 1980s than in any other country in the world, while the United States provided military assistance and massive funding for their assassins.[5] Salvadoran death squads published the slogan "Be a patriot; kill a priest."[6] Many of the people in the base communities joined armed resistance revolutions in Nicaragua, El Salvador, and other Central American countries. Others maintained nonviolence in their actions but struggled through demonstrations and community development for the same goals of economic and political justice. Military leaders saw them all as a threat, as did the United States government. The Santa Fe Document, produced by advisers to Ronald Reagan, identified liberation theology and the base communities as threats to U.S. interests. The church in Latin America became a church of martyrs not because they were defending the church's rights, but because they were defending the rights of the poor against the wealthy and powerful.

Archbishop Oscar Romero was elected to lead the Salvadoran Catholic Church because of his conservatism, but within a month the archbishop had a radical change of position under the influence of the life and death of Rutillio Grande. As the reign of terror grew under the Salvadoran military, Romero began to speak out boldly. He saw himself as the pastor of those who were being oppressed: "As a pastor, I cannot cease to accompany my people; the people give me strength and encourage me considerably to accept with them the risks of the moment."[7] In his weekly homilies Romero denounced the government's repression and called for justice for the poor. Each service was closed with a litany of the dead, reading the names and circumstances of the killing of the military's victims that week. The popular organizations Romero supported called a general strike on March 15, 1980, that saw over two hundred thousand people participating in the protests. The military responded with more killings. In his homily on March 23, Romero appealed directly to the soldiers and police:

> Brothers, you belong to our own people. You kill your own brother peasants; and in the face of an order to kill that is given by a man, the law of God should prevail that says: Do not kill! No soldier is obliged to obey an order counter to the law of God. No one has to comply with an immoral law. It is time now that you recover your conscience and obey its dictates rather than the command of sin. The Church, defender of the rights of God, of the law of God, of the dignity of the human person, cannot remain silent before so much abomination.[8]

The military government could not tolerate such a direct prophetic assault on the foundations of its repressive power, and the next day Romero was assassinated while saying the Mass. When over one hundred thousand mourners attended his funeral, the violence continued as bombs and guns were fired into the crowds, adding again to the rolls of martyrs.

Throughout the 1980s, about seventy-five thousand Salvadorans disappeared or were killed, a staggering death toll for a country numbering only five million. The vast number of casualties other than insurgents and soldiers killed in the fighting were civilians killed or wounded by death squads, army sweeps of rural areas, and a systematic aerial bombing campaign. In spite of the murders of leaders in the churches, the unions, the human rights organizations, and community groups, new people would step forward in a profoundly deep and broad-based commitment to seeking a just resolution to the conflict. One among many organizations persevering through intense repression was COMADRES (Committee of the Mothers and Relatives of the Disappeared, Political Prisoners, and Assassinated of El Salvador), which worked to publicize killings and disappearances and pressed for an end to human rights abuses. Many of the leaders of COMADRES were themselves killed, imprisoned, tortured, or disappeared, yet new leaders continued to step forward, knowing they too would become likely targets for the death squads.

In 1988, a coalition was formed of over eighty labor and farmworker federations, cooperatives, churches, and professional, university, and

business associations called the National Debate for Peace in El
Salvador. The National Debate organized a march for peace that drew
twenty thousand people. Father Ignacio Ellacuría, rector of the Central American University, addressed the marchers:

> We need to work for peace from the perspective of the suffering of
> the orphans and widows, and the tragedy of the assassinated and
> disappeared. We must keep our eyes on the God of Jesus Christ, the
> God of life, the God of the poor, and not on the idols or the gods of
> death that devour everything.[9]

Father Ellacuría was assassinated in November 1989, along with
five other Jesuits, their housekeeper, and her daughter in a massacre
that finally jarred the sensibilities of the United States Congress,
which had been numb to the tens of thousands of deaths of lesser
known Salvadorans.

During the 1980s about a million Salvadorans became refugees,
some finding their way to the United States, some internally up-
rooted, and many fleeing to Honduras or Mexico. A creative nonviolence movement began in 1987, when refugees decided to go home.
Over four thousand refugees in the Mesa Grande camp in Honduras
crossed back into El Salvador to return to their home villages, many
of which had been destroyed. Thousands more returned in later
"Going Home" repatriations. North Americans accompanied them to
provide some international solidarity and to act as a barrier to the
Salvadoran Army, which resisted the repopulation efforts. The army
harassed the returning refugees, torturing and killing many, but the
refugees were determined to reclaim their homes. They rebuilt their
villages and remained in spite of the efforts to push them back into
exile.

Argentina

The types of grassroots nonviolent resistance witnessed in El
Salvador developed at the same time in many other parts of Latin
America, where poverty and military repression were the major
realities of life. One of the earliest and most poignant nonviolent
campaigns was carried out by the Mothers of the Plaza de Mayo in
Argentina. When the Argentine military seized power in 1976, they
began a "dirty war" against leftist guerrillas, but a far broader
segment of society was victimized as the military seized tens of
thousands of people, often without telling anyone what happened to
them. About thirty thousand people disappeared, most of them under
the age of thirty and not involved in leftist politics. The mothers,
wives, and sisters of the disappeared met in the lines formed at

government offices seeking information for their loved ones, and when they received no help from the government they turned to each other for support.

After a petition calling for redress was refused, the women began a silent, illegal protest. Every Thursday they would walk one by one in a circle in front of the government offices on the Plaza de Mayo in Buenos Aires. Each one would wear a white handkerchief embroidered with the names of missing children or spouses or would carry a picture of one who had disappeared. Each carried a nail, explaining, "This is to remember the sacrifice of Christ nailed to the cross.... We each have our own Christ too, and we relive the sorrow of Mary."[10] These protesters were terrorized by the military; death threats were made against the women and their children still at home. Some of the women also disappeared, and others lost their jobs. Forty of the mothers were arrested and put in the same cell with a dead young man, recalling with horrifying directness the pain of wondering about their lost children. The women were called *las locas,* "the crazy ones," by neighbors who did not want to believe so many people were being killed. Even friends and family sometimes distanced themselves from the women.

In the early years the Catholic Church was not supportive of the Mothers of the Plaza. Only two of eighty bishops gave them any support; few would say masses for the disappeared. In 1980, though, the church began to get involved in the call for human rights, prodded by the prophetic witness and moral clarity of the mothers. Adolfo Pérez Esquivel often marched with them on Thursdays and considered his 1980 Nobel Peace Prize to be an award for the Mothers of the Plaza as well. When Argentina's defeat in the Falklands war and the declining economy weakened the military junta, it was the Mothers of the Plaza who provided the skills necessary to hold the largest of the strikes and demonstrations. As mass graves began to be uncovered and dismembered bodies found in lakes and rivers, the vindicated Mothers of the Plaza became one of the pillars of integrity for the rebuilding of Argentine society following the demise of the junta.

Chile

When General Augusto Pinochet deposed Chilean President Salvador Allende in a bloody coup in 1973, Chile entered a long period of repression under military dictatorship. The Chilean Bishops Conference publicly criticized the Pinochet regime and established a human rights organization to provide relief and counsel to victims of government-sponsored torture. Sit-ins at known torture centers, courts, and other institutions for political repression were used to highlight human rights concerns. Sometimes "lightning" demonstrations were held at busy shopping centers, informing the populace about what was going on, but disappearing before police could arrive on the scene.[11] The church's identification with the poor made it a target for paramilitary violence; priests and lay leaders were killed and church buildings bombed. Protest movements would erupt periodically, led by workers or students or the religious community, and Pinochet would respond with further repression. Eventually the political discontent grew to the point that Pinochet thought he should gain an electoral mandate to stay in power in order to defuse the protests. But the campaign to say "No" to Pinochet was dramatically mobilized by that one word, and in October 1988 the Chileans voted against Pinochet continuing in office. The strength of the nonviolent movement was such that Pinochet had to follow through with the mandate of the vote, and the army surrendered power to a civilian government.

Bolivia

In 1977 and 1978, four women in Bolivia demonstrated what the power of nonviolent courage and creativity could accomplish when their actions ignited a social movement that had a dramatic impact in that country. The women were wives of tin miners who had been fired for union activities and then imprisoned by the repressive military regime of General Hugo Banzer. They had no financial resources, little education, and were supported in their efforts only by their children and a small circle of other wives of imprisoned miners. But they had a deep faith and were politically astute.[12]

The tin miners worked in dangerous and unhealthy conditions for wages that locked their families into grinding poverty. When miners had attempted to unionize in order to better their conditions, leaders were imprisoned, beaten, or exiled. After many attempts to negotiate with authorities, Nellie Paniagua, Angélica Flores, Aurora Lora, and Luzmila Pementel began a hunger strike on Christmas Day, 1977. They demanded an amnesty for political exiles and refugees, restoration of jobs to fired workers, removal of the army from the mines, and freedom for union organizing. Archbishop Jorge Manrique allowed the women to hold the hunger strike in his own residence, which provided both security and a central stage for the political drama, since his residence was only two hundred yards from the presidential palace. The women read from the Beatitudes in Matthew's Gospel and recalled the influence the Sermon on the Mount had had on

Martin Luther King, Jr., and the civil rights movement in the United States.

On December 28, the Feast of Holy Innocents, when the children who were slaughtered by Herod are remembered, the children of the four women joined in the hunger strike. When people protested the involvement of the children, the women announced that the children would be released from the strike when adults would take their places. Quickly the strike grew, with hundreds of men and women joining the fast until almost fourteen hundred people were involved. As the days passed, the tension in Bolivia grew. Fear of army reprisals brought intense international involvement by human rights advocates. Meanwhile, the health of the women was deteriorating. Negotiations had been intensely pursued by church representatives, government officials, and a spokesperson for the women. When the negotiations broke down and some strikers and human rights observers were arrested, the four women announced they would also abstain from water until a settlement was reached.

Finally, the government acceded to the strikers demands in full, providing amnesty for nineteen thousand political prisoners and exiles, reinstating jobs for union activists with full seniority, and giving freedom for all arrested during the strike as well as freedom to organize unions in the future. Though the strike was only one step in an ongoing struggle for justice and freedom in Bolivia, it showed that the weak could employ the weapons of nonviolent action in a way that could bring even a military dictatorship into accountability to the people.

Guatemala

The Guatemalan Indians, though a majority in the country, have been targets of a genocidal war that has now killed over one hundred thousand people. Santiago Atitlán is a Tzutuhil Indian town that used nonviolence to establish itself as the country's first military-free zone. In December 1990, drunken soldiers harassed the townspeople and attempted to drag a peasant from his home. The townspeople tried to prevent them, and the soldiers fired on the crowd, wounding one citizen before retreating to their barracks. The townspeople decided they had enough, so six thousand of them marched to the army compound outside of town. The army fired on the unarmed marchers, killing thirteen and wounding twenty-three. The citizens then gathered thirty thousand signatures calling for the withdrawal of the military from Santiago Atitlán, and presented their petition to outgoing President Vincio Cerezo. He granted their request, and the army units were moved and forbidden to return. At the massacre site thirteen wooden crosses were erected where the people had died. Across the road, the military compound has been dismantled and turned into a cornfield. Thus amidst the brutality of repressive violence, Santiago Atitlán has become a symbol of hope and courage.

On May 25, 1993, Guatemala's new president, Jorge Serrano Elias, attempted to seize power in violation of the nation's constitution. He disbanded the Congress, the Supreme Court, the Attorney General's office, and other parts of the government, hoping to pull off the sort of coup engineered by President Alberto Fujimori in Peru. But the people of Guatemala responded with an immediate and widespread rejection of Serrano's seizure of power. Nearly every sector of society refused to recognize what Serrano had done, and the broad resistance made the army hesitate in supporting the president. The Guatemalan Ambassador to the United States joined the resistance, taking down Serrano's picture and claiming the embassy for the democratic forces.[13] The nonviolent forces of labor, indigenous people, business, and even the government establishment forced Serrano out of power and brought into the presidency a human rights advocate, Ramiro de León Carpio. Guatemala's situation remains very volatile, and killings and disappearances continue. But, with the growth of nonviolence movements and the leadership of people like Nobel Peace Prize winner Rigoberta Menchu, hope is getting stronger that peace and justice will have a chance.

Ecuador

Indians in Ecuador have been struggling for years, seeking land and the recognition of their cultural and political rights. During a number of nonviolent protests in 1991, the Indians were met with violence from government soldiers who fired on crowds and from oil companies whose employees drove trucks into demonstrators who were blockading roads. Then, in April 1992, thousands of indigenous people marched 225 miles from the Amazon region to the capital city, Quito. Many tribal groups joined together, as well as non-indigenous Ecuadoreans. In response to this nonviolence movement, the government partially conceded, giving the Indians surface land rights to two million acres of land they had claimed.[14] Though the concession provided for only half of the land claimed and did not deal with the volatile issue of oil, the nonviolence movement for indigenous rights is a broad and long-term struggle that will shape the life of Ecuador for many years to come.

Eastern Europe and the Soviet Union

In 1989 sweeping revolutions took place in the countries of Eastern Europe, as communism collapsed in Poland, Hungary, East Germany, Czechoslovakia, and Romania. All these revolutions were accomplished nonviolently, except that of Romania. The popular saying is that it required ten years of struggle to bring change to Poland, ten weeks in Germany, ten days in Czechoslovakia, and ten hours in Romania. Though not entirely accurate, this saying captures the snowballing effect of the freedom movements that swept the region. The policies of *glasnost* and *perestroika* ("openness" and "restructuring") initiated by Mikhail Gorbachev certainly allowed more political space for expressions for freedom to arise, but the earlier development of the Solidarity movement in Poland and the severe internal repressions under Honecker in East Germany and Ceausescu in Romania show that the changes cannot be fully attributed to Gorbachev. He was struggling to salvage a system in serious disrepair, and in his efforts he opened the way for movements that wanted to go much farther than he did. Grassroots people took advantage of the political opportunities history presented them, and in many cases created their own opportunities by taking actions to which those in power were forced to respond, usually in inadequate ways.

Poland

Poland's revolution was born in the labor movement amidst workers who were not experiencing the Marxist paradise. The workers were overwhelmingly Christian, and though the church hierarchy initially was cautious in response to the labor movement, the workers were unabashed in their expressions of spirituality in their struggle. On August 14, 1980, a strike began at the shipyard in Gdansk. Daily masses were held and pictures of the Pope were displayed, along with a huge cross. The cross became the symbol for the workers that their struggle must be free of hatred. Under the leadership of Lech Walesa, nonviolence and liberation through truth were set forth as the foundation stones for the struggle. Solidarity, the first independent trade union in a Communist country, was born. Though founded to be a trade union, it quickly grew to be an umbrella organization for a broader democracy movement that included many other sectors of society. Even when a military coup took place to try to crack down on the movement and over ten thousand arrests were made, the people continued their struggle. The leaders of Solidarity sought to live as if Poland was a free country, acting openly and setting up their own extensive network of institutions and channels of communication.

The Catholic Church served both a conservative role of providing stability and a more progressive role of being one place where Poles could speak and act autonomously in their totalitarian setting.

Father Jerzy Popieluszko, a leading figure in the campaign, often preached on Romans 12:21: "Do not be overcome by evil, but overcome evil with good." His parish church, St. Stanizlaw Kostka, seated thousands, but crowds as large as ten thousand would gather outside for special masses led by the outspoken priest. A key issue in developing a nonviolence movement is overcoming fear of the repressive powers, and Popieluszko addressed this fear:

> We have to fight our way out of the fear that paralyzes and enslaves reason and the human heart.... Our only fear should be the fear that we might ever betray Christ for a few pieces of silver. We have a duty to bear witness to the truth of what happened in August of 1980. We have a duty to demand that the hopes of the nation begin, at last, to be realized.[15]

Popieluszko was murdered by the secret police in 1984. Half a million Poles gathered for his funeral, and his martyrdom became one of the rallying points for the ongoing struggle.

Though there was no single climactic moment in the struggle, the persistence of the Polish people, the strength of the Solidarity movement even when its leaders were in prison, and the profound faith of the common people brought about a new reality that the Communist government was finally forced to accept. When martial law was ended in 1989 and elections were held, the Communist candidates were unanimously rejected. Instead, the leaders of the nonviolent movement for democracy became leaders of the state.

East Germany

In East Germany, the Christian churches were the one institution independent of the Communist state, and in the 1980s they became the dissenting voice on issues of peace, human rights, and the environment. Small groups met in the churches to study the nation's moral situation; as the groups assessed the need for peace—which was encouraged by the government—they recognized there could be no genuine peace without democracy and freedom for people to express themselves. The churches then became the training ground for democracy and the small groups became the centers for the resistance. Though they were not as deeply wedded to Christian spirituality as the people of Poland, the church's teaching did have an ethical and moral impact in the shaping of their ideas. It was through the churches and interaction with Western peace movements that nonviolence became a major component of their struggle. Glen Stassen was in East Germany in November of 1989, and commented on the impact of the church on the nonviolent discipline of the demonstrators: "They preached nonviolence, prayed for nonviolence, urged nonviolence on the authorities, and strategized nonviolent action without pause."[16]

Prayer services for peace were begun in churches in 1980 to protest the deployment of medium-range missiles in Europe. People would gather at night in one church to begin their worship and then walk to another church, holding candles. These actions symbolized their ecumenical unity as Protestant, Catholic, and Free Churches, but they also squeezed out the right to demonstrate nonviolently. When they were questioned by police, the demonstrators could respond, "We are going to worship; why is that illegal?"[17] In 1989, when thousands of East Germans responded to the lifting of travel restrictions by fleeing the country, the night prayer services in the churches resumed, and were again followed by candlelight marches. But by then the revolutionary fervor had increased, and thousands joined the marches as they spread to other cities, even though they were sometimes met with water cannons, tear gas, and beatings. Hundreds of arrests were made. By the fall of 1989, millions were involved in these protests all across East Germany. When it became clear that police violence could not stem the rising tide, the Communists began to retreat, first by holding discussions with the demonstrators and finally by resigning the government. The "Revolution of Light" had triumphed.

The churches provided much of the leadership for the new transitional government, since church vocations had been the only sector of society where people could refine their ideas by free discussion and could practice democratic decision-making. Many members of the transitional government and parliament were ordained pastors. In fact, the intense political activity of some pastors created problems for the churches in reconciling the roles of pastor and political leader.[18] Immediately following the collapse of communism, these church leaders also played a mediating and stabilizing role among the various political forces at work in the chaotic situation.

Czechoslovakia

Czechoslovakia had experienced the power of nonviolence earlier than other Eastern European countries, during the 1968 invasion by the Warsaw Pact countries led by the Soviet Union. The Soviets expected to have the situation under control within three days, but prolonged and broad-based nonviolent resistance proved far more difficult for the Soviet military to suppress than a violent revolt. It took eight months for the Soviet puppet regime to be firmly installed. Though the nonviolent resistance failed, it put up a far longer and less bloody struggle than anyone thought possible. Memories of that resistance were the seeds for the "Velvet Revolution" of 1989.

The 1989 Czechoslovakian revolution brought together Christians and humanists in a nonviolent expression of moral power. Vaclav Havel, the playwright who became president, was the leading moral voice for the resistance. He had written an open letter in 1975 proclaiming the "spiritual and moral crisis" underneath the supposedly tranquil society, marked by the erosion of moral standards, repression of dissent and artistic freedom, and order without life. His letter had been widely distributed underground and ignited the gathering of small communities of conscience. Two years later, these groups had brought about the formation of Charter 77, the human rights group that provided the initial impetus for the 1989 revolution. The church as an institution did not play as prominent a role as in the Polish and East German revolutions, but the deep commitment of Czech Christians to express their faith in their lifestyle and a willingness to suffer brought the Christian community into the thick of the struggle. Christian social ethics and humanist morality laid the foundation for a rigorous commitment to nonviolence and a demand that the truth be spoken. "Truth will prevail" became the slogan of Civic Forum, a nonviolent group that was organized in the middle of the revolution and became the main organizational vehicle for the movement.

The revolution was ignited on November 17, when students marched to commemorate a Czech student killed in the Nazi occupation fifty years earlier. With banners calling for the release of political prisoners and freedom, the current regime was clearly being addressed. The marches moved toward Wenceslas Square, singing "We Shall Overcome" and attempting to give flowers to the police. They were attacked by club-wielding police in what was later termed "the massacre," although no one was killed. Two days later two hundred thousand demonstrators gathered in a new demonstration. One soldier told of being ordered to go with his unit to Prague to crush this "counterrevolution." The soldiers talked together and decided to support Havel. "We would not go to shoot our own people. So we just went home. We disobeyed orders."[19] When the Communists shuffled the faces at the top, the protesters came out in even greater force. A general strike was called and within days the government collapsed.

A new government with a majority of non-Communists was sworn in. Not a single person had died in the revolution. When Dr. Jan Carnogursky, deputy prime minister in the new government, was asked about the peaceful nature of the revolution, he listed among its causes "the moral influence of religion and the church."[20]

Romania

The Romanian regime of Nicolai Ceausescu was notorious as being the most Stalinist government in Eastern Europe. Ceausescu was dead within ten days of the first demonstration. Hundreds if not thousands of people died in the violent repression and ensuing chaos before Ion Iliescu seized power and short-circuited the developing revolution. The spark that ignited the uprising, however, was a nonviolent protest by a pastor and his parishioners.

László Tökés was pastor of the Hungarian Reformed Church in Timisoara, located in Transylvania. Hungarians living in Romania had been victims of brutal persecution by Ceausescu, including depopulation of villages in Hungarian areas and enforced hunger. Tökés raised his voice in protest in a smuggled out interview broadcast on Hungarian television, a broadcast heard by people throughout Transylvania. The bishop of the Reformed Church in that area ordered Tökés to pastoral exile in a remote village. Tökés refused to leave and barricaded himself in the manse, protected by his parishioners. Armed men broke in and stabbed Tökés, the church building was vandalized, and a church member was murdered by security police.

The struggle came to a climax December 15–17, 1989. A moving truck came to forcibly evict Tökés, but members from Timisoara churches—Reformed, Baptist, Catholic, and Orthodox, both Romanian and Hungarian—surrounded the church to protect the man whom they viewed as the one person speaking the truth in their repressed society. On the night of the 15th police broke through the human barricade and arrested Tökés as he stood in ministerial robes at the Communion table. More demonstrators gathered, and then the police fired upon them, using machine guns fired indiscriminately from helicopters. The next day, as demonstrators cried "Give us back our dead," the police killed more civilians. The massacres triggered violence across Romania, culminating in battles between the army, which switched to the protesters' side, and the security police. Ceausescu and his wife were seized and executed. The televised view of their bloody bodies brought an end to the fighting as the police force collapsed.

However, the opposition was too fragmented and small to respond quickly to the changing events, and rather than a revolution on the scale of those shaking their northern neighbors, the Romanians watched some of the old incumbent Communists shift around and maintain power, minus the Ceausescu personality cult. The Romanian revolution was missing key ingredients for success that were evident in other Eastern European countries. The Romanians lacked the developed ideology and the time frame for maturation of the movement that the Poles had. They did not have the extensive small group experience of the East Germans. The skills in nonviolent action the Czechs had developed in their resistance to the 1968 Russian invasion were completely absent in Romania. Though the split of the army from Ceausescu was pivotal, the lack of an idea base, small groups, and nonviolent action skills limited the ability of the democracy forces to shape the flow and outcome of events.

The Soviet Union

The break-up of the Soviet Union was accompanied by both events of striking violence and ethnic strife, such as between Armenia and Azerbiajan and in Georgia, and by creative movements of nonviolence, such as in the Baltic states and the response to the attempted coup in Russia in 1991. Mikhail Gorbachev's democratization policies provided new openings for a freedom of expression, such as showing the flags of the independent Baltic states, open selection of legislative representatives, and televising the debates of the Party Congress. But the presence of the Soviet army and the occasional employment of that army in violent actions, as happened in Georgia, did not guarantee that the republics seeking independence would be able to exercise true self-determination.

Lithuania took the lead in the independence movement, where a struggle for independence had been waged against Czarist and Soviet domination for years, frequently employing guerilla tactics. By the end of 1952, over fifty thousand lives had been lost in the fighting and over four hundred thousand Lithuanians had been deported to Siberian camps. The Lithuanians then turned to nonviolent struggle, which entered a dramatic new phase with the formation of Sajudis, the Lithuanian national front, in response to the open door of opportunity presented by Gorbachev's reforms. On August 23, 1988, two hundred thousand people gathered in Vilnius to condemn the Hitler-Stalin pact that destroyed their independence. In 1989 an 800-kilometer human chain was formed throughout the Baltic states by people linking hands, sometimes in ranks three deep.

When the Lithuanians declared their independence in 1990, the Soviets imposed an economic embargo and sent in troops and tanks in a show of force. But the Lithuanians neither gave in nor resorted to violence. One Lithuanian activist said, "Our whole nation has seen that weapons could do nothing in our situation, and only trust in God could help us."[21] The Catholic Church played a key role, both in providing leadership for the movement and in teaching people about remaining nonviolent in the face of all the provocations. Under the barrels of the Soviet tanks and circling helicopters, Vytautas Landsbergis arranged for the Lithuanian Symphony to perform Beethoven's Ninth Symphony as part of a public celebration of independence. The Lithuanians lived under their own definition of political reality and nonviolently refused to accept the authority the Soviets sought to impose upon them. Finally, the Soviets had to accede to the strength of the independence movement and recognize all the Baltic states as free nations.

In Russia, nonviolence played a key role in the downfall of communism. When a coup was attempted against Gorbachev, Russian people refused to follow the instructions of the new self-proclaimed ruling group. Instead, thousands of people put their own bodies between the army and the recognized representatives of the people led by Boris Yeltsin. This struggle was brief and spontaneously organized, but a more extensive citizens' campaign was organized in Kazakhstan by people near the Semipalatinsk nuclear testing site. The Nevada-Semipalatinsk Movement (NSM) was established to bring an end to Soviet nuclear testing. Demonstrations were held in Kazakhstan and in Moscow, and NSM leaders were elected to the Congress of Peoples' Deputies to argue for a test ban. The closing of the test site was another victory for people power against seemingly overwhelming war machines.

Asia

The Philippines

In February 1986, the Filipino people stunned the world by nonviolently toppling the regime of Ferdinand Marcos, who had seemed in firm control of power only days before. Marcos had called a snap election to deflect rising criticism of his rule, but was surprised by the rapid coalescing of opposition sentiment around Corazon Aquino, the widow of Marcos' chief political adversary, Benigno Aquino, who had been assassinated in 1983. Through an election riddled with fraud and abuse, Marcos declared himself to have received the public's mandate for his rule, but the Filipinos knew better and refused to submit.

On February 22, Generals Enrile and Ramos broke from the army with three hundred troops, declaring themselves loyal to the will of the people. Jaime Cardinal Sin of the Roman Catholic Church broadcast a call for the faithful to show solidarity and support by holding a vigil at the rebel barracks. By the end of the second day, forty thousand unarmed people had gathered along the Avenue of the Epiphany of the Saints, including seven thousand nuns and five thousand priests and seminarians. The people brought food for the soldiers, including those troops loyal to Marcos who were sent to crush the revolt. The people greeted Marcos' soldiers with hugs and flowers and tied yellow ribbons (the sign of the opposition movement) around their gun barrels. When tanks were brought in, the civilians blocked the way, kneeling in prayer. "We're sitting ducks," one of the officers said. "They're psyching our troops, and we're all falling down without a shot being fired."[22] With his troops refusing to fire on the protesters, Marcos lost his ability to govern, and fled the country. The dictatorship had collapsed in a seventy-seven-hour nonviolent struggle.

But the roots for the struggle went far deeper. Inspired by the nonviolent stance of Benigno Aquino, the Roman Catholic Church in 1984 had invited Hildegard and Jean Goss-Mayr and Richard Deats of IFOR to conduct extensive training sessions on the principles and techniques of nonviolent action. Out of these seminars a new organization was formed, AKKAPKA, an acronym for Action for Justice and Peace in the language of the Tagalog people. AKKAPKA held seminars throughout the Philippines and developed grassroots groups that provided trained poll watchers and other participants in the opposition movement. When the historical moment came, the people did not react spontaneously, but out of an extensive and intentional development of nonviolent thinking and strategy.

The call for the nonviolent uprising came from the churches. Seven days after the election, the Protestant National Council of Churches issued a statement rejecting the election results, declaring, "In times like these to be patriotic means to direct our loyalty to the people and not to party or to person." Three days later the Catholic Bishops' Conference released a bolder statement, making a clear call to revolution: "A government that assumes or retains power by fraudulent means has no moral basis" and therefore "cannot command the allegiance of the citizenry." The churches thus called for nonviolence as the means for the revolution: "The way indicated to us now is the way of nonviolent struggle for justice. This means active resistance of evil by peaceful means—in the manner of Christ."[23]

The active leadership of church people played the decisive role in shaping the nonviolent character of the revolution in the Philippines. Father Jose Blanco, leader of AKKAPKA, expressed the heart of the philosophy that drove the people power movement:

> Violence addresses the aggressor and the animal instinct in the enemy or oppressor. Nonviolence searches out and addresses the humanity in the enemy or oppressor. When that common humanity is touched, then the other is helped to recognize the human person within and ceases to be inhuman, unjust and violent.... Every single human being has been created as an image of God. To recognize that image and to respect it in an absolute way is to live the Gospel radically and in a nonviolent way.[24]

When the military split, it was the civilians, armed only with the faith and songs, who stood between the military factions, thus preventing the outbreak of civil war and bringing about a peaceful transfer of power.

Burma

Economic hardship and arbitrary actions by the military dictator, Ne Win, sparked student protests in Burma in March 1988. The protests were met with severe brutality by the army and police. Over seven days the students protested, while hundreds died from army bullets, suffocation in police vans, or torture at the infamous Insein Jail. The student protests collapsed, but the anger against the repression smoldered and spread. When Ne Win formally stepped down as head of state, retaining real power behind the scenes, he appointed Sein Lwin as president. Known as "The Butcher," Sein Lwin had directed the repression of the students in March. The outrage of the students and public at large erupted in August, culminating in a general strike on August 8. Demonstrations sprang up all across the country, calling for an end to the dictatorship. The military responded again with extensive violence, gunning down hundreds of unarmed people, including many Buddhist monks who had joined the movement. When doctors and nurses at Rangoon City Hospital joined in a demonstration to try to stem the flow of dead and wounded being brought in, the army fired into the crowd, killing scores more. Yet in spite of the rising level of violence from the army, the number and size of protests and strikes continued to grow.

On August 24 the army appeared to back off. Martial law was lifted and the soldiers returned to their barracks. Demonstrators began organizing grassroots democratic structures to manage everyday affairs in the cities. Pro-democracy papers and magazines sprang up.

Many government functionaries and even some military personnel joined the democracy movement. Democracy forces organized for direct political action as hope grew among the populace. In early September they called for the government to resign, an interim government to be installed, and elections to be scheduled. Instead, on September 18 the army emerged from their barracks in a systematic attack against the population, massacring thousands, arresting students and other demonstration leaders in house-by-house sweeps, and causing thousands of students to flee to the jungle areas under the control of ethnic minority insurgents.[25]

The new ruling junta, with the Orwellian name SLORC—State Law and Order Restoration Council—called for an election. Aung San Suu Kyi, daughter of the leader of the Burmese independence movement, had risen to the fore in the democracy movement, and she became the leading political figure for the opposition, calling for a persistent campaign of nonviolence to restore democracy and human rights to her country. Suu Kyi's politics emerged from a deep Buddhist spirituality of nonviolence. Suu Kyi spoke particularly about freedom from fear:

> Fearlessness may be a gift but perhaps more precious is the courage acquired through endeavor, courage that comes from cultivating the habit of refusing to let fear dictate one's actions, courage that could be described as "grace under pressure"—grace which is renewed repeatedly in the face of harsh, unremitting pressure.[26]

Suu Kyi demonstrated her grace under pressure during her campaign tours around Burma, which violated SLORC's decree against political meetings of more than four people. While marching with some of her supporters, they were stopped by an army captain who threatened to fire if they advanced. Suu Kyi told her companions to turn aside while she walked down the road alone, insisting that only one life be put at risk. At the very last moment a major intervened and countermanded the order to shoot. Suu Kyi and her companions went on with their march and rally.[27]

When the crowds continued to grow at Suu Kyi's rallies, SLORC moved to decimate the National League for Democracy, Suu Kyi's party. Suu Kyi and thousands of other NLD leaders were arrested in July of 1989. Though under house arrest, Suu Kyi continued her nonviolent witness by refusing exile. When the election was held in May 1990, the NLD won over eighty percent of the votes, even in army districts with their repressive restrictions on the campaign. Nevertheless, SLORC refused to turn over power to the elected legislature and stepped up their repressions. When Aung San Suu Kyi was awarded the Nobel Peace Prize in 1991, however, international attention was focused on Burma and pressure for change began to mount.

Many Christians were involved in the democracy movement in Burma, including some who spoke at rallies in Rangoon and other cities, though as a country with a Buddhist majority, Buddhists played a larger role in the protests. Many monks were in the forefront of demonstrations and were among those gunned down by the troops. Months after the crackdown some monks refused to receive alms from soldiers, thus denying soldiers one of the ways Buddhists can earn spiritual merit. The military responded by raiding many monasteries and finally coercing a reluctant submission from the Buddhist leadership. However, the organization, numbers, and spirituality of the monks will probably again rise as a factor in future resistance movements.

China

The Chinese students began their dramatic nonviolent vigil for democracy in Tiananmen Square in May 1989. Political space for less restricted freedom of expression had been opened by the liberal wing of the Chinese Communist party, which had permitted large character posters to be put up on what was called the "Democracy Wall." In the spring of 1989 students began to organize and demonstrate against corruption and for educational reform; when they were ignored by Communist Party leaders, the protests expanded and the issues they raised became more fundamental. Students gathered at Tiananmen Square, where thousands began total fasts. Within days the entire country was electrified by the student protests, as over two thousand dehydrated students were rushed to hospitals, their places at the protest being taken by new students. Strategy was developed through *ad hoc* committees that established links via fax machines to Chinese organizations around the world. The global media attention and a previously scheduled visit to the Chinese government by Mikhail Gorbachev in the midst of the protests increased the sense of drama and the political tension around the demonstrations. Thousands of workers joined the students in Beijing, Shanghai, and other cities.

The government ordered the army into Beijing to restore order. The students, many of whom had been in the army for their mandatory service, made direct links to the soldiers, saying the peoples' army could never attack the people. The soldiers were given food along with political instruction by the students, and the army sent to quell the demonstrations was immobilized nonviolently. Then, on June 3 and

4 another army, drawn from rural provinces and isolated from the news of the student activities over the past weeks, moved into the city. Shooting erupted along the approaches to Tiananmen Square. Changan Avenue became a shooting gallery as the advancing tanks and soldiers sprayed machine gun fire into crowds of students, workers, and other civilians, many of whom responded by throwing stones and bottles. Some demonstrators turned over armored personnel carriers and beat and hanged some soldiers, but most of the carnage was directed by the army at unarmed protesters. The confrontation was most vividly captured on video when a single unarmed man stood in front of a column of tanks, moving to block their way as they tried to go around him. His courage and determination against such superior might symbolized the moral superiority of nonviolence, even as the army regained control of Tiananmen Square and its bloodied side streets. Nobody knows how many people were killed in the crackdown, through estimates range between two and four thousand. Thousands of other students, workers, and intellectuals were arrested, some to be executed and most imprisoned. Many leaders of the democracy movement fled the country and are continuing their efforts abroad to bring democracy to China.[28]

Though the nonviolence movement in China, as in Burma, did not triumph, the story is not finished. The struggle for freedom and justice continues, and through nonviolence both of these movements have shaken powerful regimes that could very easily have dispatched any violent resistance. As the efforts to overcome repression in Poland took many years, activists in Burma and China are prepared for a long struggle in their quest for freedom.

Indonesia

The Indonesian invasion of East Timor has received little attention in Western media, but at least two hundred thousand people—one third of East Timor's population—have died in a campaign that can only be called genocidal. After years of guerrilla resistance, a nonviolence movement has sprung up. Protest banners are displayed. Activists have smuggled documents to Amnesty International detailing human rights violations, even though their actions can lead to imprisonment, torture, and death. In November 1991, the Indonesian government launched a campaign against students, including the raiding of churches that had provided sanctuary for activists. When a rally was held to commemorate one of the men killed by soldiers, the army opened fire on the assembly, killing over a hundred people, while many others "disappeared." Rally organizers have been imprisoned for long terms, though they proclaimed their commitment to the principles of nonviolence and peace.

Thailand

In Thailand, the military—a perennial force in Thai politics—seized power from the parliamentary government in February 1991. As the military tried to reconstruct the government with its own people in key positions, people who were notorious for corruption and abuse, a nonviolent campaign began, heavily influenced by the Fellowship of Engaged Buddhists. The Fellowship had been begun by Sulak Sivaraksa, a Buddhist layman, and through it the core leaders of the demonstrators had received training from Quakers and Mennonites over the previous fifteen years. Though Sulak had been exiled because of his public criticism of the coup, a disciplined cadre of nonviolence leaders remained and was in place to carry on the resistance.

The nonviolence demonstrations for democracy began in the spring of 1992, and included prayer, fasting, and meditation over a period of seven weeks. In May the demonstrations grew, and the military brought in the tanks. Scores if not hundreds of people were killed, and the revulsion of the country toward the military violence was so swift and thorough that the military had to step back and restore the democratic government. The demonstrations strengthened the power of the nonviolence movement, and the people of Thailand continue to seek a government that is responsive to the concerns of the populace and not just the interests of business.

Africa

South Africa

The struggle of blacks in South Africa against the system of apartheid has been a major focal point for world attention. For Christians apartheid represents a shameful legacy, for it began as an explicit doctrine around the Communion table in the mid-nineteenth century.[29] It then became the political platform of the National Party and was buttressed by the Dutch Reformed Church's theology. The leading opposition group against apartheid, the African National Congress (ANC), began as a nonviolent organization, with its leader, Chief Albert Luthuli, receiving the Nobel Peace Prize in 1960. But following the Sharpesville Massacre that same year, where over sixty unarmed protesters were gunned down by police, the ANC initiated a campaign of armed struggle. ANC violence, however, never approached the massive and systematic violence inflicted daily by the white police upon black civilians.

The churches either sanctioned the violence of the government or piously and passively pleaded for an end to the violence without engaging directly in the struggle for justice. Only a few courageous prophetic voices were heard from the church, including those of Desmond Tutu, Alan Boesak, and Beyers Naude. Under the leadership of Archbishop Tutu, the South African Council of Churches began a ministry of seeking justice for the oppressed, which brought it more and more into conflict with the government. Tutu was awarded the Nobel Peace Prize in 1984, yet apartheid was no closer to being dismantled than when Luthuli had received the award twenty-four years earlier.

In February 1988 a major change took place in the struggle against apartheid. The government banned seventeen organizations, including the United Democratic Front, and restricted the largest labor federation, the Congress of South African Trade Unions, from political activity. That effectively left the churches as the only sector of society in a position openly to press the protests. They responded days later with an unprecedented "Parliament March," led by twenty-five church leaders from various denominations and five hundred clergy and laity, who carried a petition demanding the restoration of the right for peaceful protest. They were met with water cannons and police violence, and the church leaders were arrested.

The response of the South African Council of Churches, under their new executive secretary, Rev. Frank Chikane, was to invite IFOR staff for extensive training in nonviolence. They devised a campaign called "Standing for the Truth." The churches were known for their statements against the "heresy of apartheid," but now the time had come to make a stand, even if the church would be martyred. Chikane said, "I've talked about honest and dishonest nonviolent disciples. Dishonest nonviolent disciples raise nonviolence to stop people from resisting the system. But honest nonviolent disciples want to see nonviolent protest working."[30] It was time for the churches to become honest disciples of nonviolence. Their first action began with a church service where young people stood bound and gagged at the altar, symbolizing the plight of the country. Archbishop Tutu went to each one, removed the bonds and gags, and led them in a procession, carrying a huge cross. They then marched to the police station to demand the release of a church steward who had been seized by police during the service. Similar actions were undertaken all across South Africa, maintaining the nonviolent discipline that had been missing in the 1985 protests. In every event, church leaders were in front, dressed in robes and cassocks, along with crowds of parishioners from every walk of life.

The Standing for the Truth campaign was a major factor in changing the political climate in South Africa, bringing about the political pressure that released Nelson Mandela, the leader of the ANC, from prison. With Mandela's release and the lifting of the ban against the ANC, the prospect of a nonracial form of government became a realizable goal, though the white power structure continued to resist the demands of the majority every step of the way. With the formation of a new constitution in 1993, the end of racist apartheid regime was in sight. Nonviolence and the willingness of church leaders to join the people in their struggle broke the logjam of confrontation and repression that allowed apartheid to remain in place.

Other African Nations

Many other African countries have seen nonviolent movements develop, though in very different contexts from that of South Africa. Nations that had achieved independence from colonial powers in the fifties and sixties became one-party states that often slipped into corruption and brutality. African people in many nations began to rise up and demand human rights and participation in the political process. Democracy movements developed in Tanzania, Kenya, Zaire, Cameroon, Mali, Togo and Zambia, Mauritania and the Ivory Coast. Old heroes who had become new tyrants have been forced by a younger generation to allow multiparty elections. Sometimes protests have been nonviolent, even when met by military violence; at other times rioting has broken out. Political pressures have been building in Africa due to the declining economies of many nations and the inspiration of the democracy movements that swept across Eastern Europe.

Liberia's brutal civil war brought the traumas of that country to the world's attention, but prior to that war becoming a news story, nonviolent protests against the oppression and corruption of the government of Samuel Doe had been led by church officials. Methodist Bishop Arthur Kulah led two major peace demonstrations, including one of more than fifteen thousand people who marched in the capital Monrovia to call for Doe's resignation. Pentecostal Bishop Dixon, head of the Liberian Council of Churches, also played a leading role. When the government soldiers met the demonstrators, Bishops Kulah and Dixon knelt in prayer. The soldiers then allowed the demonstrators to pass, and violence was avoided.

Church people in Zaire were active in the efforts to replace the brutal and exploitative rule of Mobutu Sese Seko with a democratic form of government. In September of 1991, unpaid soldiers rioted in Kinshasa and social order collapsed, while Mobutu stayed securely protected in his armored yacht on the Zaire River. Efforts were undertaken to negotiate some form of constitutional rule through the establishment of the National Conference on Democratization, but Mobutu kept undercutting the attempts to establish any government which would limit his power. In February 1992 the frustrated religious community held worship services throughout Kinshasa, then marched on the central square from their various churches. The marchers were met by gunfire and bayonets. Scores died, hundreds were injured. Church leaders have played a key role in presenting the philosophy of nonviolence, including forming a political party with nonviolence as one of its foundational principles. Church leaders have also served in pivotal positions on the National Conference, most notably its chair, Monsignor Laurent Monsengwo Pasinya, Archbishop of Kinsangani. It remains to be seen what the shape of the new Zaire will be, arising from the misery of decades of colonial and dictatorial exploitation.

In Zambia, nonviolent movements brought about the peaceful transition of power from Kenneth Kaunda to opposition candidate Frederick Chiluba. Kaunda was the leader of the independence struggle against the British when the colony was known as Northern Rhodesia. Under Kaunda, Zambia became a one-party authoritarian state. Strengthened by a vibrant labor movement, opposition forces were able to pressure Kaunda to legalize political activity in late 1990 and hold multiparty elections the following year. Even in losing power, however, Kaunda boosted his reputation in history by not only bringing his country independence but also agreeing to multiparty democracy, sparing Zambia the degeneration witnessed in countries like Zaire.

Kenya's Daniel Arap Moi, following the electoral defeat of Kaunda in Zambia, vowed he would crush Kenyan demonstrators "like rats."[31] But Moi's defiance did not stem the rising tide of political activism in Kenya. Protestant and Catholic church leaders led the way in the nonviolent protests, for the church was the only institution that remained in Kenya with the capacity to speak and to challenge the abuses of Moi's dictatorship. They began speaking out against corruption and human rights abuses. Though Moi, a churchgoer himself, accused the churches of being agents of foreign powers, the church leaders made the initial calls for a multiparty system. One of the leading critics of Moi, Rev. Alexander Muge, was killed in a suspicious car accident. In December 1992, multiparty elections were finally held, which Moi won due to the splintering of the opposition. However, it is evident that the political awakening of Kenya will continue, with the church playing a strong prophetic and advocacy role.

The Middle East

The Middle East is one of the most volatile regions of the world, with the Israeli/Palestinian conflict at the heart. Numerous wars have been fought and countless acts of terrorism have been committed. Late in 1987, the Palestinian Intifada began, a new form of struggle by Palestinians in the occupied territories of the West Bank and Gaza. "Intifada" literally means "shaking off," to signify for Palestinians the shaking off of their own fears and then the shaking off of the Israeli occupation. Jean Zaru, a Palestinian Quaker, stated:

> We started by affirming one another. All of us felt empowered. We had a sense of our own inner power and worth, young and old, men and women, rich and poor. This affirmation and morale building helped us to think clearly and gave us the confidence to take creative action.[32]

The Intifada has continued since 1987 and has been a major factor in opening up what opportunities there were for peace in the midst of a protracted and bitter conflict.

Most media presentations about the Intifada have focused on the stone-throwing of the Palestinian youths, but the vast bulk of activities are nonviolent and intentionally so.[33] Palestinians have engaged in strikes, store closings, boycotts, tax resistance, marches, sit-ins, passing out leaflets, fasts, flag displays, and other nonviolent forms of protest. They instituted their own daylight savings time one month before or one month after the Israelis did. Israelis responded by checking watches, breaking them if they were on Palestinian time, making youths stand against a wall for the hour, but the Palestinians continued on their own time. The most significant aspect of the Intifada was rejecting the imposed institutions of the occupation and establishing Palestinian institutions. When the Israelis closed the schools, the Palestinians responded by setting up their own illegal tutoring system in people's homes. The Palestinians began to live in line with the future dream of an independent state, which was more threatening to the Israeli government than the earlier acts of terrorism.

Mubarak Awad is a Palestinian Christian who established the Palestinian Center for the Study of Nonviolence in Jerusalem. He was a leading organizer of the Intifada until the Israelis exiled him. Ironically, when the Israelis threw him out of the country, nonviolence was given a boost in Palestinian eyes: if it made the Israelis that upset, there must be something to it! Palestinians prefer to talk of "civil disobedience" or "civilian struggle" rather than "nonviolence." The passivity in "nonviolence" is accentuated in Arabic, whereas the Intifada is an activist movement to make the physical and moral costs of governing the occupied territories unsustainable.

Beit Sahour, a middle-class, predominantly Christian town in the West Bank, played a leading role in the Palestinians' extensive campaign of tax resistance. In a published statement the townspeople said, "We will not finance the bullets that kill our children, the growing number of prisons, the expenses of the occupying army. We want no more than what you have: freedom and our own representatives to pay taxes to."[34] The people of Beit Sahour redirected their resources into helping families hurt by the boycotts and demonstrations, setting up anti-crime programs and an alternative education system. The Israelis sealed off the town from September 22 to October 31, 1989. Phone lines were cut, property confiscated, businesses and homes destroyed, and tax resisters jailed. One woman pleaded for the army to leave her refrigerator as everything was being taken from her house, saying, "I have small children, and the milk will rot outside." The army officer offered to leave the refrigerator if she would pay 50 shekels (about $20). She refused to bargain, appealing instead to the officer's humanity. When the officer negotiated down to one shekel, tempting the mother to give up her part in the resistance, she defiantly said, "Take the refrigerator!"[35] When the soldiers left on November 1, the residents celebrated, proud of their steadfast resistance. The townspeople have also welcomed Israeli peace activists into their homes and churches for dialogues and joint peace demonstrations.

Among the Israelis there have also been nonviolent movements to oppose the occupation or military service in the occupied territories. Hundreds of Israeli women conduct weekly vigils; these "Women in Black" vigils periodically swell into the thousands and sometimes unite with Palestinian women also demonstrating for peace. When one march of five thousand Israelis and Palestinians was going through Jerusalem, a Palestinian flag was unfurled. Police then attacked the demonstrators with tear gas and clubs. The next day twenty-five thousand protesters forming a human chain were again met by police violence. Though the Palestinians were accustomed to such treatment, it set off a debate among the Israelis about the brutality of their police forces.

Soldiers by the hundreds refused to serve in the occupied territories, sometimes going to prison. *Yesh Gvul* is an organization of resisters from the Israeli military that began in protest of Israel's invasion of Lebanon in 1982 and has continued to organize against the repressions in the occupied territories. Rabbis for Human Rights was organized in response to the Intifada and currently has a membership of about eighty rabbis. They have worked to gather information about human rights abuses and to uphold the principles of freedom, justice, and peace for all the inhabitants of the area. When the Israeli government expelled 415 Palestinians in December 1992, the rabbis organized a food convoy to the Lebanon border for the exiles in their makeshift tent village. The Israeli soldiers blocked their convoy, so the rabbis joined Palestinians in a protest in front of the Knesset building, living in tents for a couple months. Palestinians see the nonviolence of the Intifada as a way to help Israelis as well as themselves. Zoughbi Elias Zoughbi said, "Through nonviolence we not only seek the liberation of our nation, but also seek the liberation of our enemy by alleviating Israeli fears of an inevitable Palestinian state."[36] The hopeful prospects of the Israeli-PLO peace accord are a fruit of what Zoughbi envisions.

Over a thousand Palestinians have died in the Intifada, many shot by soldiers or settlers; many more have suffered the effects of tear gas, including hundreds of miscarriages. Tens of thousands have been hospitalized and more tens of thousands arrested. Some Israelis have been killed by scattered acts of violence, but the systemic violence has been directed at mostly unarmed Palestinians. Many Palestinian youths have thrown stones. Some people argue that the stone-throwing harms the Palestinian cause because it gives the Israelis justification for their repression as well as fueling their memories of the Holocaust. Others see the stone-throwing as an emotional outlet which is nonlethal and has helped maintain a low level of violence in the uprising, since the Palestine Liberation Organization (PLO) issued orders restricting and prohibiting the use of guns in the Intifada. The rise of violent Palestinian organizations such as Hamas have been fueled by Israeli intransigence and violence, but the majority of Palestinians in the occupied territories continue to support nonviolence and the peace process.

The Intifada draws broad support among the Palestinians and has changed the political landscape in the Middle East. In 1987 the Palestinians had been pushed to the sidelines, with the Palestine Liberation Organization battered from the war in Lebanon and the focus in the Middle East moving to the Iran-Iraq war. The forgotten people of the occupied territories seized the leadership, both in tactics and in stating how a way could be found to bring about peace with Israel. The PLO, with some mediation assistance from Jewish peace groups and the Swedish government, made a statement that renounced terrorism and recognized the right of Israel to exist, thus pursing a peaceful settlement to the conflict along the lines of United Nations resolutions 242 and 338. This statement cleared the way for the opening of contacts between the United States and the PLO. The Israeli government also felt domestic pressure from the Intifada, which brought about the collapse of the governing coalition and forced new elections. The Middle East peace talks that began in 1992 resulted in part from the growing strength of the Palestinian community coming from the uprising. At that time Zoughbi said,

> "Whenever I become frustrated and think that the uprising is not gaining any ground, I remind myself that nothing in Israel's forty-year history has stopped it for two years as the Intifada has done. Had the Palestinians used real violence against the Israelis, the Intifada would have been over in a short time." [37]

The Palestinian willingness to endure suffering rather than commit acts of terrorism cracked open a door of hope in that troubled region.

North America and Western Europe

Europeans and North Americans were engaged in the 1980s in massive efforts to halt the nuclear arms race. Two major focal points emerged: a nuclear weapons freeze and the deployment of medium-range missiles in Europe. At the beginning of the decade, the Strategic Arms Limitation Treaty (SALT) II was dying in the face of Congressional opposition in the U.S. The Soviet Union had invaded Afghanistan, and Ronald Reagan came to the White House intent on a massive build-up of U.S. military forces. The planned deployment of Pershing II and Cruise missiles in Europe was threatening to destabilize an already tense superpower standoff in Europe. Fears of nuclear war, aided by loose rhetoric by U.S. officials, swept the U.S. and Europe.

The European peace movements took the lead, mobilizing demonstrations of hundreds of thousands of people against the "Euromissiles." The Dutch Interchurch Peace Council (IKV) had formed in the 1960s as an ecumenical project to address issues of human rights, development, and peace. IKV provided the educational and organizational base for the protest movement against deployment of the Pershing II's and Cruise missiles. They mobilized an international campaign to hold protests in European capitals, the largest of which was four hundred thousand people coming to Amsterdam. Every bus in the country was used to bring demonstrators to the city, and twenty extra trains had to be scheduled. One Dutch activist said, "That is what this movement is all about—ordinary people rediscovering the power to make peace a reality."[38] The Dutch people not only wanted to keep the missiles out of their own country, they wanted to bring an end to nuclear armaments altogether, so in their drive for peace they spread throughout the continent, spurring the formation of other anti-nuclear protests.

The rejection of the U.S. nuclear umbrella by the people of the Netherlands prompted the U.S. Defense Secretary to coin the word "Hollanditis" as the disease of nuclear pacifism. Evidently the disease was highly contagious, as the protests escalated. Women in Great Britain began an encampment at the gate of Greenham Common Air Force Base, where some of the missiles were scheduled to be deployed. In spite of harassment and arrests, the women maintained their encampment over the years until the missiles were finally removed under the provisions of the INF (Intermediate Nuclear Forces) Treaty. The women of Greenham Common inspired similar women's peace encampments at other bases in Great Britain and Europe, as well as an encampment at the Seneca Army Depot in New York, where the U.S. maintained its missile stockpile for eventual shipment to Europe. The encampments maintained a continual witness against nuclear weapons and were the organizing point for demonstrations and civil disobedience actions. Public protests played an important role in shaping the negotiating positions which eventually resulted in the INF Treaty.[39]

In the United States, the idea of halting the arms race was crystallized in a simple idea that captured the imagination of the frustrated public. Why not just stop? Senator Mark Hatfield introduced an amendment to the SALT II Treaty calling for a bilateral moratorium on nuclear weapons production in 1979. The proposal for a mutual, verifiable nuclear weapons freeze as a first step toward disarmament sparked public imagination in western Massachusetts and was presented at town meetings in New England, where American democracy is experienced in its most fundamental and direct form. The freeze campaign spread across the country at the grassroots level through petition drives, lobbying efforts, and demonstrations. During the United Nations' Second Special Session on Disarmament in 1982, almost a million people marched through the streets of New York calling for an end to the arms race.

Organizations proliferated in occupational groups, churches, and local communities. Many municipalities and institutions declared themselves Nuclear Free Zones as an exercise of local sovereignty regarding issues of their own survival. Blockades by canoes and other small craft were organized to prevent Trident submarines from sailing into their bases. A network sprang up along the rail lines to protest the shipment of nuclear warheads from the Pantex factory in Texas to various sites around the country. Thousands of individuals withheld their taxes to protest military spending, some losing cars and even homes when the Internal Revenue Service cracked down on these protesters. Others formed communities, living at low income levels to reduce their tax assessments. Regular vigils and acts of civil disobedience were held at the Nevada nuclear test site and at weapons-producing corporations and research centers. Wherever the nuclear arms system was locally present, activists would bring their presence into the open and make it the focus of persistent campaigns of resistance. The slogan "Think globally, act locally" expressed the strategy to make the global issue of nuclear war a tangible one in local communities.

One of the most controversial forms of protest was the destruction of nuclear weaponry in what were called "plowshares" actions, taking the name from the biblical passage "they shall beat their swords into plowshares" (Isaiah 2:4). The first such action took place at the General Electric Aerospace plant in King of Prussia, Pennsylvania, on September 9, 1980, when eight religious peace activists damaged two Mark 12A nuclear warhead casings with hammers. Other actions were taken against nuclear submarines, missile silos, and other weapons-production facilities. Though some people questioned whether their action was nonviolent, the protesters were usually deeply religious and intentional about avoiding harm to human beings. Their actions were taken in part to apply international laws embodied in the Charter of the United Nations, the Geneva and Hague Conventions and the Nuremberg Principles to governmental activity in the preparation for nuclear holocaust. They compared their action morally to the destruction of the Nazi gas chambers, though most judges refused to allow defenses based on the Nuremberg principles. Cases were tried on narrow grounds of criminal trespass and malicious destruction of property, overlooking the horrifying destructive capability of the weapons systems. Some plowshares activists were sentenced to prison terms as long as ten years.

At the same time as the nuclear arms race was moving into high gear, the U.S. government was also concerned about revolutionary movements in Latin America. In Nicaragua, the Somoza dictatorship was overthrown, and the leftist Sandinista movement came to power. The Nicaraguan revolution brought new hope to movements for justice throughout the region as well as severe consternation to U.S. policymakers. The Central Intelligence Agency gathered the remnants of Somoza's National Guard and other anti-Sandinista elements and launched a brutal war of attrition and terror upon the Nicaraguan people. Civil war broke out in El Salvador, and the United States pumped millions of dollars into the Salvadoran army, whose sweep-and-destroy campaigns and "off-duty" death squad activities forced thousands of Salvadorans to flee the country. Their story was repeated in Guatemala, where the military waged a genocidal campaign against the indigenous people. The proximity of Central America to the United States, the ease of travel, the flood of refugees, and the support of the U.S. government for groups and governments engaged in systematic and horrifying abuses of human rights all worked together to spark an extensive movement of solidarity and resistance among people in the United States.

Tens of thousands of Americans visited Nicaragua and El Salvador to learn about the conflicts. With the credibility gained by first-hand experience, they became the persistent voice against the views presented by the U.S. government. One of the early tours led to the inauguration of a new form of nonviolent action for peace. A tour group from North Carolina arrived in the farming community of El Porvenir in Nicaragua the day after Contras (as the U.S.-supplied anti-Sandinista insurgents were called) had destroyed it. Survivors heard stories of sadistic killings, rapes, and executions where sons were forced to pull the pins on grenades hung round their father's necks.[40] Though Contras were still roaming the area, no attacks were made where the American group was located. This generated the idea of establishing teams of "witnesses" who would rotate into Nicaragua for two-week periods. They would live in the war zones with people under threat of Contra attack, learn from the people about the war, and work alongside them. When they returned to the U.S., they would speak out against the war and provide the hard data and specific stories of the atrocities committed with the funding of the U.S. government. Four thousand Americans participated in Witness for Peace in Nicaragua.

Out of a retreat of religious peacemakers in 1983 a contingency plan was developed to resist an expected U.S. invasion of Nicaragua. It eventually took shape as "The Pledge of Resistance," expressing the commitment by signers to engage in or support acts of civil disobedience in the event of an invasion. Over seventy thousand people signed the pledge, and Pledge groups were formed in four hundred cities and towns in all fifty states. If the U.S. was to invade, the government would simultaneously have to imprison tens of thousands of its own citizens. President Reagan signed the "National Security Decision Directive," which envisioned the president declaring a "State of Domestic National Emergency" and instructing the Federal Emergency Management Agency to round up undocumented Central Americans and U.S. citizens on a classified "Administrative Index" and hold them on U.S. military bases. When U.S. policy emerged as a "low-intensity conflict" of a grinding guerrilla war, targeting mainly Nicaraguan civilians and the economic and social infrastructure, the Pledge network focused on the appropriations votes in Congress to provide support to the Contras. In 1985, when Congress voted to send "humanitarian" aid to the Contras, four thousand people were arrested for committing civil disobedience. In Boston, 586 arrests were made when demonstrators nonviolently occupied a federal building to hold a town meeting protesting U.S. policy in Central America. Similar actions were held across the country.

It is hard to tell what role such massive and visible protests played in shaping U.S. policy, but the policy of low-intensity conflict that emerged was intended to minimize awareness among the U.S. population of its government's involvement in the wars in Central America. The Pledge and other solidarity groups had to shift their strategy to keeping the issue before the American people through education campaigns and demonstrations. In one such campaign "Crosses of Sorrow and Hope" were planted in public parks and the lawns of homes and businesses, inscribed with names of the dead from Nicaragua and El Salvador.

When refugees from the wars in El Salvador and Guatemala began to cross into the U.S., the Immigration and Naturalization Service (INS) began to deport them since they fled from countries whose governments were supported by the U.S. A movement within the religious community sprang up, beginning along the U.S./Mexico border and stretching across the United States into Canada. Churches and synagogues declared themselves "sanctuaries," providing safe havens for refugees. A network developed to help bring refugees across the border and transport them to sanctuary churches or to Canada. Though the U.S. Refugee Act of 1980 and the United Nations Protocol Accords of 1967 say that no person can be deported who has a grave fear of persecution if returned to their homeland, the INS refused to acknowledge the political violence the refugees were fleeing. Stories of relatives being killed, of refugees being tortured or threatened with death, and of the killing of many who were returned did not move the INS. However, thousands of people heard these first-hand reports of the horrors perpetrated in El Salvador and Guatemala as the sanctuary churches became places for the stories to be told to a wider public. Eventually some three hundred churches and synagogues, twenty U.S. cities, and the state of New Mexico publicly declared that they would provide sanctuary to Central Americans fleeing persecution.

The U.S. government harassed churches, sanctuary workers, and peace advocates, infiltrating and secretly recording Bible studies and worship services and using paid informers. Eleven sanctuary workers, including two Catholic priests, a Presbyterian minister, and a Catholic nun, were arrested and tried in Tucson, Arizona. While the judge refused to hear evidence about the conditions the refugees were fleeing, international or U.S. refugee laws, or the religious motivations of the defendants, he did allow a government case based on infiltration, threats, deceit, and nondisclosure of evidence. When seven of the Sanctuary workers were found guilty, Sr. Darlene Nicgorski commented, "If I am guilty of anything, I am guilty of the gospel."[41] The Sanctuary movement continued as long as the refugees came, and during the Persian Gulf war the same concept was used to welcome soldiers and members of the National Guard who refused to go to the Gulf.

Actions in solidarity with the anti-apartheid movement in South Africa were seen in a variety of forms in the United States. On college campuses, demonstrations were held to demand that endowment funds be removed from businesses related to South Africa. A major disinvestment campaign was undertaken to counter the reluctance of the U.S. government to enact or enforce comprehensive sanctions against the apartheid regime. Churches and unions submitted shareholder resolutions calling for corporations to withdraw from South Africa, backed by demonstrations at corporate sites. The South African embassy in Washington, D.C., was a focus for many demonstrations and civil disobedience actions.

Nonviolent actions in one form or another were used on behalf of issues of justice and peace or to resist governmental or community oppression, sometimes arising from a philosophy of nonviolence and sometimes merely as a tactic of protest. Movements in support of the environment, gay and lesbian rights, and Native American rights employed nonviolent action in their struggles, as did pro-choice, pro-life, anti-racism, and labor movements, and campaigns to reclaim vacant housing. Americans have come to use such tactics extensively. A national holiday was declared, though not without controversy, on the birthday of Martin Luther King, Jr., identifying him as a great American who repeatedly committed civil disobedience in response to a vision and moral obligation higher than national law or governing authorities. In spite of the heavy militarization of the U.S. as the world's superpower, nonviolent action has found a strong and extensive place at the grassroots level in the efforts to shape national policy.

Portraits

Martin Luther King, Jr., once said, "In the nonviolent army, there is room for everyone who wants to sign up. There is no color distinction....Nonviolent soldiers are called upon to examine and burnish their greatest weapons—their heart, their conscience, their courage and their sense of justice."[42] Most of the people who participate in nonviolent movements for peace and social change will never get their names in history books, but they are the ones who through their courage, creativity, and community with others in the struggle turn the flow of history in a more positive direction.

In Latin America there is a custom to remember those who have died by someone calling out the person's name and all responding, *"Presente!"* Through the following portraits of several ordinary peacemakers we can say a *"Presente!"* for the millions who have struggled nonviolently, including those who gave their lives so others could know freedom, peace, or a greater measure of justice. All of the individuals in these portraits are Baptists, for those happen to be the ordinary folks I know, but their courage and creativity is found in many people of many faiths in many lands.

Maria Cristina Gomez lived in San Salvador, El Salvador. At one time she had been a Sunday school teacher, helping to develop a new curriculum called *Nueva Vida en Cristo* for the Baptist churches. She was also a grade school teacher, and on April 5, 1989, armed men burst into her school room and dragged her away into a Jeep Cherokee, the favorite vehicle of the Salvadoran death squads. An hour later her bullet-riddled body was found with acid burns on her face. Maria Cristina Gomez had become one of the seventy-five thousand killed or disappeared in El Salvador's civil war.

Why was Maria Cristina killed? Two weeks before her death she had been a leader in the opening of the first women's clinic in El Salvador for victims of rape and other abused women, acting against the violence perpetrated upon women. She also had marched against the violence of the government and the death squads. Friends recalled her as the one who was unafraid to speak out, who took the bullhorn so her voice and message could be clearly heard. When a friend warned her to be careful, Maria Cristina replied, "If we don't talk, who is going to do it?" She helped organize women office workers to form their own union. Wherever she could, she was involved in the struggles for justice amidst the slaughter sweeping El Salvador.

Though she had once been a church leader, her activism drove her beyond the churches. Many in the churches did not want to be associated with her out of fear. One friend said she was "living ahead of her time." But her faith was always the driving force in her work for justice. At a memorial service a statement was read by one of those whose life she had shaped: "If someday I die in this war, don't cry; remember that I'm only a seed that someday had to die to grow up and give fruits of love and peace. Now I feel stronger because I have more hands next to mine working for peace."

Maria Cristina Gomez: *Presente!*

When Moscovites woke up on August 19, 1991, to learn that a coup had ousted Mikhail Gorbachev, **Vera Kadaeva**, a Ukrainian woman who works as a volunteer in a Christian charitable ministry, teaches the Bible to children in a Moscow orphanage, and writes letters of encouragement to prisoners, thought that opportunities for free religious expression would be closed. When she saw the tanks and armored personnel carriers on the street, she took some New Testaments and went to Red Square. Vera approached the soldiers and gave them each a Testament. "I have come to you with a word from God," she said. "'Thou shalt not kill.' That is God's commandment. Life is a gift from God, and no one has a right to lift a hand against his neighbor."

Then she approached the tank crews surrounding the Russian Parliament building where Boris Yeltsin was protected by a barricade of buses and people standing arm-in-arm. Vera went directly to the soldiers with the same message, telling the officers, "God says to you, 'Thou shalt not kill.' This commandment is above all your orders." As she saw the young soldiers, she remembered her own nineteen-year-old son who had just been called up to join the army. She prayed, "Lord! Save these children! Save Russia!" Vera's prayers and the prayers of many others were answered in large part through the nonviolent courage of those who put themselves between the tanks and the targets of the coup plotters.[43]

Phineas Mapheto, pastor of the Mpho Baptist Church in South Africa, had a son imprisoned at Robbin Island for his activities in the black freedom struggle. The ferry to Robbin Island was segregated, with whites sitting on the top deck with the view and blacks seated below. Though there was no law for this segregation, the regulations stated that one had to obey the master of the ship, who consistently carried out the apartheid policies on board. After many visits to the island, the sixty-year-old Mapheto decided that "God does not expect this from me. God does not expect this from any of His children. I will refuse to follow this policy."[44]

Rev. Mapheto seated himself on the ferry's upper deck, which created consternation among the ship's crew. When the shipmaster was informed, he came with an authoritative chill in his voice and warned Mapheto that he must leave or else be removed from the ship. Mapheto politely refused: "The only reason why you are asking me to move is because I am black." He offered to go below if all others on the upper deck would move also. By now the confrontation had attracted the attention of the other passengers, and in frustration the shipmaster finally walked away.

On the return trip, Rev. Mapheto again proceeded to the upper deck to find a seat. A young white official yelled at him, and Mapheto calmly rebuked him, "If you want to speak with me, you must address me as your elder." When ordered to go below, he again bluntly confronted racism as the only reason for the order and refused to obey. After more sputtering and fuming, the ferry officials finally gave up, leaving Rev. Mapheto to enjoy the upper deck for the entire journey.

Ken Medema is a Christian musician from San Francisco. He participated in a demonstration against the nuclear weapons design program at the Lawrence Livermore Laboratory. His involvement in the protests began when his church, the Delores Street Baptist Church, let a group use their facilities to hold nonviolence training. As he and his wife listened to the sessions, they "heard gospel" and decided to form an affinity group in their congregation to join in the movement.

The early morning of the next demonstration found Ken sitting on the road, blockading the laboratory, and he was one of the first arrested. His blindness added extra anxiety to the confusion of arrest and imprisonment. He was separated from his friends and put in a cell with other demonstrators whom he did not know. In the cell, he was engulfed with loneliness and questions about whether he had done the right thing. But in the three days leading up to their arraignment, the prisoners got to know each other, and their time in jail was spent teaching one another and singing. Ken taught them a song he had written, "When All the World Shall Feast Again," to the tune of "When Johnny Comes Marching Home." The entire group was processed as one case, and they asked Ken to present their statement to the judge. Ken led them in singing their witness about their action:

When all the world shall feast again, hurrah! hurrah!
Injustice and crime are ended then, hurrah! hurrah!
All the valleys with joy shall ring
And all the folk on earth shall sing,
And we will not rest till all the world shall feast!
When weapon is plow and hoe again, hurrah! hurrah!
Shall justice like rivers flow again, hurrah! hurrah!
And darkness shall be done away,
And we shall see salvation's day,
And we will not rest till weapon is plow and hoe!

Far from the deep loneliness and anxiety of three days earlier, in the courtroom Ken and his fellow prisoners experienced a profound sense of solidarity and exultation. After a long silence the judge said, "Well, what do you make of that!" They were sentenced only to the three days they had spent in jail.

Nan Zing La is a pastor who earned his living as a lawyer in Myitkyina, in the Kachin State of Myanmar, formerly known as Burma. He was the first Kachin to graduate with a law degree. He was imprisoned in 1958 for political activities, then released in 1963 when Ne Win granted an amnesty for political prisoners. During the 1988 democracy uprising, Nan Zing La called for democratic reforms at the demonstrations in Myitkyina. When the military crackdown came, he was arrested and not allowed any visitors for over six months. Amnesty International adopted him as a prisoner of conscience along with Bawk La, another Kachin Baptist pastor/lawyer who had given speeches at the demonstrations. Nan Zing La was released along with many other political prisoners in mid-1992 as part of conciliation gestures offered by the military regime, due in part to negotiations under way through Baptist individuals seeking to mediate between the army and ethnic insurgents.[45]

Sixto Ulloa served as a Sandinista representative in the Nicaraguan legislature. This layman played the key organizing role from the Nicaraguan end for Witness for Peace. He was excited at the idea of a prayer vigil for peace in the very middle of the war, and worked tirelessly to arrange logistical matters between the North American delegations and the Nicaraguan government and church leaders. Sixto was also involved in producing the prophetic pastoral letters from the Nicaraguan Baptist Convention to churches in the United

States and to President Reagan, letters which called for an end to the U.S.-sponsored Contra War against Nicaragua.

George Williamson was in Iraq as part of a Fellowship of Reconciliation delegation in the months just prior to the outbreak of the U.S. war against Iraq. This Ohio pastor attended an event to commemorate Iraq's dead from the Iran-Iraq war, and was appalled to see a highly militaristic ceremony involving hundreds of children in military dress chanting slogans of hate: "Yes, Yes, Saddam! No, No, Bush!" George broke out of the bystanders and began walking down the ranks of children like an officer reviewing the troops. One reached out to touch his hand, and George warmly took it. The soldiers orchestrating the demonstration didn't know what to do and helplessly followed him as he shook hands with the children.

The chanting faded away as the children began practicing English phrases, "Good morning!" and exchanging names with George. When he pulled out some Polaroid photos of children in his church to give to these Iraqi children, all semblance of order evaporated as the children eagerly reached for the pictures. Then a child called out, "I love you." George called back, "I love you." Touching and hugging, he made his way down the tangled lines of children to a new chant of love.

When he was finished and the soldiers had restored "order," George went off by himself to weep, knowing that for one brief moment he and the children had risen above the war fever which gripped their two countries and sought to make them enemies. They had built a bridge of love amidst the chants of hatred.

As Ceausescu's army closed in on Rev. László Tökés in Timisoara, Romania, **Daniel Gavra**, a young railway worker, joined the other young people who were making a human chain around Tökés's church to protect the besieged pastor. He showed his own pastor, Rev. Peter Dugulescu, the bundle of candles he had brought for the demonstrators to keep lit throughout the night. When the army fired on the unarmed crowd, Daniel was severely wounded and had to have a leg amputated. He told his pastor from his hospital bed that "he had lost a leg, but he had lit the first candle."[46]

Of such heroes, heroines, and martyrs is the nonviolent army composed. Whatever presidents, prime ministers, and secretary generals may have to say about shaping a new world order, these people are also stating their case, often so strongly and so clearly that the political leaders have no choice but to accede to their call for true peace with justice.

Chapter 5

Conflict Resolution
and Mediation

The ring of the telephone jolted me out of my immersion in a theology book. I was in seminary, taking a heavy load to make up for some lost time in my academic plan. Our pastor, Merle Pimentel, was on the other end of the line. My wife, Sharon, had come to his office that night, and Merle told me I had better get down there quickly. Without a clue as to the problem, I headed for the church. Sharon was very upset as I took a chair next to her. Merle related to me that she had come to him to talk. Our young marriage was under severe stress because of our heavy schedules, especially my overload of studies and student pastoring, plus the half-time job I had so I could pay tuition. Our relationship was the easiest part of our life for me to overlook under all the demands of my other commitments. For weeks Sharon had been trying to break through my academic concentration to let me know how absent I was becoming to her, but I wasn't picking up her signals. Even her blunt messages were shrugged aside. Finally, in desperation, she had turned to our pastor.

Having a third person involved in the process was at first an embarrassment to me; I had to admit then that Sharon and I had a serious problem and needed some help. As one who tends to avoid conflict rather than face it with creativity, I needed Sharon's bold action to confront me with the stress I was bringing to our relationship through my choices. I had developed a mental grid to explain away or devalue all Sharon's messages to me about the issue, but a third person—our pastor in this case—was able to get through to me because of his objectivity and my respect for and trust in him. He related to me what Sharon had said to him, and I heard it in a fresh, though painful way. When she then spoke directly to me, my interpretive grid had been disengaged so I could finally hear what she had been trying to say.

Once the communication had been opened up, Sharon and I then had to deal with the situation and the new (at least for me) perception of the state of our relationship. Again the third person helped us.

Merle helped us analyze our situation so we could see the choices we had made and the choices still before us. He suggested actions we could take to change our situation and to work directly at strengthening our relationship. Though we ended up not taking many of the options he suggested, his concrete proposals released our creativity to work on our own mutually satisfactory solutions. I dropped some of my courses and took an extra year to go through seminary, and we made more time to be together as a couple. Not only did our marriage survive graduate school, it was strengthened as a result of our self-discoveries through the conflict and through the assistance we received from our pastoral mediator.

Conflict has been resolved with the help of mediators throughout human history and in a variety of cultures and forms. In China, Confucius developed a system of dispute resolution by means of "moral persuasion and agreement rather than sovereign coercion."[1] Every year hundreds of thousands of disputes are settled using Confucian mediation. Each culture develops its own ways of handling conflict—some more through avoidance, but others through a wide range of methods to bring about resolution. In the past two decades, however, some significant changes have happened on a global scale that are bringing conflict resolution and mediation into the center stage of peacemaking. In this chapter the development of those changes as well as the basic principles of conflict resolution and mediation will be briefly explored, along with some stories of how mediation has helped to end wars in various countries.

The Development of Conflict Resolution as a Discipline

Conflict resolution as a discipline has roots in many fields of study and practice. The development of the social sciences brought the rigor and scope of academic methods to an exploration of human behavior, and conflict as a basic and universal human experience has been examined in the fields of anthropology, psychology, sociology, and political science. Ways that human individuals and social groups deal with conflict, from making war to creating a process for resolution, have become major topics of inquiry. But the academic field is still in its early stages of development. Dean Pruitt, purposefully exaggerating a bit, assessed the state of the discipline in this way:

> Negotiation and mediation today can be likened, in some respects, to medicine and surgery in the early eighteenth century. Both sets of fields consist almost entirely of practitioners; training is heavily in the direction of the apprenticeship; practitioners operate more or less intuitively, each with a distinct individual style; and the litera-

ture in both fields, to the extent it exists, derives mainly from the experience of practitioners and consists largely of aphorisms about appropriate action.[2]

Since Pruitt wrote those words in 1986, the field of conflict resolution has continued to grow as a scholarly pursuit, with more work being done on theory and analysis both to reflect on past experiences and to provide more thorough training for practitioners in dispute resolution.

A second major stream in the development of conflict resolution has come from the field of labor/management relations. Following the process of industrialization in the West, workers began to organize to improve their lot. In the early 1900s a number of industries took steps, in response to union concerns, to set up grievance procedures. The coal industry developed an umpire system, and one Chicago factory instituted an impartial chairman system to handle disputes. The labor union struggles of the 1920s and 1930s led to collective bargaining processes that were supported by the National Labor Relations Act and various institutions to undergird negotiations. In World War II, the National War Labor Board was established to maintain stability in industry during the war through mediation and voluntary arbitration in labor disputes. Then in 1947 the federal government became directly involved in mediation through the formation of the Federal Mediation and Conciliation Service. Many of these practitioners in labor mediation and negotiation have gone on to provide leadership in the broader field of conflict resolution.

The racial conflict in the United States in the 1950s and 1960s also provided experience for conflict resolution. In conjunction with the nonviolent campaigns for civil rights, negotiations were conducted in hundreds of communities regarding racial justice and community peace issues. The 1964 Civil Rights Act established the Community Relations Service, which served to mediate racial conflicts without litigation. In many communities multiracial coalitions were established to try to diffuse conflict and address the underlying issues of racism and economic injustice.

Police departments have also worked creatively through negotiation to resolve potentially violent confrontations peacefully. Many departments have developed negotiation teams to handle hostage situations, achieving a high rate of success in terminating such incidents without further violence. Domestic quarrels are one of the most explosive situations a police officer has to face. When the New York City Police Department set up a Family Crisis Intervention Unit trained in third-party intervention, they saw a dramatic reduction in the number of officers killed while responding to domestic crisis calls.[3] Many police departments have also assigned community relations officers to work with neighborhoods in conflict management and community negotiation in order to diffuse potential crisis situations.

The legal system in the United States has formally incorporated "alternative methods of dispute resolution" as a part of its efforts to reform itself in the face of an explosion of litigation, court costs, and case backlogs. The alternative methods address some of these problems by removing cases from the courts to mediation or arbitration settings. Local bar associations and courts have set up community centers staffed by lawyers and other professionals, many of whom are volunteers, to deal with lower level disputes and face-to-face conflict resolution. Sometimes in nonviolent crimes the victims can receive compensation, and the offenders are forced to see up close the harm they have done as well as pay back the victim and the community, under the supervision of the local court. These resolutions cut the time necessary to handle a case, clear up the court docket for more serious cases, and provide an opportunity for solutions to be found to conflicts that are more likely to solve the problems than straight adjudication on the points of law.

Schools have also been prime sources of conflict resolution development, focusing on training children in effective ways to handle conflict and to mediate conflicts with peers or younger children. The Neighborhood Dispute Resolution Program in San Francisco began working in conflict management training in the early 1980s in a program which eventually spread to over one hundred schools. Children were taught role playing, assertiveness, listening skills and mediation techniques. Then teams would work on the playgrounds to help their classmates in the conflicts that involved pushing, name calling, and other disputes at that level. Principals in the participating schools reported that they spent less time on discipline, the atmosphere of the school was calmer, and teachers could give more time to teaching. The children found their new skills helpful not only at school but also at home. Schools in the Republic of Ireland and Northern Ireland have also adopted conflict resolution curricula, with a view to addressing the larger violent social conflict in which many generations have grown up. The hope is that a new generation with extensive skills in nonviolent means of handling their disputes will be able to address more creatively the issues that have plagued Northern Ireland with political violence for so long.[4]

International diplomacy has also been an area of growing understanding of conflict resolution. With improvements in communications and travel, efforts to build international community have become both necessary and possible. Following World War I, the League of Nations was established as a forum to address international issues, but with the rise of fascism the League's fatal flaws were revealed. In spite of its inabilities to stop the militarism of the fascist states, the League of Nations was a step in the right direction. Out of the ashes of World War II a stronger international body was formed, the United Nations. It, too, had critical weaknesses, which were revealed in the deadlocks in the Security Council when the vetoes of the antagonistic superpowers blocked effective action in any conflict in which they had a stake. However, major progress was made in developing international structures for handling conflict in ways that are nonviolent. The International Court of Justice in The Hague, the Netherlands, has become an important forum for adjudication of international disputes. Regional and global treaties have been negotiated in a wide range of issues, from disarmament to the access to resources in the sea and Antarctica. In many cases, conflicts have been resolved before they got to the explosive stage. In addition to the United Nations, regional bodies such as the Organization of African Unity, the Organization of American States, and the Association of South East Asian Nations have helped countries find common ground, work on issues of mutual benefit, and resolve many conflicts through negotiation. Though the number of wars has remained horrendously high, the infrastructure to work on international conflict resolution has been under a careful and steady process of development as modern technology has shrunk the size of our world.

A final stream feeding into the new interest in conflict resolution has been the work of religious communities, particularly the historic peace churches. For many years Quakers, Mennonites, and the Church of the Brethren have developed conciliation ministries. They have aided churches in conflict, provided their services to communities, and in some cases played important roles in seeking resolutions to international conflicts or civil wars. Quakers organized communication assistance missions to bridge the gaps between warring parties in the Middle East following the 1967 war, between India and Pakistan in 1965, and during the Nigerian civil war in 1968–1970.[5] The Mennonite Central Committee's Conciliation Service has provided conflict resolution training and mediation assistance as an expression of their peace witness. Conflict resolution has entered many of the mainline denominations and ecumenical structures through the fields of pastoral counseling, peace advocacy, and organizational management. The consistency of the goals and techniques of conflict resolution with the Christian gospel has provided both a spiritual basis for conciliation practitioners and practical methods for the person of faith seeking to bear witness to God's love in a tangible way.

The development that has so dramatically energized the field of conflict resolution in recent years is the linking of all these different areas of human interaction. Academic institutions have developed courses and even degree programs in conflict resolution. Special institutes have been established at some universities, bridging the diverse disciplines of sociology, psychology, political science, criminal justice, and business administration. The studies being undertaken draw from innovations and experiences in these various areas and then feed back to them, causing a cross-pollination of ideas. After an extensive campaign by a broad coalition of advocacy groups, the federal government established the U.S. Institute for Peace, popularly known as the "Peace Academy," a decentralized network of academic institutions and research centers established to study peacekeeping, peacemaking, and conflict resolution. Professional journals and newsletters devoted to the field have proliferated, disseminating ideas and case studies to the growing circles of interested academics and practitioners. Professional organizations have been established, with rapidly growing memberships among institutions and individuals, and at times hosting large national conferences to address rising issues in conflict resolution.

The opportunities presented in the development of conflict resolution point to a world with a greater measure of peace. Through broad-scale education and participation in conflict resolution processes there is the possibility of a profound change in American society and perhaps in the global community. The adversarial and confrontational mode of operation which has dominated in the West may shift to include more collaboration and partnership in problem-solving. This change in consciousness about how conflict can be approached is more possible now because training in the skills for dealing creatively with conflict is more broadly available. If the majority of American school children could learn specific conflict resolution skills, the social impact as they matured and moved into positions of leadership in society would be profound. Whether they were in the role of a conflicted party or mediator, they would be better able to express themselves, listen to others, develop a range of alternatives, and negotiate, and they would have a sense of empowerment in the face of conflict. Instead of being armed with handguns, people would be armed with the skills to untangle the knots of their conflicts.

On a societal level, education in conflict resolution might help a culture that currently enshrines as heroes the tough males who solve conflict by defeating—usually killing—their opponents to learn to lift up new paragons of virtue, those who use courage and creativity to help resolve conflicts peacefully. Success might be redefined from beating one's opponent to working out mutually satisfying agreement. On a global level, as we face a shrinking planet with increasing pressures from population and resource limitations, conflict resolution skills and structures will be absolutely necessary for the maintenance of human existence. With the weapons of mass destruction humanity now has available, an inability to resolve conflict can lead to extinction. Conflict resolution provides a ray of hope for finding the way to the next stages of our political and social development as human beings.

But there are risks in the field of conflict resolution, risks which must be addressed if the hope it brings is to be actualized. Conflict resolution which does not address fundamental power imbalances among conflicted people or groups can become an instrument of injustice. It can be a way to negotiate the survival of the status quo and undercut necessary reforms or even revolutions. Traditional power structures are better organized and have more access to resources than those which are poor or have been denied access to power for one reason or another. Negotiation can lead to a resolution which provides a superficial solution that might make survival more viable for the disadvantaged party, but which fails to attend to the deeper issues which caused the conflict in the first place.[6]

Furthermore, in mediation apart from the legal system, the codification of important social norms may be lost because the challenges to current laws or precedents never get recorded and adjudicated. Conflict resolution could then become a ghettoized form of "second-class justice," where those who cannot afford lawyers resort to alternative systems unprotected by the sanctions available from the courts. On the other hand, conflict resolution could be used by those with power and money to set up their own system for handling disputes, leaving the public courts in an increasing state of decay and dysfunction.

Finally, there is the question of moral wrongs becoming negotiable. In the wars following the breakup of Yugoslavia, for example, is it acceptable for a conflict resolution process to confirm the results of ethnic cleansing? If negotiation achieves a substantial ratification of gains made by a policy of genocide against other ethnic groups, then serious questions need to be raised about whether that negotiation was a tool for peace or for injustice. If the latter, then conflict is not resolved, but is merely suppressed by negotiated means.

These and other risks in the field of conflict resolution will be examined more fully at the close of this book. Though there are concerns to consider, conflict resolution has nonetheless brought about significant achievements for peace and reconciliation and provided deeper understanding of the tools and processes for the peaceful handling of our disputes, and it is to these processes that we now turn.

"Getting to Yes": Processes for Conflict Resolutions

Roger Fisher and William Ury of the Harvard Negotiation Project gave a tremendous boost to the field of conflict resolution with the publication of their book *Getting to Yes: Negotiating Agreement Without Giving In.*[7] Their bestseller was translated into eighteen languages and has become a classic work on negotiation. A brief summary of their methodology will serve to present some of the major themes in conflict resolution in general.

Fisher and Ury contrast *positional* negotiation with *principled* negotiation. Positional negotiation refers to the widely practiced form of bargaining, in which each side makes an offer neither expects to be the final one, and they then trade and compromise until a middle position is found. For example, if I want to buy a house offered for sale at $160,000, I might offer $135,000 and eventually settle on $150,000. Positional bargaining is often inefficient, since it creates an incentive to stall for a better deal rather than come to a solution. It also puts the relationship at risk, since the negotiating parties are in a win/lose situation: for one party to gain, the other has to make a concession. Such a process can also produce unwise agreements, because more attention is paid to each side's position and the investment of ego in defending it, rather than in resolving the underlying needs. The more parties that are involved in a conflict, the more complex and the less resolvable the conflict is through positional negotiation.

Principled negotiation pursues a different course, in which negotiation is based on the merits of the situation. Fisher and Ury identify four basic points in the process of principled negotiation. The first is to separate the people from the problem.[8] In most conflict, people's emotions are tangled with the problem. The first step is to separate the people from the problem, not by ignoring the people inside of the conflict but by dealing with the problem directly and intentionally. Misperceptions can be addressed by having each side "try on" the other side's point of view, working to at least understand if not agree. If both sides can have a stake in the outcome, they are more likely to be involved constructively in the process. The proposed solutions should also be consistent with the values expressed on each side, so that each can "save face" and feel positive about the outcome. Emotions can be acknowledged explicitly and labeled as legitimate, but with certain rules set about emotional display during the negotiations. Perhaps it can be contracted for one person or side to "let off steam" at a time while the other side makes no comment or response. Communication is vital to the negotiating process, but it should be assumed that the other side will almost always hear something different from what was said. Active listening, rephrasing what was heard, and trying to speak in the terms used by the other side all aid the communication process. The work done on the relationship can shift the parties from an adversarial mode to being partners in problem-solving, working together in a hard process to find a fair agreement advantageous to each side.

The second component of principled negotiation is to focus on interests, not positions.[9] Because "the basic problem in a negotiation lies not in conflicting positions, but in the conflict between each side's needs, desires, concerns and fears," these interests are the moving causes in the conflict, which positions taken in negotiations attempt to protect. But for every interest there is a range of positions which can satisfy it, and some underlying interests on opposing sides are compatible even if their stated negotiating positions are not. To uncover the interests, one can ask why the particular decisions embodied in each side's position have or have not been made. Each side will have multiple interests, and in the process those interests need to be identified and acknowledged specifically as part of the problem. Adequately addressing the other's interests is part of the negotiator's problem, because a solution will not be found if it is not satisfactory in some way to both parties. This will help the conflicted parties move beyond blaming each other for what happened in the past. Instead, the parties can look forward to options that will address the interests each side has.

The third component of principled negotiation identified by Fisher and Ury is to invent options for mutual gain.[10] If a negotiator is thinking in terms of a single answer to the conflict, then a range of alternatives is foreclosed which might have addressed the underlying interests. Fisher and Ury recommend inventing options to widen the range of solutions to select from and also to create partnership in the process of shaping the solution. It begins by separating *inventing* from *deciding*—what is commonly known as "brainstorming." In a setting separate from the decision-making process, every conceivable idea is elicited without any criticism. After the brainstorming, the most promising ideas are highlighted, with everyone working to improve them, perhaps incorporating elements of some rejected ideas. In the process, options with contrasting strengths and weaknesses can be evaluated, and the options that provide the best mutual gain can surface.

Fisher and Ury's fourth component of principled negotiation is to insist on using objective criteria.[11] Battles of will are costly, so a critical phase of the negotiation is to develop agreed upon standards of fairness to assess the viability of any proposed solution. The principles should be agreed to first, then all issues can be weighed in terms of those principles. Fisher and Ury call for negotiators to use reason and to be open to reason, but not to give in to pressure. Bribes, threats, manipulation of trust, or intransigence should be countered with requests to explain the reasoning behind what is being done, with objective criteria relevant to the issue.

The principled negotiation process that Fisher and Ury present can be practiced by both negotiators and mediators. The goal is to find win/win solutions that will result in a genuine resolution to the conflict. Even if one party is not interested in following this approach, the process can be turned around by consistent and persistent refusal to play the positional game and by pressing to deal with interests and objective criteria.

Another factor to consider in the development of processes for peacemaking is the cultural context. The technical field of conflict resolution has developed in the context of Western culture and sometimes is built on assumptions that may not be valid in other settings. Conflict resolution in North American is based on formal patterns of handling conflict, with designated settings for the process, an objective or even professional mediator, and face-to-face, issue-oriented communication in an effort to achieve agreement on the issues. But other, more traditional cultures, both within the United States and in other countries, are more relationship oriented, and the resolution of conflict requires the presence of interpersonal relationships built upon trust with the mediator. In these cultures the conflict issues need to be discussed in the context of the connections of people and history and hopes to the core situation. Communication may be handled in these cultures more appropriately through indirect means, using a mediator as a surrogate, rather than talking directly to the opposing party. Because of the vast differences in cultural assumptions, it is important for anyone involved in cross-cultural mediation to be sensitive to the frame of reference for the disputants.

John Paul Lederach calls this sensitivity "contextualization," or knowing "how a person interprets the boundaries and context of the conflict":

> Contextualization helps the mediator decide on an appropriate style and format of intervention. She must be sensitive to the parties' potentially varying preferences for formality, temporal organization, pace and sequencing in the different phases of the interaction, and to the context of their wider social networks.[12]

With appropriate sensitivity, the mediator can access the strengths and resources for conflict resolution from his or her own culture and elicit the strengths and resources of the disputants and their culture.

In one such contrasting culture, for example, John Paul Lederach identifies some of the basic elements to conflict resolution in Latino culture from his own study and experience in Central America, providing a very different perspective from that presented by Fisher and Ury.[13] Lederach found that *confianza*, *cuello*, and *coyuntura* are fundamental to resolving conflict in Central American settings. *Confianza* means "trust" or "confidence," and refers to having people upon whom one can depend, thus providing the relational security necessary for a mediator to be acceptable. *Cuello* refers to "having connections," networks of people who are important in dealing with the problem. Whereas Anglo models of conflict resolution value a neutral outsider in the mediating role, the valuing of *confianza* and *cuello* indicate the importance of a mediator who is closely related and trusted by the disputants in Latino models. *Coyuntura* refers to the larger context, including the timing of events. It indicates a sensitivity to relationships and fluid situations that must be ripe before resolution can take place. *Coyuntura* requires the mediator to be available and present on a long-term basis, so that at the right time the conciliation work can proceed. Lederach's study in Central America shows that each culture has its own variations in style and structure and relational assumptions in handling disputes, and these dynamics will need to be identified and built upon by anyone seeking to aid in a conflict resolution process.

Mediators

Mediators have functioned in resolving conflicts in a wide variety of ways in the rich range of human culture. David Augsburger holds that conflict is "intentionally and productively—or automatically and dysfunctionally—triangular" in structure, drawing in other people as victims, allies, or mediators.[14] When the third party refuses to form a coalition with the conflicting party, the neutral person or group can assist those in conflict to find a mutually satisfactory solution. The addition of the third party dramatically increases the power of the opposing parties to change through providing the support and stability necessary to deal constructively with the relational imbalances of the conflict. The third party can help maintain symmetrical relationships of motivation, power, communication, and tension levels, as well as a balanced sequence of movement through the stages of negotiation.[15] Cultures institutionalize mediation in various ways, but recent developments in the study of conflict resolution and the growing interdependency of the global community have brought mediation to new levels of necessity and understanding.

Governments often play mediating roles. Henry Kissinger's shuttle diplomacy in the mid-1970s sought to bring peace between Israel and Egypt, a process which was taken to a partial resolution by President Jimmy Carter at Camp David. Sometimes governments have tried to work in partnership as a mediation team, as the Soviet Union and the United States did in a failed attempt to convene Arab-Israeli talks in Geneva, also in the 1970s. Superpower mediation, however, is seldom neutral, for the government acting as mediator also has its own policies that it is trying to advance. James Laue points out that although many American diplomats would say they are mediators in certain conflicts, structurally they are advocates representing the interests of the U.S. government.[16] If resolving a conflict between two other nations improves the situation for the mediator, then the convergence of interests can be beneficial to peace. Governmental mediators also have access to resources to provide infrastructural support to negotiations and can use promises and threats to add to the stake the parties have in a successful resolution.

Nations which are not superpowers may also provide mediation services because of their regional relationships and respect from both sides. President Oscar Arias Sanchez of Costa Rica played the role of convener and mediator in a peace process among five Central American nations that were affected by the civil wars in three of those nations. Costa Rica itself had camps of Nicaraguan Contras in their border areas, refugees fleeing war zones, and political pressure from the United States to bring Costa Rican policies in line with U.S. regional objectives. Because of Costa Rica's own relative stability and efforts to remain neutral, Arias was able to work with his counterparts in the other Central American countries to set up a process which ultimately led to peace accords in Nicaragua and, indirectly, in El Salvador. Earlier, Panama, Mexico, Venezuela, and Columbia established themselves as the Contadora Group to pursue Central

American peace. The United States undermined this mediation effort (which had produced a draft treaty) because it was outside the U.S. policy framework. Yet in spite of U.S. diplomatic subversion, Contadora laid a basis of diagnosis and an outline for resolution that were later picked up by the Esquipulas process, which Arias mediated.[17]

In the efforts to resolve the civil war in Sudan in the early 1970s, mediation was undertaken by church groups, while Emperor Haile Selassie of Ethiopia played a critical role at two stages in the peace process in strengthening the mediation and providing a site for the peace talks.[18] Ethiopia again played a mediating role in 1993, hosting peace talks among the various clan factions in Somalia in efforts to end the fighting in their neighboring country. The difficulty of any government involvement in mediation is that political considerations—either internally for the mediating government or in the relationship between the nations—can further complicate the situation by adding other factors into the already complex nature of the conflict. Many countries do not want to even consider the mediation of another government if the conflict is a civil war, on the grounds that the matter is an internal affair and their sovereignty would be compromised.

An alternative to governments serving as mediators has been the use of intergovernmental agencies as conveners of peace processes. The United Nations, most often through the office of the Secretariat, has been called upon to mediate many international conflicts, such as the Iran-Iraq war, the war in Afghanistan, and the decolonialization wars in Africa, as in Namibia. More recently, the U.N. has shifted its stand against involvement in civil wars and has assisted in mediation where its services were requested to end internal conflicts. The U.N. mediated the peace talks between the government and insurgents in El Salvador, which led to the peace accords signed in early 1992. Regional intergovernmental agencies have also played roles as mediators. The Economic Community of West African States (ECOWAS) mediated a cease-fire between guerrilla factions struggling for power in Liberia after the factions had brought down the government of President Samuel Doe. ECOWAS also sent a multinational peacekeeping force that occupied the capital of Monrovia and opened channels for relief supplies to be brought into the country. However, an interim government set up by ECOWAS then became yet another faction in a dispute that has yet to be resolved.

Non-governmental organizations (NGOs), including religious bodies, have also been utilized extensively for mediation. In a conflict where official communication has become impossible or politically problematic, and where diplomatic channels are suspect because of concerns for national sovereignty, NGOs can serve as a link between warring groups or governments. These unofficial diplomats have as their major strength their independence from governmental bodies. They are not accountable for national policy and they do not have to report to any government, though they often make reports to relevant parties in order to keep them appraised of their activities. The non-official links between sides through NGOs can provide an opportunity to test new ideas or proposals at minimal risk. If the response is positive, then the peace process can advance. If the response is negative, or if the opposing side seeks to manipulate the proposal for its own advantage, then the process can be disavowed without a loss of face. The NGO mediator must understand this function and remain vulnerable to failure; an NGO third party is more likely to assume that risk of failure in order to bring peace than governments are. NGOs can also bring new perspectives into a conflict since they are not limited by the interpretation of facts or policy objectives in which governments get invested. NGOs can confront negotiating parties with facts they wish to ignore or press for them to face issues they are refusing to address adequately. NGOs can also pursue a variety of channels for informal contact in order to establish an atmosphere supportive of a formal negotiation process.

Recently an NGO and a government combined for one of the most remarkable mediation efforts in history. A peace accord between Israel and the Palestine Liberation Organization was finally achieved by secret talks in Norway that allowed the parties to get around some of the political barriers that had proved insurmountable in the public glare of the Middle East peace talks. A research team from the Norwegian Institute for Applied Science had developed contacts with Israeli officials while working on a report on conditions in the occupied territories. Norway's State Secretary for Foreign Affairs, Jan Egeland, followed the work of the research team. When one of their key contacts, Yossi Beilin, was made deputy foreign minister in the new Israeli Labor government, Egeland visited Beilin to suggest that Norway could help create a secret contact between Israel and the PLO leadership.

In January 1993, the first meeting of unofficial representatives of the two sides was set up by the Norwegian research team at a secret location in Norway. The atmosphere was very positive and the talks picked up momentum when Israel repealed the ban on contacts with the PLO. The remote suburban home of Marianne Heiberg, a member of the research team, and Johan Jorgen Holst was the host site for the small delegations to share. In this intimate setting, with Egeland and Holst (who became Foreign Minister in April 1993) mediating, the agreement was reached that burst into public view that fall. The relaxed atmosphere was even assisted by four-year-old Edward Holst playing at the delegates' feet while the negotiations were taking place.[19] The low-risk contacts of an NGO, the willingness of a neutral government to assist, and the offering of a quiet context in which to grapple with the complex issues were all critical elements of the process to achieve this peace accord.

NGOs are often dismissed—sometimes rightfully so—as amateurs. They have limited access to information and may not understand various governmental policies. If NGOs are humble enough to recognize their limitations and shape their roles accordingly, this weakness can be turned to a strength, while arrogant amateurism, particularly in cross-cultural mediation, can complicate the conflict and deepen the distrust. NGOs may also be manipulated and used for purposes of disinformation. Communication can be used to achieve greater understanding between the parties, or it can be a tool of deception. The limited knowledge of many NGOs makes them more liable to manipulation by one side or the other. Jesus' admonition to "be wise as serpents and innocent as doves" (Matthew 10:16) is sound advice to mediators inserting themselves between deadly adversaries. NGOs can also be used by one or both sides as a tactic to delay getting involved in formal talks. If an informal channel can be strung along with risk-free promises, a government or opposition group can give an appearance of wanting peace while stonewalling any genuine process. Any NGO in a mediating role will have to be aware of these risks and assess whether the process it is involved in is a valid one or not. If it is being used to extend the conflict and not resolve it, the NGO should break off or perhaps use the threat of disengagement to force a more serious negotiating posture from the offending side.

Through their work in the process of mediation in the resolving of conflict, John Paul Lederach and Paul Wehr have learned to distinguish between two differing types of mediators.[20] The most commonly recognized is the "outsider-neutral," a third-party who by his or her external position is viewed as more objective and who can impartially moderate the negotiation process. Once the conflict is resolved, the outsider-neutral usually leaves. The "insider-partial" mediator, on the other hand, is much more intimately connected to the conflict. The effectiveness of the insider-partial is based on his or her relationship to the conflicted parties over a long period of time, which has led to trust being established. The insider-partial mediator emerges from the setting of the conflict, and so brings to the mediation process a knowledge of that setting and the people involved. The insider-partial mediator also is respected not for any technical expertise in conflict resolution, but because of who he or she is in the network of relationships in the context of the conflict. Local religious leaders are often in a strategic position to play this role, for they bring a vital network of relationships and a moral stature to a conciliation process that few other NGOs can claim. In many of the peace processes, a team of insider-partials and outsider-neutrals was developed, bringing the strengths of both identities to the negotiations. This was the case in Nicaragua, Burma, and El Salvador.

Whatever their identity, mediators can undertake a variety of activities to assist the parties in their conciliation efforts. They can gather information, for example. Many times the facts of a conflict are so clouded by rhetoric and propaganda that it is difficult to know what is really going on. Gathering information and making objective reports can help each side have an opportunity to make its case, correct misrepresentations, and perhaps hear how it sounds to outsiders. Mediators can also assist in communication, especially when the emotions of the conflict have made it very difficult for the parties to communicate directly. Mediators can carry messages, interpret actions or interests, or establish procedures for more formal discussion. In that context mediators can "float" proposals from one side or the other, or put forward their own proposals to overcome gaps between the negotiating parties or to provide a more concrete focus for discussions. Whatever the specific role is which the mediator plays, it should be agreed upon by the parties early in the process.

We will now turn to two cases of mediation involving church leaders as "insider-partial" mediators and one case in which a government served as mediator in a peace process. The events in Sudan illustrate the involvement of an international church body. The events in Nagaland did not get much world attention due to the remoteness of the region and the Indian government's policy to isolate the area, but they show the importance of an insider-partial mediator at critical stages in a peace process. The Arab-Israeli negotiations at Camp David mediated by U.S. President Jimmy Carter and his staff are an example of a government serving as mediator. Carter's work was motivated in large part by his own Christian convictions, and the successes of Camp David became a springboard for his later work as an NGO leader in conflict resolution.

Solitary Chinese democracy demonstrator stops a line of tanks on Changan Avenue, approaching Tiananmen Square on June 4, 1989. (Associated Press/Wide World Photos)

Henry Hodgkin of Great Britain (left) and Friedrich Siegmund-Schultze of Germany, co-founders of the International Fellowship of Reconciliation. (IFOR archives)

Muriel Lester, founder of Kingsley Hall in London and IFOR's traveling secretary. (Courtesy of FOR)

Hildegard Goss-Mayr conducting a nonviolence training session in Ivory Coast. (IFOR archives)

Mahatma Gandhi setting out on his famous Salt March in which he nonviolently defied British colonial control of salt production. (IFOR archives)

Rosa Parks sitting on a Montgomery bus, the action that sparked a yearlong nonviolent campaign to end segregation in that city's transit system. (BPFNA archives)

Members of the FOR's "Journey of Reconciliation" prepare to board a bus in violation of Southern Jim Crow laws in 1947. (Courtesy of FOR)

A teacher from the Highlander Folk School in Knoxville, Tennessee, an institution to educate local activists to work for social change. (Highlander Research and Education Center)

Fred Shuttlesworth, Ralph Abernathy, and Martin Luther King, Jr., marching for civil rights in Birmingham, Alabama, in 1963. (Birmingham Public Library, Dept. of Archives and Manuscripts)

Israeli Women in Black during their weekly vigil calling for an end to the occupation of the West Bank and Gaza. (Buttry)

Members of Witness for Peace carry "crosses of sorrow and hope" with names of civilians killed by Contras in Nicaragua. (Vicki Kemper, courtesy of *Sojourners* magazine)

Mothers of the Plaza de Mayo silently march in Argentina to bear witness to their disappeared loved ones. (Eric Wheater, courtesy of *Sojourners* magazine)

Illegal conference of Polish human-rights activists in basement of the Church of God's Mercy in Warsaw in 1987. (Polly Duncan, courtesy of *Sojourners* magazine)

Women from the antinuclear encampment at the Greenham Common Air Base in Great Britain surround the base in an effort to halt deployment of cruise missiles in Europe. (Courtesy of FOR)

A Soviet Baptist hands copies of Scripture to tank crews facing the Russian Parliament building in Moscow during the August 1991 coup attempt, urging them not to kill anyone. (Boris Yablakov/Foreign Mission Board, SBC)

George Williamson, president of Baptist Peace Fellowship of North America, disrupting militaristic demonstration with Iraqi children during peace trip to Iraq. (Courtesy of George Williamson)

(From left) Desmond Tutu, Alan Boesak, and Frank Chikane refuse police orders to disperse following a march and prayer rally against apartheid in South Africa. (Adil Bradlow, courtesy of *Sojourners* magazine)

The Berlin Wall crumbling before the assaults of nonviolent citizens. (Courtesy of Doug Hostetter)

Polish people in silent vigil at the grave of martyred Father Jerzy Popieluszko. (Polly Duncan, courtesy of *Sojourners* magazine)

Ken Sehested of the Baptist Peace Fellowship praying at a vigil at the Nevada nuclear test site. (Paul Obregon, courtesy of BPFNA)

A Burmese student refugee in Bangkok calls for human rights while undertaking a hunger strike, displaying photos of Aung San Suu Kyi. Sign reads: "Give me no food; give me no water; give me human rights." (Source unknown)

(From left) Saboi Jum and former President Jimmy Carter with the author during discussions of the Burma peace initiative. (Buttry)

Saboi Jum with a child soldier at the insurgent headquarters inside Burma. (Saboi Jum)

Negotiations in insurgent headquarters during Burma's civil war in 1980.
(Saboi Jum)

Members of the Burma Peace Committee are welcomed by Brang Seng of the
Kachin Independence Army at insurgent headquarters in a remote area of Burma.
(Saboi Jum)

(From left) Saboi Jum, author,and Brang Seng meeting in an Asian hotel room in secret negotiations for a peace process in Burma. (Buttry)

Author (standing) speaking at negotiation session with leaders of insurgent groups in Burma's civil war. (Buttry)

Demonstration in San Salvador sponsored by the National Debate for Peace. Banner reads: "The product of justice will be peace, the fruit of equality perpetual security." (Courtesy of Debate Nacional por la Paz en El Salvador)

Edgar Palacios (front) speaking at a National Debate for Peace rally in El Salvador. (Courtesy of Debate Nacional por la Paz en El Salvador)

President Carter, President Sadat, and Prime Minister Begin shake hands at the Egyptian-Israeli Peace Treaty signing ceremony. (Courtesy of the Jimmy Carter Library)

Delegations from opposing sides of the Ethiopian civil war meet with Jimmy and Rosalyn Carter for peace talks at the Carter Center. (Rick Diamond, Atlanta, Ga.)

Nicaraguan President Daniel Ortega (left) and American Baptist missionary Gustavo Parajón discussing peace issues in Nicaragua. (BPFNA archives)

Longri Ao, Baptist leader who mediated peace efforts between Indian government and Naga insurgents. (Board of International Ministries, ABC)

Author at memorial for United Nations peacekeepers from Austria killed during peacekeeping operations in Cyprus. (Buttry)

Participants at the National Urban Peace and Justice Summit flash their new peace sign: "Together, not separate." (Jeffry D. Scott/Impact Visuals)

Prayer vigil in Kansas City in support of the "Gang Summit" and an end to neighborhood violence. (Jeffry D. Scott/Impact Visuals)

Union coal miners block coal truck during the Pittston strike. (Brian Jaudon, courtesy of *Sojourners* magazine)

Adolfo Pérez Esquivel of Argentina, the 1980 Nobel Peace Prize recipient for his work linking nonviolent struggles across Latin America. (James Forest, courtesy of IFOR)

Miguel Tomás Castro, pastor of Emmanuel Baptist Church in San Salvador, El Salvador. (BPFNA archives)

Jonathan Buttry (author's son) in front of National Rifle Association headquarters at rally to end handgun violence. (BPFNA archives)

The World Council of Churches and the Civil War in Sudan

In the early 1970s the World Council of Churches (WCC) and its related organization, the All Africa Conference of Churches (AACC), played a mediating role that culminated in an agreement ending a civil war that had raged in Sudan since 1955.[21] Sudan emerged from the colonial era with two distinct regions in the country. Northern Sudan was the larger and more developed region. Ethnically, the people in the north consider themselves Arabs and are predominately Muslims, with strong ties to Egypt and Mecca. Southern Sudan was poorer, with a less educated population ravaged by centuries of slave trading. The people there are non-Arab blacks from a number of different tribes who are primarily Christians and animists.

British colonial policy exploited the differences between north and south while doing little to create a unified sense of national identity. The tensions created by the movement toward independence were dramatically increased by the economic, educational, and racial differences between north and south. A series of incidents, including a mutiny of southern troops in 1955, resulted in an armed insurgency in the south. For a long while the guerrillas were small in number and disorganized, but northern repressions added to the insurgents' numbers. The civil war grew from scattered actions to persistent insurgency and government counter-insurgency campaigns. Over five hundred thousand people lost their lives in the war as its intensity and scope grew.

When Colonel Gaafar al-Numeiri came to power and Joseph Lagu became the head of the Southern Sudan Liberation Movement (SSLM), an opening developed for peace initiatives. Numeiri was interested in peace talks with the southerners, and Lagu had established unified control over the once-fragmented insurgency. The World Council of Churches, in partnership with the All Africa Conference of Churches, approached the government about exploring the possibilities for peace as a step in providing relief for the hundreds of thousands of refugees displaced by the war. Informal contacts were also made with Sudanese exiles who stayed in communication with the insurgents. After initial positive responses from the government, the Presbyterian Church in Sudan sent a formal invitation for a joint AACC/WCC team to visit Sudan to investigate the situation. The delegation met with government officials and offered their services as intermediaries for a process of reconciliation. The government agreed, and plans were made to contact the leadership of the SSLM. General Lagu agreed to talks, and a preliminary meeting between the two sides was set up in Addis Ababa, Ethiopia.

The mediating team was made up of Burgess Carr, the General Secretary of the AACC; Kodwo Ankrah, Africa Secretary for the WCC's Commission on Interchurch Aid, Refugee and World Service; Leopoldo Niilus, a lawyer who directed the Commission of the Churches on International Affairs of the WCC; and Samuel Bwogo, General Secretary for the Sudan Council of Churches. As a team they had different sympathies toward the parties which helped establish bonds of trust to the two sides. They utilized their diverse skills in a way that divided up the labor, yet maintained a strong cohesiveness among the mediators. Carr also used symbols which strengthened his authority as intermediary. He dressed in traditional African attire, wearing the headdress and carrying the stick of a chieftain. He drove a big car with the AACC flag on it, something which might have been viewed as ostentatious in another setting but in this context gave him added credibility to the two delegations.

When the talks began, the atmosphere was tense and hostile; whenever tempers flared in this first face-to-face encounter, Burgess Carr would remind the participants of the purpose for their meeting and the urgency of working on peace. Later in the day the two sides had dinner together, which generated a more informal atmosphere. The delegates began to build relationships, which enabled them to talk more comfortably with each other. At the preliminary talks enough trust was established between the two sides regarding the seriousness of the other's intentions that they set a date for official negotiations to begin. Agreement was also reached on the principle of one Sudan, placing on the agenda for the official talks the issue of ensuring that southern interests would be sufficiently addressed in the negotiated accord.

During the peace process the AACC/WCC team assisted the SSLM side in their logistics and in providing some direction so they could be more realistic and technically prepared. The insurgents lacked the experience, resources, and diplomatic stature to enter the process on an equal basis with the Sudanese government, so the AACC/WCC team helped the SSLM in preparation of their statements by communicating the range of government options, paid their travel expenses to the negotiations, and helped broker legal assistance for the SSLM delegation. Though their assistance could have been viewed as favoring one side, the government was not offended since the AACC/WCC aid was helping the process as a whole to more effectively address the central issues to the war.

Between the preliminary talks and the official negotiations, a tragedy took place that was turned into a trust-building transforming initiative. A Sudan Airways plane crashed in SSLM-held territory. The survivors were handed over by the SSLM forces to the Red Cross, including those who were government officers in uniform. Seriously injured survivors were given medical treatment by the rebels until they were sufficiently recovered to be moved. The media in Khartoum, Sudan's capital, discussed the story in a favorable way, helping to alter the public opinion of the SSLM as "terrorists": if the rebels were human after all, perhaps they were capable of making sincere agreements.

In February 1972, the official negotiations were opened in Addis Ababa. When Emperor Haile Selassie of Ethiopia indicated that it was not possible for him to chair the talks, representatives from the two sides selected Burgess Carr to "moderate" the talks, thus putting the church leaders into a role more pivotal than just serving as communication links and facilitating the meeting. Carr began with a sermon from the Old Testament and the Koran, setting a tone for the work and moving the talks to a search for peace based on the moral principle of reconciliation, rather than a compromise based on the perceived weaknesses and strengths of the two sides. Throughout the process Carr gave sermons and led prayer sessions that appealed for both the Christians and the Muslims to transcend the immediate conflict, to forgive, and to work together to rebuild the war-ravaged land. Each time the parties agreed on any of the negotiated points, Carr closed the session with a time of silent prayer. Though the northerners were Muslims, the Christian composition of the mediation team did not alienate them because Carr spoke on the basis of shared Christian and Muslim teachings, and the Muslims respected the spiritual leadership of the church leaders. As a result, what could have been viewed as a divisive issue (and in Sudan's history religion had often been exploited by one side or the other for the sake of economic or political gain) became a moral imperative that helped keep the two parties at the negotiating table.

After the opening round of talks in which each side presented more extremist proposals, an agenda was set up of the issues to be negotiated. The mediating team clustered them into the areas of political and human rights, economic, and military/security issues. The less controversial issues were handled first, a decision which ended up creating a "benevolent cycle"[22] as the negotiators began to build an increasing base of agreement: when the talks became heated, Carr would either call a break or adjourn the meeting and the members of the mediation team would then shuttle back and forth between the two sides to explore possible ways to bridge the gap. Sometimes they would draft a proposal after listening to the concerns each delegation voiced and then present it to the reconvened group. The compromise drafts would clarify the issues and focus the discussion, and many were adopted with only minor changes. The mediating team also set up small committees to work on more detailed issues, such as selecting the trained economists from each delegation to cover issues of taxation, control of resources, trade, and revenue-sharing. The small groups allowed for more efficient negotiation, especially with the lessened participation of the politicians in the technical problem-solving.

Through the relationships built by working in small groups and by socializing, and through the reconciling spirit promoted by the spirituality of the mediation team, a remarkable dynamic began to be seen. At times in the talks some northerners would side with southerners against their own delegation or would make arguments about what was fair to the other side, sometimes causing confusion as the delegates became more empathetic toward one another. When the agreement was finally achieved, Carr led them in prayer, weeping as he prayed. Various members of the delegations were crying, too, and one general from the north confessed his remorse for the slaughter between brothers all these years. One of the ministers in the government's delegation lifted Carr into the air in jubilation.

But signing the accord did not signal the end of the process. Ratification was difficult as more extremist elements on both sides reacted negatively to the accord. Numeiri ratified the agreement quickly, but General Lagu began to draw back from the agreement his representatives had signed. A final intense meeting between Carr and a representative of Haile Selassie convinced Lagu of Ethiopia's guarantees for the security of the repatriated insurgent forces, and the peace accord was officially ratified. The intermediaries continued to work with the process, monitoring the steps taken in compliance with the peace agreement and assisting in refugee relief and resettlement.

Eleven years after the peace accord was signed, civil war broke out again in Sudan as the political landscape shifted. Allies in the first conflict became enemies in the second, and once again hundreds of thousands of Sudanese people suffered from war, famine, and exile. Mediation efforts have been made to end this second civil war, most notably by Jimmy Carter and the International Negotiation Network, but as of this writing such efforts have not achieved an end to the bloodshed.

Christian Peacemaking in Nagaland, India

Under British colonial rule, many tribal groups were united into one administrative region in North East India. During the independence struggle many of the tribal peoples, including the Nagas, believed they had been promised complete independence by Gandhi and Nehru. The Naga National Council (NNC) had participated in the movement against British colonial rule, but when Naga independence was not granted after the British left India, the NNC began to agitate against the new Indian government. Longri Ao was a Baptist teacher and church leader who had joined the NNC as a student and was known as a "fiery" speaker in the nonviolent struggle led by Gandhi.[23] When the NNC decided to follow the policies of leaders advocating violence, Longri left the NNC and became more involved in church work.

In the mid-1950s, Naga guerrilla activity began to intensify, and Indian troops were sent into the Naga Hills. The "undergrounds" or "Federals," as the insurgents were called, drew many of the Nagas to the hills, including young people from the churches. Since the Nagas were predominately Christians or animists rather than Hindus, the churches were viewed as centers of rebel sympathy and targeted by Indian repressive measures. Many churches were burned and pastors were arrested, and a number of Baptist deacons were tortured and killed.

As the situation deteriorated, a group of Naga church leaders formed the Naga Church Ministers' Mission for Peace. The ministers, led by Longri Ao, preached peace and nonviolence in churches and other public meetings. They traveled to underground camps to talk peace with the armed resistance. Longri wrote of these efforts:

> We had been this whole year moving about in quest of lasting peace in Nagaland, often in rain and in scorching sun, cutting our way through thick jungles, and having meetings and prayers with our underground fighters inside deep forests and with those in prison.[24]

Of one church whose congregation had suffered from the war, Longri reported:

> I spoke of the love of God in Jesus and of forgiveness. But the people could not understand. I knelt with the parents of a young man who was killed by the underground soldiers. They wept bitterly and said they could never forgive. However, when our team returned the second time, the father attended all our meetings and told how God was helping him to forgive.[25]

The government demanded that the ministers hand over the undergrounds to the army, but they refused, insisting that their mission was to "call them to peace."[26]

Kijungluba Ao was a Baptist pastor who worked as part of the Mission for Peace. He was a quieter man than Longri, but was very influential with the Indian government, meeting with the governor of Assam, military officers, and Prime Minister Nehru in a search for peace. Once, when Kijungluba was away, Indian soldiers burst into a church meeting and lined up and shot all the deacons. Upon his return, Kijungluba went to the commander of the army unit to surrender. "All my colleagues were killed for being elders of the church. You must want to kill me, too," he said. The commander was so moved by Kijungluba's courage and nonviolent witness that an investigation was initiated and changes made in army operation policies.

At the Naga Baptist Convention held in early 1964 a "Peace Mission" was established to press for a cease-fire. Rev. Michael Scottan from Great Britain, an activist in the cause of racially oppressed groups around the world, was invited to participate. He had hosted a Naga insurgent leader in India and was also a friend of Jawaharlal Nehru, India's prime minister. J. P. Narayan of the All India Sarvodaya Movement and B. P. Chaliha, chief minister of Assam, added stature to the Peace Mission from the Indian side. With the logistical groundwork laid by Longri Ao, the negotiations through the Peace Mission went on for five months. In September 1964, the cease-fire agreement was reached between the Indian government and the major groups in the Naga insurgency.

The cease-fire did not bring an end to the conflict, though for the Naga people the relief from the war was welcome. The rebels still wanted independence, and some of them went to China in search of arms and training. The negotiations for a peace accord dragged on and on, and the cease-fire was periodically extended. Then, in 1972, the undergrounds attempted to assassinate the chief minister of Nagaland. In response, the Indian government revoked the cease-fire and declared all underground organizations unlawful. Longri Ao used all his moral force to keep the violence from erupting out of control. He publicly criticized the Indian government for reneging on their moral obligation to persuade the insurgents to give up violent means in their conflict. He called upon the army not to move into the jungles and for the insurgents not to attack. In the absence of a cease-fire, these prophetic and pastoral appeals were the thin thread holding peace together.

In 1974, the churches joined the effort to obtain a state government whose aims were more conducive to peace, and the United Democratic Front came to power on a peace platform. In this more favorable context, the Nagaland Peace Council was formed by the Baptists, with Longri Ao as president of the Liaison Committee, the main working group. The Liaison Committee began to shuttle between the insurgents and the government, finally bringing them together in August 1975 at the Chedema Peace Camp. At that time the two sides were only able to agree that the solution be acceptable and honorable for both sides. The insurgents agreed not to insist on discussing independence, and the government likewise refrained from insisting on a solution within the framework of the Indian Union.

A further round of talks were later held at Shillong that resulted in a peace agreement after three days of negotiations. The Indian government removed the war measures. The major factions of the Naga insurgency disarmed, a process overseen by the Nagaland Peace Council. Longri Ao participated in many of the arms collection trips to the distant villages. He and his colleagues held prayer services in which he spoke of the love of God and of the peace agreement as God's doing. At the conclusion of the services there were often tearful scenes of veteran guerrillas handing over their arms to the team members.

When Longri Ao died in August 1981, his body was taken to his home village of Changki. All along the way crowds gathered, with thousands spilling into the streets of Kohima, the capital of Nagaland, for a funeral service. The words on his simple grave marker read: "Man of Peace. Here Lies Rev. Longri Ao, God's Humble Servant."[27]

The political tensions in Nagaland have not been fully resolved, and some rebel groups are still in the jungles. But the Nagaland Peace Council continues its work to hammer out a lasting reconciliation in the context of just relations between the Nagas and the Indian government.

Jimmy Carter and the Camp David Agreement

Governmental diplomacy for the sake of peace was taken to a new level with the efforts of U.S. President Jimmy Carter to mediate between Egypt and Israel in the late 1970s. The Arab nations and Israel had fought four wars in twenty-five years, interspersed with acts of terrorism, embargoes, boycotts, incursions, and other forms of conflict. Hundreds of thousands of refugees had been pushed during those years from one Middle Eastern country to another. Numerous efforts were undertaken to open peace talks, but all floundered upon the entrenched positions and deep hatreds of the two sides, giving rise to a prevalent feeling of hopelessness as the world sat on a powder keg of Middle Eastern politics.

When Carter took office, one of his top priorities was meeting with the leaders of the Middle East.[28] President Anwar Sadat of Egypt was the first, coming to visit Washington in April 1977. Following the formalities of the visit and official discussions, Carter invited Sadat to a private conversation upstairs in the White House. These private opportunities for frank discussion and the building of relationships in which options and openness could be explored without the political vulnerability of premature publicity or posturing became a key part of Carter's approach. A bond of trust was established between the two leaders that became a major ingredient in the peace process. Later, Carter met privately with Prime Minister Menachem Begin of Israel, and after their meeting Carter believed compromise positions were possible, if a format for talks could be worked out.

As efforts to get peace talks going in Geneva kept stumbling over one political obstacle after another, a psychological breakthrough occurred when Sadat stunned the Egyptian parliament with an announcement of his willingness to go to Jerusalem. Begin responded days later with an invitation sent via Carter for Sadat to address the Knesset, Israel's parliament. Sadat came to Jerusalem on November 19–21, 1977, and his visit was viewed by many as one of the most momentous and symbolically significant events since the founding of the state of Israel. Thus speaking directly to "the enemy," Sadat presented Israeli leaders with their own enemy in a bold yet hopeful encounter. He stated bluntly what Arab requirements were for peace, exhibiting by his presence his own willingness to take steps to achieve that elusive dream.

Sadat's transforming initiative breathed new life into the peace process, but soon old patterns of conflict reasserted themselves. As the weeks dragged on without progress, the volatile situation seemed to be heading toward yet another war. With normal diplomatic efforts proving fruitless, Carter decided to make what he thought of as "one last major effort":

> There was no prospect for success if Begin and Sadat stayed apart, and their infrequent meetings had now become fruitless because the two men were too personally incompatible to compromise on the many difficult issues facing them. I finally decided it would be best, win or lose, to go all out. There was only one thing to do, as dismal and unpleasant as the prospect seemed—I would try to bring Sadat and Begin together for an extensive negotiating session with me.[29]

Invitations were extended for the two leaders to come to Camp David, the presidential hideaway in Maryland, and they enthusiastically accepted.

Alone in the Maryland hills, the three leaders and their staffs began a negotiation process with no time limit and no press contact except a minimal report through one spokesperson. The intimacy and the relaxed atmosphere of Camp David provided a setting in which the seemingly intractable issues of the Israeli/Arab conflict could begin to be untangled. Carter knew that in addition to discussions of the political, economic, and military/security issues, the meetings would be intensely personal, so he studied extensive biographies of Sadat and Begin, seeking answers to questions about what made them who they were. This personal approach was to pay high dividends at critical junctures in the process.

After initial meetings separately with Carter, the three leaders gathered to begin the work of negotiation. Extreme positions were presented, which led to a dramatic increase in tension. By the third day all restraints were gone, and though they had identified a long list of issues both major and minor, they were so polarized that the prospects for success seemed extremely dim. At one point when Sadat presented his counter-proposal to Begin, Carter said to Begin that if he would sign it as written, it would save them a lot of time. They all broke out in laughter at the ludicrousness of the idea. But by the end of their joint meetings anger and resistance to compromise predominated. Carter was desperate, as the two men seemed ready to walk away from the table. "They were moving toward the door," Carter recalled, "but I got in front of them to partially block the way. I urged them not to break off their talks, to give me another chance to use my influence and analysis, to have confidence in me. Begin agreed readily. I looked straight at Sadat; finally, he nodded his head. They left without speaking to each other."[30]

The next ten days were spent in an intense series of meetings between Carter and his advisors, alternating between the Israeli and Egyptian delegations. Between these sessions the Americans worked on trying to narrow the gaps between the two sides, providing draft compromises on the various points to be negotiated. Twenty-three versions of the "Framework for Peace" were made in those ten days, demanding a staggering amount of energy, creativity, and clerical speed from the mediation staff.

Carter played an activist role in the process. When Begin and Sadat had been face-to-face, Carter tried to minimize his involvement and let the Egyptian and Israeli leaders interact directly. With them separated, he had to become an interpreter of each party's interests and needs to the other, which often included affirming the integrity, good faith, and honorableness of the other. When the two sides seemed deadlocked, Carter reviewed the consequences of failure and, as agreements were reached on some of the lesser points, was able to plead with them not to throw away the successes they had achieved because of unresolved issues. Though the hard work of negotiation involved many details and arguments over fine semantic distinctions, Carter also repeatedly stirred the dreams for peace among the participants. Sadat expressed his own dream eloquently: "With success at Camp David, I still dream of a meeting on Mount Sinai of us three leaders, representing three nations and three religious beliefs. This is still my prayer to God!"[31] Carter's combination of passion for the over-arching vision for peace and persistence to work on the details that kept the parties ensnared in the conflict were essential to the success of the peace process.

Yet success seemed an impossibility for most of those thirteen days at Camp David. Carter's advisors often set low expectations and tried to prepare for failure. On day eleven, with discussions about the Israeli settlements in the Sinai at a deadlock, Sadat was about to leave. Carter, a deeply committed Christian, excused his staff and alone prayed fervently "that somehow we could find peace."[32] He then met with Sadat and, building on the trust they had established as friends, was able to keep Sadat involved in the process, and the next day it seemed the final compromise had been reached. Then, on the final day, Begin announced he would not sign the document because he repudiated a letter of understanding from the United States to Egypt about Jerusalem which had been agreed to the night before. The situation once again seemed hopeless.

Photographs had earlier been prepared of the three leaders, which Sadat had already autographed. Begin had requested them for his grandchildren. Carter's secretary, Susan Clough, suggested that the President obtain the names of Begin's grandchildren and personalize each one, which Carter did. He then walked to the porch of Begin's cabin to talk with the distraught and nervous Prime Minister. Carter gave him the photos, with his granddaughter's name on the top one. Carter later recalled:

> He spoke it aloud, and then looked at each photograph individually, repeating the name of the grandchild I had written on it. His lips trembled, and tears welled up in his eyes. He told me a little about each child, and especially about the one who seemed to be his favorite. We were both very emotional as we talked quietly for a few minutes about grandchildren and about war.[33]

They then pressed on to the details of the latest disagreement. Carter left Begin with a new version of the disputed letter, then waited with his staff and the dejected Egyptian delegation. Minutes later Begin called, accepting the letter. Exhausted but ecstatic, Carter's staff raced to complete the documents. They all flew back to the White House, and late that evening the "Framework for Peace" was signed.

Following Camp David, the effort to turn the "Framework for Peace" into formal treaties bogged down as confusion reigned in Israeli politics. Begin almost immediately began making provocative statements, and the Israeli cabinet demanded a redrafting of the agreements. Many Arab states and the Soviet Union were highly critical of what had taken place. Carter made a trip to the Middle East to meet directly with Begin, the Israeli cabinet, and later with Sadat. Once again new issues were raised which had to be resolved, and the treaty seemed to be dying a death by degrees. But persistence and the relationships established by Carter with both Begin and Sadat finally bore fruit when agreement on the last points was reached between Carter and Begin on the way to the airport in Tel Aviv. In fact, reporters had believed the talks had collapsed because at the press briefing a few hours earlier Jody Powell, the President's press secretary, had been so pessimistic when everything seemed to be unraveling.

Sadat and Begin came to Washington to sign the peace treaty on March 26, 1979. The treaty was only a partial solution to the conflicts in the Middle East, failing to address adequately the issue of the Palestinian people. But it did resolve the military conflict between the two largest military powers in the area and pointed the way for future negotiations. In spite of the assassination of Anwar Sadat, changes in the Israeli government, two major wars in the region, and the continued building of settlements by Israelis in the occupied territories, Egypt and Israel have not gone to war again.

Chapter 6

The Hard Work of Negotiating the Peace

As I stooped over the humming fax machine, it seemed an electrical current was surging through my own body as well. For over a year I had been working with Saboi Jum from Burma, struggling to develop a peace process to end the civil war in his country. We sent initial proposals for peace talks to the military government and some of the ethnic insurgent groups, but it felt like talking to blank walls. Then Saboi called me with good news. He had just received a response from the government via a member of our Burma Peace Committee in Rangoon. He would fax it to me immediately.

The pages groaned their way out of the machine, and I read each line as it emerged. The government was interested in pursuing the talks from a position that included a cease-fire, insurgents retaining their arms and territory, and insurgent participation in whatever political process would be established to deal with formation of a constitutional government. I knew there would be a lot of concerns connected to all these points, but they were certainly within the framework of a legitimate negotiation process. We had our first positive response! Now the challenge was how to build the peace initiative step by step so the various sides could hammer out a mutually satisfactory agreement. At least the journey had now begun.

The efforts in which Saboi Jum and I have been engaged in Burma are just one of many mediation initiatives undertaken in the past decade throughout the world. Diplomatic initiatives by the United Nations, superpower nations, or regional international organizations make the news with increasing regularity. The United Nations has been called upon to help bring an end to conflicts, establish peacekeeping missions, and monitor elections in more countries in the period from 1989 to 1992 than from its inception through 1988. Less visible but no less critical has been the role of non-governmental organizations, including churches, in negotiating peace. Religious leaders have often been the mediators or the moral voice calling political factions or warring parties to the negotiating table. Some of these stories of the hard work of negotiating the peace in today's world are told in this chapter.

Mediation in Nicaragua

The war in Nicaragua was a conflict on which the world focused its attention in the 1980s. The triumph of the Sandinista revolution in July 1979 inspired hope among many other poor countries who were seeking to assert their nationalist identity in the face of neo-colonialist economic powers and to provide justice for their impoverished people. At the same time, U.S. President Ronald Reagan viewed the success of the Nicaraguan revolution as a threat to American values and to the United States' economic and political control of the Western Hemisphere, and he used Cold War rhetoric to describe to American citizens the threat Nicaragua posed to them. The polarization of the United States and Nicaragua was intensified by the Marxist rhetoric of some Sandinistas and the development of relations with Cuba and the Soviet Union. Under CIA direction, the U.S. began training and providing supplies for the insurgent forces against the Sandinista government. These forces, known as the "Contras," often targeted civilians and the social infrastructure in what became a brutal war of attrition.

A parallel conflict developed between the Sandinistas and the Indians of the eastern coast of Nicaragua. Whereas the Contra war was centered on social ideology and political power, the war with the Indians was over ethnic autonomy. The Sandinistas were predominately from the Spanish-speaking west coast, and they sought to unify the country and impose their social programs on the English-speaking Indians (Miskitos, Ramas, and Sumos) and Creoles. The Indians resisted, misunderstandings escalated, and armed conflict finally broke out. The Indian insurgents usually kept a distant relationship with the Contras, but added to the strain on the Sandinista government and army.

In 1987, Costa Rican President Oscar Arias led a peace process with the presidents of Nicaragua, Guatemala, El Salvador, and Honduras to develop a regional solution to the conflicts tearing Central America apart. Their Esquipulas agreement (named for the Guatemalan town where the negotiations were held) began a process that eventually led to the ending of the Contra war in Nicaragua and provided some pressure to end the war in El Salvador. The central structure of the Esquipulas process involved the formation of national reconciliation commissions within each country. In Nicaragua four people were chosen: heading the commission was Cardinal Obando y

Bravo, who, though hostile toward the Sandinistas, was selected for his spiritual authority. Obando's mediation proved critical as the process unfolded, especially at key points in the negotiations that resulted in breakthrough agreements.[1] Also appointed to the National Reconciliation Commission to fill the category of "outstanding citizen," was Dr. Gustavo Parajón, pastor of the First Baptist Church in Managua and president of CEPAD (Evangelical Committee for Aid and Development), a Protestant ecumenical council originally set up as a relief agency. Under the commission's facilitation, talks were held between the government and the Contras which led to an accord to demobilize the insurgents and hold new elections.

Prior to the success of that peace process, however, a separate mediation effort involving the Sandinista government and the Atlantic Coast insurgents resulted in the first cease-fire along the way to ending the war. The Moravian Church was the major religious body among the Atlantic Coast Indians, and the earliest pro-Indian organization was made up mainly of Moravian pastors, which led to the church suffering in the Sandinista-Indian war.[2] The Moravian Provision Board worked with the Sandinista government to improve communications and facilitate consultations, which placed them in a prime position to mediate when the context became more favorable.

In September 1987, the various factions of the Indian resistance formed an umbrella organization, YATAMA, and contacted Moravian church leaders, led by Andy Shogreen and Norman Bent, about possible steps toward reconciliation. They invited John Paul Lederach, a missionary with the Mennonite Central Committee who had earlier done conflict resolution workshops among the Moravians, to join them, and sent a request for assistance in opening dialogue to Dr. Parajón on the National Reconciliation Commission. In the ensuing discussions between the church leaders and the Indian leaders on the one hand and Interior Minister Tomas Borge of the government on the other hand, a Conciliation Commission was set up to facilitate the negotiation process, consisting of Andy Shogreen, three other Moravian pastors, Parajón, and Lederach. The Moravians were close to the Indian leaders; Brooklyn Rivera of YATAMA had once lived with Shogreen during their student days. Parajón was trusted and respected by Borge and President Daniel Ortega, as well as by the Moravians, with whom he had worked in CEPAD. Lederach provided consulting assistance on conflict resolution and handled many details of logistics and communication.

As the Conciliation Commission began to make progress, it became evident that some parties did not want to see a peace process succeed.

Lederach was warned by a Miskito Indian who had joined the Contras of a plot by a CIA operative to kidnap his three-year-old daughter.[3] It was decided that his pregnant wife and daughter should return to the United States, but when rumors of his own assassination were heard, Lederach returned to the U.S. as well, where he continued as a central link in the communication process even while moving his family from Colorado to Pennsylvania:

> During the same days we were moving our belongings east some of the most important and difficult aspects of the entry negotiations were worked out....Since Norman [Bent] often had difficulty getting phone lines out of Nicaragua, our line of communication was for me to call Norman [in Managua], then call Brooklyn Rivera [head negotiator for YATAMA, in San José], then call Norman back. The phone bill documents the process: from Boulder, Burlington, Colby, Kansas City, St. Louis....On several occasions I called from phone booths outside, in freezing temperatures, to transmit the latest message or proposal to one side or the other.[4]

In January 1988, Lederach returned to Nicaragua for the first round of talks held following the rounds of communications to establish the conditions for the talks and for the entry of the Indian delegation into the country.

When the Indian delegation flew into Managua, the process almost broke down while they were still in the airport terminal. The Sandinistas informed them that the meetings would be held at Borge's office at the Ministry of the Interior, which was viewed as hostile territory by YATAMA. For an hour and a half the delegation stayed on the tarmac, demanding a neutral site. The parties finally agreed to met at the Office of Protocol, and Borge then took Rivera and his delegation out to dinner at his restaurant in Managua. In the meetings the relationship between Borge and Rivera grew, and with that small trust generated, significant progress was made on the substantive issues. Parajón and Shogreen mediated the sessions, with four members of the negotiating team from each side around a table. The parties had agreed that no foreigners could be present at the table, so Lederach sat outside the curtains that defined the space, keeping track of the proceedings with his computer and creating the documents needed as the meeting progressed.

A second round of talks was held the next month followed by an agreed-upon tour of the Atlantic Coast communities by Rivera and the Conciliation Commission. At Puerto Cabezas a rally was scheduled at the local baseball stadium where Rivera was to speak. About two thousand Miskitos had gathered, but the participants were attacked by seventy or eighty Sandinista supporters wielding clubs and chains. Rivera was escorted back to his hotel by a crowd of his supporters, but the commission members were assaulted in their truck. The windows were smashed, two members required stitches for their cuts, and one suffered a broken wrist before they could escape the mob.

The commission members saw their role as not to work on matters of substance—that was for the parties in the conflict to resolve—but to facilitate the procedure of the peace process. This included being a go-between for communications, arranging for travel visas and tickets for undocumented exiles, arranging accommodations, and advocating strongly for face-to-face encounters. They also helped the various factions within YATAMA to come to a more unified position by traveling to the various locations within and outside Nicaragua where leaders of the factions were based.

By late 1988, agreement was reached on over half of the issues, and a cease-fire was established between YATAMA and the Sandinista government. Though the CIA and Contras tried to undermine the agreement with further threats of kidnapping or assassination, the commission members continued their work. When an impasse developed in 1989, former President Jimmy Carter offered to mediate in discussions over the remaining differences, including the issue of Indian resistance leaders returning to participate in the electoral campaigns. In September 1989, full agreement was publicly acknowledged between the government and YATAMA, bringing a formal end to the war with the Atlantic Coast people. Carter also played an important role in certifying the integrity of the 1990 election and monitoring the transitions in government from the Sandinistas to the National Opposition Union (UNO) following Violeta Chomorro's victory in the polls.

Following the conclusion of the peace agreements, the church leaders continued to play mediating roles in the process of implementing the accords. In addition to the ongoing work of the Conciliation Commission and National Reconciliation Commission, many Protestant and Roman Catholic leaders also participated in local "peace commissions" that sought to end fighting between independent units of former Contras and former Sandinista soldiers who continued to clash and attack civilians in the rural areas. They also assisted in the reconciliation work of resettling former insurgents in war-devastated communities. Though the difficult work of hammering out peace agreements has been finished, the healing of the country and its people will take a long time.

The National Debate for Peace in El Salvador

On January 16, 1992, a peace accord was signed by the government of El Salvador and the insurgent Farabundo Marti Liberation Front (FMLN), formally ending the civil war which over a decade had brought some seventy-five thousand deaths as well as untold horror and suffering to the people of El Salvador. Celebrations broke out across the country, tempered with a sober realism about how difficult the process of fulfilling the peace accords would be. The peace was not the result of one side or the other establishing a military advantage. It had not come about primarily from a concerned international community demanding an end to the violence. Rather, the major force for peace had been generated from Salvadorans at the grassroots level who said *"No mas"*—"No more"—to the war plaguing their land.

In August 1987, peace talks began between President Napoleon Duarte and the FMLN as a result of the Esquipulas II agreements among the Central American presidents, mediated by President Oscar Arias of Costa Rica. The process did not last long in El Salvador, and the talks were indefinitely suspended. Archbishop Rivera y Damas, successor to the assassinated Oscar Romero, called for an assembly of organizations from a broad span of the social sectors to examine the fundamental problems in the country and to seek a means of bringing the government and the FMLN back to the negotiating table. Out of that assembly, held in September 1988, the National Debate for Peace was born. Initially it included sixty organizations representing labor unions, peasants, marginal communities, small- and medium-sized businesses, universities, women, professionals, indigenous peoples, humanitarian groups, and churches— what the Salvadorans called the "social forces." The religious community played a leading role with people from the Baptist, Lutheran, Episcopal, and Roman Catholic churches and base communities. Eventually the National Debate grew to over eighty organizations representing over one million members, the broadest and most democratic group in all of El Salvador.

Rev. Edgar Palacios, pastor of the Shalom Baptist Church in San Salvador, was chosen as the general coordinator for the Debate. In addition to his theological training, Rev. Palacios had studied political and social sciences extensively, so he was able to relate to the variety of organizations forming the National Debate and articulate their consensus to Salvadoran society, the government, and the FMLN. As the Debate grew, it had to expand its organizational complexity, and Ramon Diaz Bach, a businessman, joined Rev. Palacios as co-coordinator. Lutheran bishop Merdardo Gomez played a leading role in the

Debate as well, having risen as a major prophetic voice in the country following the assassination of Archbishop Romero.

The immediate goal of the Debate was to bring about peace through negotiations between the government and the FMLN. But participants in the Debate had an even larger vision for their work. They hoped to stimulate and contribute to the formation of a new social pact by means of consensus-building among the social forces of El Salvador. A cease-fire would not be enough. The solution to the war lay in establishing social justice, genuine democracy, and a demilitarization of the country. Under this agenda, the Debate not only undertook the task of urging the government and the insurgents to come to the negotiating table, they also worked at educating and providing a forum for people at the grassroots level to participate in the shaping of a postwar El Salvador.

When the National Debate for Peace was organized, the military considered it a crime even to speak of negotiations with the FMLN, in spite of what had happened at Esquipulas II. The leaders of the Debate and all the member organizations were taking a huge risk as they began to make their case both to the warring parties and to the general society. They held their first march on November 15, 1988, though they remembered how the marches in the late seventies and early eighties were met by National Guard violence that left hundreds dead. The church people led the way, carrying banners with Bible verses such as "Justice and peace will kiss" (Psalm 85:10). The Debate sponsored assemblies, forums, press conferences, and international conferences to move the society toward a consensus for a negotiated solution to the war. Whenever an action was taken by one side or the other, such as the FMLN proposal that its supporters be allowed to participate in the 1989 elections, the Debate would publicly comment and support any moves toward a genuine peace process and social justice.

After the election in July 1989, in which the FMLN was not allowed to participate and which was won by the ARENA party, the Debate issued its "Political Platform for Peace," calling for "the de-escalation of the war, the humanization of the conflict, an indefinite cease-fire... the respect of fundamental human rights and an end to the repression." The government and FMLN began the negotiations in September, but they collapsed when the National Police bombed the office of FENASTRAS (The National Labor Federation of Salvadoran Workers, a member of the National Debate), killing ten people.[5] The Debate issued another call for national reconciliation, including social justice, respect of human rights, demilitarization, and an end to political repression. When the FMLN launched an offensive days later, the military accused the Debate of being a front organization for the FMLN. Six Jesuit priests, including Ignacio Ellacuría, who had spoken at Debate marches, and Segundo Montes, who worked closely with the Debate leadership, were murdered by the military, along with their housekeeper and her daughter. Rev. Palacios and Bishop Gomez fled the country when their names were also broadcast with death threats, and many offices of Debate member organizations were closed.

Nevertheless, the work of the Debate continued with visits to the United Nations, the embassies of countries represented on the Security Council, and the U.S. Congress calling for international pressure to end the war via negotiations. Rev. Palacios and Bishop Gomez traveled openly to Panama to meet with the FMLN leaders to urge the resumption of peace talks. They returned to El Salvador, and in March 1990 the Debate held a national forum with over eighty constituent member organizations. It was nearly unanimously agreed that "the Armed Forces, together with the United States, has been one of the greatest obstacles confronting the dialogue process," while "the FMLN overall has demonstrated the greatest will to negotiate."[6] The following day, members of the Debate marched in San Salvador to commemorate the tenth anniversary of Archbishop Oscar Romero's assassination and to call for peace talks. Two weeks later, with the assistance of the United Nations, the government and FMLN both agreed to begin the negotiations once again.

This time the negotiations stayed on track, culminating with the signing of the peace accords almost two years later in Mexico City in January 1992. During the negotiations, the Debate sponsored many forums to continue educating the social forces and the Salvadoran people about the peace process and the root issues of the war. They marched a dozen times to express the national will for peace. They called for parallel negotiating sessions with the social forces and political parties, which resulted in a series of consultations with these groups, the government, and the FMLN. As a result, the Debate had direct input regarding the issues to be discussed and the solutions to be proposed. Some of the final agreements were taken directly from Debate proposals. The Debate also aggressively pursued lobbying efforts to get the U.S. Congress to halt its military aid to the Salvadoran government, calling consistently for the total demilitarization of the society. They also urged Salvadorans to participate in elections in March 1991 not by voting for parties, but voting for persons who support "the popular project"—the agenda of peace, social and economic justice, human rights, and demilitarization. When the peace accords were close to completion and right-wing elements were increasing their opposition to the process, the Debate mobilized tens of thousands to march in the streets of San Salvador demanding a cease-fire.

When the peace accords were finally signed, the people of El Salvador could genuinely claim the credit. They had demanded the cease-fire; they had persistently pursued their goal in spite of threats and even killings; they had persevered in the face of a superpower that was still supporting a military solution. Rev. Edgar Palacios was fond of saying, "Peace is not a gift from the stars. Peace must be conquered every minute of the day!" That persistence finally saw the peace process through to a successful conclusion in the signing of the accords. That persistence is also still at work as the National Debate monitors the steps taken to comply with the peace process and maintains popular pressure for implementing the agreements to move toward social, political, and economic change, the restructuring of the military, and the preservation of human rights.

Mediation in Burma

In 1980 a Baptist pastor, a Catholic priest, and a few other concerned individuals began to contact government and insurgent leaders in Burma about talks to end the civil war in their country. Burma had achieved independence from British colonial rule in 1948, but some of the minority ethnic groups incorporated by the British into Burma almost immediately began to fight for complete independence. Later, religious and cultural oppressions by the dominant Burmese incited still more minority ethnic groups, including the Kachins, to join the insurgency. By the early 1960s, civil war raged in all the ethnic minority areas. A coup led by Ne Win brought the military to power in 1962, deposing an inept parliamentary government. The military strengthened itself to fight the civil war and to gain dominance over every aspect of Burmese society.

The Kachin insurgents in the northern hills of Burma had been fighting the government since 1962. The Kachins are mainly Christian, with Baptists being the largest denomination. The religious persecution they faced at the hands of the Buddhist majority was a major factor in provoking their uprising. All missionaries had been expelled in 1966 as part of a broad effort by Ne Win to remove all foreign influences from Burma, and the churches had been forced to stand on their own in a harsh environment since that time. Some Christians chose to join the guerrillas in the jungles; others sought to merely endure, praying to be allowed to live and worship in peace. Few had any vision of a more activist approach in bringing an end to the conflict.

Rev. Saboi Jum, a Kachin Baptist leader, did have such a vision and a strong sense of determination. He wrote to both Ne Win and the head of the Kachin Independence Army (KIA), calling them to meet for peace talks. He traveled back and forth between the capital of Rangoon and the jungle headquarters of the KIA. After months of talking with officials and guerrillas, direct talks were finally initiated. A cease-fire between the military and the KIA was instituted while the talks were held for a more permanent accord. After nine months the agreements were generally in place except for some minor details, when fighting broke out again, reportedly provoked by Communist guerrillas who still hoped for a complete revolution in Burma. Rev. Jum and the others who had worked on the peace process had to keep a low profile amidst the political rubble resulting from the breakdown of the peace process.

In 1987, Rev. Jum first made contact with me at my office in the headquarters of the American Baptist Churches in Valley Forge, Pennsylvania. When we arranged for him to speak at the International Baptist Peace Conference held in Sweden the next year, he electrified the conference with his story of the travails of his country and pleaded for help from the international Baptist community to assist in bringing peace. "I believe, and I have a conviction, that it is the responsibility of the church to make peace in our country," he said.[7] In response to his appeal, he and I spent four days in January 1989 drawing up a strategy for getting the peace process going again.

We contacted John Paul Lederach of the Mennonite Central Committee for advice and counsel, and he gave us a realistic perspective on the basis of his work in the peace process in Nicaragua. Then we traveled to Atlanta, Georgia, to meet with the staff at the Carter Center and later with Jimmy Carter himself. Carter agreed to participate in the mediation process if we could get both sides to invite him. This promise gave us greater credibility as Saboi Jum began forming a Burma Peace Committee, initially made up of all Baptist Kachins. After months of putting out feelers to the two sides, we finally received positive responses about opening communication to explore the conditions for holding peace talks. Direct conversations were held between the Burma Peace Committee and the government on the one hand, and with some of the insurgent leaders on the other. This process culminated in the first face-to-face meeting between the two sides in almost a decade. Only the Kachins were present from the insurgent side, but the talks achieved an agreement to expand the discussions to include all the armed insurgents.

During the time this peace process was germinating, a democracy movement erupted in Burma and was met with the harsh repression I have described earlier, in Chapter 4. The peace process was already complicated by the cultural and political diversity of the ethnic insurgents, and the agenda of the democracy movement, both the political opposition and the students' demands, added to its complexity. Some groups were interested in peace; some thought any talks with the army regime were a sell-out; others were open to negotiation but were unwilling to risk direct involvement themselves.

An international group was formed to advise the Burma Peace Committee and explore diplomatic means of supporting a peace process. People from nongovernmental organizations (NGOs) in the United States, Canada, Thailand, Germany, and Great Britain participated in various aspects of the process. When conflicting opinions among the opposition groups caused a postponement of scheduled talks with the government, the international group met with all the key leaders of the ethnic insurgency and the democracy movement who had fled to the insurgent areas. A fragile consensus was achieved to continue pursuing the peace process, though with some groups still keeping a wary distance until substantial actions were taken by the government to show their good faith, such as the release of political prisoners.

Then the process was put on hold. Externally, the military launched major offensives against the insurgents, including a drive toward their central headquarters in Manerplaw. Internally, the Burma Peace Committee was struggling to add more representatives from other ethnic groups, which required building new relationships of trust. The institutional support of the process was also under strain. Religious groups, denominations, and ecumenical mission agencies had provided most of the funding and staffing to support the process. Because of concerns over appropriate action for such religious bodies and general funding decreases, some of the key institutional support was cut, which led to the termination of my own direct involvement. The grassroots networks, led by the Baptist Peace Fellowship of North America, picked up the administrative support, and Rev. Jum continued to press ahead in spite of drastically reduced finances. But the Burma Peace Committee, which had always operated on a shoestring budget and prayer, was in an even more precarious state.

In the spring of 1992, major changes took place. There was a shake-up in the ruling junta, followed by some gestures of conciliation by the military. Some political prisoners were released, though Nobel Prize winner Aung San Suu Kyi remained under house arrest and thousands of other political prisoners continued to languish in jail. Through the mediation of the Burma Peace Committee, the army called a cease-fire in July. Many suspected this was a ploy to achieve some relief from the international pressure against the regime, but when the dry season began, no major offensives were undertaken in spite of sporadic fighting in some areas. The cease-fire had not been formally negotiated, so there were a number of structural problems. In the fall, direct talks were again held between the army and the Kachins, who viewed themselves as speaking on behalf of the entire insurgency. The communications channels were strengthened and momentum built up for the next round of talks to deepen the process and solidify the cease-fire.

By 1993, the Burma peace process had been completely separated from its international support. The process moved forward between SLORC and the KIA, but a deep rift began to develop between the Kachins and other groups in the insurgency. Rather than achieving a comprehensive peace agreement, as of this writing it appears that the opposition is in danger of fracturing. If the military is sincere in its proclamations for peace, the cease-fire with the Kachins will be extended across the entire country. But if the military uses its respite from fighting the Kachins to make major assaults on other ethnic groups and the student democracy leaders, then the military will have used peace talks as a diversion to enable its strength to be concentrated against the remaining ethnic and student insurgencies. That would be a tragedy for all the people of Burma.

A number of lessons have emerged out of the process. Peace in such a complex conflict will not be quickly or easily achieved. Neither side can militarily defeat the other, so one course is to let the war simmer interminably. This has been the story for over forty years. Many people inside and outside of Burma profit from the war, though the vast majority of people and certainly the nation as a whole suffer from it. A great infusion of energy is necessary to overcome the inertia of the conflict and move it toward a constructive and conciliatory resolution. This energy must come from citizens of Burma as well as the international community, but so far the investment in peace has been minimal.

What has been achieved is due in large measure to the persistence of Rev. Saboi Jum, who has pursued the dream of peace even when the funds were drying up, death threats were being made, and suspicions were rampant. He is driven by both a pastoral concern to ease the suffering of his people and a theological understanding of the centrality of the work of reconciliation in the Christian ministry. He has been supported in both financial and advisory capacities by the international NGOs, but at critical points the funding and personnel commitments have been too limited to provide the intensive backing necessary to strengthen the peace process and undertake the organizing efforts to diversify and broaden the forces for mediation. In spite of all the weaknesses of the peace initiative in Burma, a cease-fire has been achieved, fragile and poorly structured as it may be. It will take a great deal of courage, wisdom, and political will to keep the peace process on a constructive track. The prospering of a peaceful Burma will require a deeper investment by all parties and by the international community in moving toward a just settlement of that country's political and cultural turmoil.

Jimmy Carter and the International Negotiation Network

The day the peace treaty between Israel and Egypt was finalized, President Jimmy Carter wrote in his diary, "I resolved to do everything possible to get out of the negotiating business!"[8] That was one resolution Carter failed to keep as the dream to make peace in a conflict-torn world grew to a calling following Carter's departure from the presidency.

At the Carter Center, which he established at Emory University in Atlanta, the former president used his international stature, connections, and experience to form the International Negotiation Network (INN). Realizing there was no organization focused on resolving intra-national or civil wars—which constitute the major portion of wars in the modern world and account for the greatest amount of death and suffering—Carter organized the INN to connect global resources for conflict resolution with the disputing parties seeking a way out of their wars. The INN Council was formed, and participants in the council have included such eminent world leaders as Oscar Arias Sanchez (former president of Costa Rica and Nobel Peace Prize recipient), Prime Minister Gro Harlem Brundtland of Norway, General Olusegun Obasanjo (former president of Nigeria), Lisbet Palme of Sweden, Sir Shridath Ramphal (former secretary-general of the Commonwealth of Nations), Marie-Angelique Savane (U.N. High Commissioner for Refugees), Archbishop Desmond Tutu (South African Nobel Prize recipient), and Andrew Young (former U.S. ambassador to the U.N.). The INN Council and staff offer their services to parties in conflict, providing mediation, monitoring existing and emerging conflicts, and helping the disputants find potential third parties, necessary experts, and funds to assist in peace processes.

Since its inception, the INN has participated in efforts to resolve conflicts in countries throughout the world. Carter himself played a significant role in mediation to help end the war between Ethiopia and the break-away province of Eritrea, and he worked unsuccessfully to assist the parties in the second civil war in Sudan. He helped the Nicaraguan government and the East Coast Indian resistance overcome the last hurdle in their peace process, and monitored the 1990 election and the peaceful transfer of power following the election. Carter and the INN monitored elections in Panama, Haiti, and Paraguay.

A major project of the INN has been an effort to facilitate a peace process in Liberia, a country that has been devastated by a vicious civil war since December 1989. Carter was invited by all parties to observe the elections, and he was able to negotiate the release of prisoners of war and refine the discussions of the peace process. Frequently, the INN was the primary communication channel between the sides. The Economic Community of West African States provided the peacekeeping forces and has convened the peace process, drawing upon the INN for support and assistance.

Through his direct involvement in the mediation of civil wars and by serving as a catalyst for yet other efforts beyond his direct involvement, Jimmy Carter has raised a crucial challenge to the global community to develop an international infrastructure that could assist in establishing peace. The world's resources and human expertise have been poured into efforts to make war, but the global community is still in the early stages of learning skills for resolving conflicts peacefully. The United Nations continues to develop as an international institution for peacemaking and peacekeeping, but it is limited by the political boundaries of sovereignty of its nation-state members. Jimmy Carter is providing one very creative and highly visible way that nongovernmental bodies, often in partnership with international political bodies and governments, can effectively organize to support peace processes and initiatives. The INN program is helping peacemakers move from the mediation of civil wars on an *ad hoc* basis to the creation of an adequate infrastructure that can maintain consistency, offer academic perceptiveness, and provide access to global resources.

The United Nations and Conflict Resolution

Though nongovernmental groups, including religious organizations, have played important roles in mediation, international conflict resolution in the past decade has seen the emergence of the United Nations as the major player on the world stage. The Charter of the United Nations sets forth as a basic purpose of the U.N.:

> To maintain international peace and security, and to that end: to take effective collective measures for the prevention and removal of threats to the peace, and for the suppression of acts of aggression or other breaches of the peace, and to bring about by peaceful means, and in conformity with international law, adjustment or settlement of international disputes or situations which might lead to a breach of the peace. (Article 1, paragraph 1)

For decades, while the conflict between the United States and the Soviet Union blocked most opportunities for conflict resolution in other countries, the U.N. itself became a diplomatic battleground for the superpowers. Since the rapprochement between the United States and the Soviet Union in the mid-1980s, the U.N. has been called upon to mediate in many conflicts that had once been Cold War proxy battlefields. The number of requests for U.N. assistance has dramatically escalated: from 1948–1987 the U.N. undertook thirteen peacekeeping operations, while from 1988–1992 U.N. peacekeepers have been called upon for thirteen new missions while maintaining five of the earlier operations.[9] In many other situations, the U.N. has taken nonmilitary action to initiate, stimulate, support, or monitor peace processes.

The particular roles of the United Nations in conflict resolution can be broken down into three categories: peacemaking, peacekeeping, and peacebuilding. Peacemaking involves all the efforts to bring conflicted parties, either nations at war or government and insurgent groups, to a settlement. In the Security Council, resolutions are passed which reflect the global community's basic assumptions about the conflict. For example, in the conflict between the Israelis and the Palestinians, Resolution 242 laid out the "land for peace" formula that eventually came to be recognized by all parties as the basis for negotiation. Though many resolutions are ignored in the heat of battle, they still have a significant impact in diplomatic circles, especially when the sides finally decide they must find a way out of their conflict.

More pro-active peacemaking occurs through the diplomatic efforts undertaken by the U.N. secretary-general. The phrase "good offices" is used to described the behind-the-scenes relational diplomacy in which the secretary-general uses persuasion to encourage the parties to enter negotiation or carries messages between the parties when they refuse to talk directly with each other. This third-party role often evolves into a more formal negotiation effort. The U.N. secretary-general may act as a convener of the talks or take on a more mediatorial role. For many years the U.N. served as third-party only to nation-states at war, such as Iran and Iraq, or between colonial powers and indigenous liberation movements, such as in Namibia. More recently, however, the U.N. is being called upon as a mediator in civil wars which have caused regional instability, forced refugees across national borders, or led to such horrific suffering that the world cried out for peacemaking intervention, as in El Salvador and Somalia. Though the United Nations often bears the burden of political biases, its identity as the one international body reflecting almost the entire community of nations gives the U.N. a measure of objectivity and mediatorial clout that can be a strong glue holding the parties together in a negotiation process.

Peacekeeping is a unique role played by the United Nations in which personnel are provided to assist in disengaging combatants and providing a buffer between them. When a cease-fire agreement is reached, the Security Council may authorize a peacekeeping operation to observe the adherence of the sides to the cease-fire arrangements. If disarmament agreements are reached, the peacekeeping soldiers may monitor assembly points for military units to gather, assist in demobilizing those units, or store weapons that are turned over to U.N. control. As people in the middle between two sides that had only recently been trying to kill each other, the U.N. peacekeepers have a very delicate task to perform. Small provocations and even accidents can trigger volatile reactions that can quickly explode into warfare, so peacekeepers must often interpose themselves and engage in grassroots mediation to resolve these dangerous incidents peacefully. Being in the middle is very risky, and over the years several hundred U.N. peacekeepers have been killed in these operations.

When a peacekeeping operation is authorized, nations that would be viewed as neutral by the warring parties are asked to contribute personnel to the U.N. mission. Military units are the most publicized, but police officers and civilian administrators also are frequently brought into peacekeeping operations. The police relate to the civilian population concerning matters of community law and order, usually in those contexts where the national police had been part of the conflict or had become too militarized. The interposition of the peacekeeping forces helps the warring groups to cool down as they work on the remaining issues of a comprehensive peace accord or until all the phases of their disengagement have been accomplished. In recognition of their pivotal role in resolving many conflicts around the world, the U.N. peacekeepers were awarded the Nobel Peace Prize in 1988.

The third type of conflict resolution initiatives undertaken by the U.N. are efforts to build the peace. In these activities the U.N. assists in moving toward a post-conflict situation, helping the warring groups to work out new structures and ways of relating that address some of the concerns that fueled their war while providing a foundation upon which to build a peaceful future. Elections have been a frequent component of peace settlements, so the U.N. has provided monitors and sometimes even personnel to run the elections so that all the parties will know they had a chance to present their cases to the people. When a faction does not like the results of the election and returns to fighting, such as UNITA did in Angola, the weight of world recognition can shift to support those chosen through a free and fair process to lead a country. Then the validity of the case of those who resume military action is undercut, leading to a loss of allies and credibility. Establishing an electoral process can strengthen nations in the practice of self-determination and in nonviolent ways to handle political differences.

Peacebuilding involves restoration of war-damaged lives, societies, and environments. Because the U.N. system is so extensive, covering a wide range of global concerns, many different program resources can be brought to bear in the rebuilding process. Refugee programs can assist in resettling displaced persons. Health and development projects can help people return their lives to some semblance of normalcy. Confidence-building measures, such as transparency about military information or establishing impartial judiciary procedures, can be taken to encourage people who had been at war to stick with peaceful means of settling political disputes.

The Persian Gulf war raised a possible fourth area of involvement of the United Nations in the future: peace-enforcement. Peace-enforcement means that the U.N. endorses or participates in military action to overcome a nation that has acted against the international order. When Iraq invaded Kuwait, its action was condemned in a number of Security Council resolutions. When Iraq refused to leave Kuwait, military action was authorized by the U.N., under U.S. leadership. The conflict in Bosnia had led some to call for similar action to be taken to halt Serb aggression and the practice of ethnic cleansing.

Peace-enforcement, however, can be also viewed as a euphemism for engaging in warfare under the same criteria offered in the just war doctrine. The United Nations or U.N.-authorized coalitions become a party to the conflict, and a solution then cannot be mediated by the U.N., since it is no longer a neutral third party. Who will take up the role as mediator once the U.N.'s credibility as an impartial peacemaker is undermined by its active participation in wars? Since the Security Council's terms for a cease-fire are imposed as demands from outside, the defeated side is not likely to view the terms as having lasting validity. Iraq's resistance to complying with the U.N.'s cease-fire terms illustrates the shallow nature of a peace imposed by force rather than negotiated by equals. The U.N. is now viewed in Iraq as an antagonist, not an arbiter. The issue of peace-enforcement will no doubt be debated for the next few years, especially since the ending of the U.S./U.S.S.R. standoff has opened the possibility for major U.N. military action.

A brief examination of the conflict resolution processes in a few specific cases will show how the various facets of U.N. peace efforts can work together. In Central America, pivotal mediation was done first by President Oscar Arias Sanchez of Costa Rica and by the Conciliation Commission in Nicaragua. The U.N. was then brought in to provide observers for the election in Nicaragua and to monitor the cease-fire. In El Salvador, pressure from the National Debate for Peace helped to persuade the insurgents and the government to return to negotiations, and the United Nations then mediated the talks. In both countries, the U.N. has supervised demobilization processes.

Angola's search for peace was a direct beneficiary of the ending of the Cold War. Complex negotiations between the governments of Angola, Cuba, and South Africa, under U.N. and U.S. sponsorship, led both to the independence of Namibia and to an agreement to withdraw Cuba's fifty thousand troops from Angola. The U.N. sent military observers to monitor and verify the Cuban withdrawal. Then Portugal, the former colonial power in Angola, with the support of the Soviet Union and the United States, mediated talks between the Angolan government and the National Union for the Total Independence of Angola (UNITA). A peace accord was achieved in 1991, and the United Nations was called upon to verify the compliance with the terms of the accord. The U.N. set up observation teams to work with the demobilization of soldiers and the proper custody of weapons. Police observation teams monitored the neutrality of the Angolan police. When elections were held in 1992, the U.N. provided technical assistance to the Angolan government for conducting the elections, then monitored the process to assure fairness. When UNITA placed second to the governing party and decided to take up arms again, the

U.N. certification of the election as free and fair was a major factor in the decision by the United States to abandon its long-standing support of UNITA and recognize the government of Angola as legitimate.

The war in Cambodia (sometimes known as Kampuchea) has been through many stages, from the U.S. bombing during the Vietnam war and American support of the military takeover, to the Khmer Rouge's victory and the horrors of their genocidal policies, to the invasion by the Vietnamese and the installation of a puppet regime, to the grinding insurgency of the Khmer Rouge and other factions against the Vietnamese-supported government. Because the United States, Soviet Union, and China all supported different factions in the war, the Security Council could take no action. However, Secretary-General Javier Pérez de Cuéllar used his "good offices" to open communications between the various sides in the conflict, identifying some points of convergence which might lead to negotiations. By 1988 the global political context had improved, and Pérez de Cuéllar put forward a proposal as a framework for peace talks. The negotiations were held with the assistance of Indonesia and France. The U.N. secretary-general actively mediated, seeking to bridge the differences between the negotiating positions of the factions and dispatching envoys on fact-finding missions. The five permanent members of the Security Council (United States, Soviet Union, China, United Kingdom, and France) were involved in helping to shape the basis for an agreement, which both strengthened the hand of the U.N. and assured that the Cambodian factions would stay in the negotiation process.

In October 1991, an agreement was reached, and the U.N. began to mobilize for its largest peacekeeping operation to date. A total of over twenty thousand people were eventually deployed by the United Nations in Cambodia. Human rights conditions were monitored, a civilian administration was set up for national defense, finance, public security, and information. The U.N. developed the infrastructure and provided training for a national election supervised by U.N. personnel. Close to fifteen thousand military personnel were deployed to verify the withdrawal of foreign forces, supervise demobilization, store arms and equipment, and assist in releasing prisoners-of-war and clearing mines. After delays due to lack of funding and walk-outs by the Khmer Rouge, the elections were finally held in May 1993, and a new and peaceful future is now dawning on that long-suffering land.

Though the United Nations is being called upon to help resolve conflicts to a greater degree than ever before, there are severe internal constraints that are keeping the U.N. from responding fully to the new peacemaking opportunities. Each peacemaking venture is put together on an *ad hoc* basis; the funding and personnel are organized for each specific mission authorized by the U.N. Security Council. Frequently, insufficient funds are raised to carry out the tasks agreed upon in peace accords. For example, the U.N. was delayed in setting up its administration in Cambodia for months because of lack of funding. The peace agreement ending the civil war in Mozambique was jeopardized when, five months after their scheduled deployment, U.N. peacekeepers still had not arrived. Only the determination of the Mozambicans to leave their war-torn past behind kept the peace process on track. Long-term peacekeeping missions are also at risk because of financial short-falls. Cyprus has had a U.N. force monitoring its conflict since 1964. Though no peace agreement has been reached and tens of thousands of troops are still deployed on each side of the U.N. buffer zone, the U.N. budget for the peacekeeping operation is totally exhausted. Only the voluntary contributions by nations who have committed military or police contingents keep the operation viable, and in 1993 the thinly stretched peacekeeping contingent suffered the pull-out of one of the remaining countries in the operation.

Clearly, the global community is going to have to address these matters in a structural way if U.N. peacekeeping and peacemaking are to face the challenge adequately. Secretary-General Boutros-Ghali has called for the establishment of a stand-by peacekeeping force so that new forces do not need to be organized with each request for their deployment. A stable funding mechanism needs to be established, with adequate funding provided from the U.N. member states. The world's political leaders send a double message when they ask for U.N. help in resolving conflict after conflict but then fail to pay their assessment for the U.N. core budget or peacekeeping operations. In recent years, the United States has become the largest delinquent nation in unpaid assessments.[10] Peace comes at a price, and the global community is going to need to pay the money to support conflict resolution if the U.N. and other international agencies are to be effective in their work of making, keeping, and building the peace.

Chapter 7

Peacemaking
at the Local Level

The church next door to our house cut down a huge tree one day during the summer. The wood was left in the churchyard over the weekend, cut into two-foot lengths, some two or three feet in diameter. The neighborhood kids, including my two sons, found the woodpile, and their creative energies were turned loose. They constructed an elaborate clubhouse, with stockade-style walls, a door with an architecturally-sound lintel, a couple of windows, and a roof made of scrap plywood scrounged from who knows where. Some of the smaller pieces of wood became seats inside. They even used some branches to mark out a walkway up to the front door. All in all, it was a striking achievement for the young builders. They got some cups and Gatorade and seemed well on their way to enjoying their new clubhouse.

Then their summer's daydream began to unravel. The big kids decided to make the club an exclusive one and kicked the younger boys out, even though they had all participated in building the clubhouse. Insulting signs were even posted outside the clubhouse to keep the younger ones from returning. The injustice left the younger kids seething, frustrated, and focused on revenge. Late in the evening, they got their chance when the big kids were playing somewhere else. They came back and began to demolish the clubhouse, breaking the Gatorade bottle, pulling apart the logs and branches, hacking the plywood with shovels, and writing their own obscene graffiti as editorial comment on their former buddies. What was still left standing they demolished early the next morning.

As I was puttering around the kitchen later that day, I watched my kids playing in the backyard with some of their friends (others in the younger set). Suddenly the older boys stormed into the yard, obviously fresh from their discovery of the ruined clubhouse. Since the U.N. peacekeepers weren't available, I raced out of the kitchen before violence could erupt. I used my superior force as an adult to require the adversaries to enter mediation on the spot. Though the decibel level was high, each group began to tell their side of the story. I worked carefully to listen and explain to each side how the other side felt. We analyzed the situation and came to see that injustice lay at the root of the conflict, but that a destructive response had not helped any-body. The "Clubhouse War" had led to the unsalvageable ruin of the one thing that everyone valued. We then talked about the recent Persian Gulf war and how when it comes to conflict adults do not do much better. Were there other solutions we could work out? We ended with apologies and forgiveness all around, and by the end of the day the whole group was playing together again.

Peacemaking is a serious and necessary affair not only at the international level, but also in the backyard and neighborhood. Con-flicts have similar patterns of genesis from the local to the global level, and the same type of skills are needed to forge peace, whether a parent or the U.N. takes on the peacemaking mission. Peace educa-tion and peacemaking need to begin locally. Children who learn effective conflict resolution skills and nonviolent ways of expressing their concerns or resisting injustice will be better equipped to contrib-ute to the ongoing effort to build peace and justice as they move into adulthood. People in local communities who face the issues of racism, political and class divisions, crime, and poverty are the front line of the struggle for viable social covenants which, if they break down, can lead to large-scale calamities such as in Somalia and the former Yugoslavia. So in this chapter we move from the stories of historical importance to the mundane, from the international scale to the communal. Ultimately, however, both for the reign of God and the forging of deep peace in the world, these stories are as pivotal as the great movements sweeping the nations.

Transforming Initiatives One-on-One

Peacemaking can take place at the level of our individual relation-ships by taking transforming initiatives. We can break out of the scripts assigned to us, whether as victim, combatant, dominator, or bystander. Changing the script changes the direction of the play, which in a conflict situation can open up new possibilities for the relationship, including reconciliation.

Roger and Claire Dewey are a couple who have given their lives to years of urban ministry in Boston. Many of those years were spent with an organization Roger founded called Christians for Urban Justice. One day when Roger was unloading some cartons of the latest issue of their magazine, a young fellow about sixteen years old offered to help. Roger accepted his help, though he was a bit suspicious when the youth slipped into the bathroom. He came out with his hand held in his jacket as if he had a gun and said to Roger, "This is a stickup!" "No, it's not," Roger replied. The teen insisted, "Yeah, yeah, this is a stickup!" Again Roger said, "No, it's not." As the confused would-be mugger tried to press his case, Roger told him he had the wrong guy and would not be there if he knew what they were about at C.U.J. The youth gave up. "Yeah, you're right. Can you help me get a job?"

Roger led the young man to a back office, where they talked for a while about life, about trust, about how to make something of oneself in a hard world. Roger gave him a copy of the C.U.J. magazine before he left. Later, in a subway station Roger was again approached by muggers and thought he would try the same line, "No, it's not." This time the response was more serious. "Listen you (a few choice words deleted), we mean business!" Roger told them, "You're welcome to look, but I have no money." He was left unharmed. The words are not magic, Roger assured me, and the drug plague in the inner cities has added to the unpredictability of such encounters. Another time Roger was in the C.U.J. thrift and craft shop when he was accosted by a knife-wielding robber. When he tried to talk, he got a superficial slash across his chest. "I don't know when to shut-up sometimes!" Roger commented.

Claire often was in the store as the manager and had to deal with occasional robberies. One robber grabbed the money and was stopped when Claire proclaimed, "This is God's money; you don't have any right to it!" She explained how the store marketed crafts for cooperatives in poor countries, returning all the profits to the craftspersons. "They need the money more than you do," she said. When the robber refused to leave the money, Claire halted him again and insisted he take a brochure about the store which explained their Christian ministry and vision of economic development. "Take it, read it, come back and buy something. Do something good with your life," she admonished.

Roger and Claire refused to follow the victim script, and their choice of a different script allowed their own humanity to come creatively into play. They also refused to follow the hatred or vengeance script that dehumanizes the criminals who assault us. They knew the poverty, joblessness, and despair tempting many to a life of crime, and in their faith they knew the transforming power of God. So as Jesus had instructed in the Sermon on the Mount, they took transforming initiatives in the unpredictable context of criminal action. Whether or not their money was taken, a direct human relationship was established with the robber, with the potential for reconciliation.

The nonviolent responses of Roger and Claire Dewey in the face of potential violent crime mirror the actions of Robert Barclay, a seventeenth-century Quaker writer. Barclay was stopped in England by a pistol-wielding highwayman who demanded his money. Barclay's response was firmly yet gently to tell the robber that he was not his enemy but a friend willing to help if needed, but that he was not intimidated by the highwayman's weapon. Barclay said he did not fear death because he believed in immortality. He then asked the man threatening him if he could actually shed the blood of one who had no enmity for him and who was willing to befriend him. Confused by Barclay's response, the highwayman fled.[1]

Rabbi Michael Weisser in Lincoln, Nebraska, was being harassed by Larry Trapp, Grand Dragon of the Ku Klux Klan in the state. Trapp sent packages of hate mail and made threatening calls, leading Weisser to have a phone tap installed. Then Weisser decided he had to confront both the fear and the anger in himself and in the Klansman seeking to instill that fear. So Weisser tried to call Trapp. He got the answering machine, with a ten-minute recorded message of hate against Jews and blacks. When he could finally leave his own message, he asked Trapp to think about the hatred inside him because one day he would have to face God with it. Another time he told Trapp that the Nazis exterminated those with physical disabilities, so why did he love the Nazis so much since Trapp himself was confined to a wheelchair?

After Weisser had left many messages, one day Trapp picked up the phone demanding, "What do you want?" Weisser rewrote the script by calmly saying he knew Trapp had a hard time getting around and thought he might need a ride to the grocery store. Trapp got very quiet, the anger draining from his voice. He said, "I've got that taken care of, but thanks for asking," and hung up. Weisser's transforming initiative worked its way deep inside Trapp, and he called back later asking for help to get out of the Klan and away from all the hate eating him inside. Weisser and his wife, Julie, took dinner over to Trapp's house. Julie Weisser thought of Trapp's own apprehensions about this meeting and decided to take a silver ring as a peace offering. When Michael Weisser walked in and touched Trapp, the Klansman burst into tears. When Julie gave him the silver ring, Trapp removed the two swastika-emblazoned rings from his hand and gave them to her. "I want you to take these rings; they just symbolize hatred and evil, and I want them out of my life," he said. From this encounter the Weissers and Trapp began to work educating Nebraskans about hate groups. Trapp's liberation from racial hatred through the Weissers' peacemaking changed them all personally and gave a new sense of direction in life to the former Klansman.[2]

Individuals can take transforming initiatives, not only as people engaged in the conflict in some way, but also as third parties. Kenneth Morgan, a professor from Colgate University, witnessed a striking example of mediation in Damascus, Syria. He was strolling along the marketplace when a man came through the crowd on a bicycle with a basket of oranges balanced precariously on the handlebars. Another man, bent over with a heavy load, bumped into the bicycle, knocking it over and spilling the oranges into the street and nearby stalls. Yells and curses led to a confrontation, with excited onlookers gathering. As the bicyclist moved toward the porter, a tattered little man came out of the crowd, took the raised fist in his hands, and kissed it. The watchers murmured their approval, and the antagonists relaxed. The little man disappeared, and everyone began to help pick up the oranges.[3]

Roger Dewey once intervened in a confrontation between gangs of white youths and black youths in Wainwright Park in the Dorchester area of Boston. The park was white turf, but black families had moved into many of the streets coming into the park from the west. Roger's home overlooked the park, and he saw the white kids threatening the black kids with rocks. He raced outside and placed himself between the two groups. He said to the white kids, many of whom he knew, "You are my friends, but these are my friends, too," gesturing toward the black youths. "If you want to get to them, you will have to go past me." One of the teens taunted him, "You can get awfully bloody that way!" Roger replied, "Of course, but Jesus is standing right here with me. He's disgusted with what you're doing. Put down the rocks and get out of here!" Being good Catholic kids from St. Mark's parish, Roger later recalled, they could not attack Jesus, so they left.

Stories such as these could fill many volumes, each one challenging us to develop the kind of thinking patterns that will be creatively open to the unexpected. Telling such stories can free us to throw away worn-out conflict scripts that lead to domination and victimization. The community of a local congregation can be a place where such stories are shared if the congregational life encourages participation rather than audience passivity. The stories of Roger and Claire Dewey were shared in the context of our church in Boston, which helped us all think more creatively about the violence in our neighborhood, which most of us had experienced.

Conflict Resolution in the Neighborhood

Wainwright Park was the focus for much of our neighborhood conflict in Dorchester, and it became the scene of a fairly successful process of conflict resolution. The racial turf war exploded when the city's housing authority moved three black families into a triple-decker on a predominately white street on the east side of the park. The public housing apartments of the black families were being remodeled, and the situation was supposed to be temporary, but quickly the tension began to build. The black families were harassed by whites throwing snowballs and yelling racial epithets. Then a molotov cocktail that mercifully failed to ignite was thrown at the house, and the next night the triple-decker was firebombed, causing only minor damage but awakening the community to the seriousness of the situation. That weekend the larger neighborhood, working through block organizations and churches, mobilized people to undertake an around-the-clock vigil over the weekend at the targeted triple-decker. Many of us spent our hour shifts in the middle of the night sitting on the front porch as a sign of community commitment to resist racist violence.

A meeting was then held at the Lutheran church near the park. Black and white adult neighbors, the white teens who hung out in the park, and the community relations officer of the police department attended. Rather than beginning with laying down the law, the meeting started with people expressing their concerns. Many spoke of the need for a safe neighborhood. Others spoke of how the city had allowed the park to deteriorate. The white teens spoke of how blacks moving in would mean they would lose their homes. They had historical experience to back them up: many of them had lived in an area not so far away which had been white until black families started moving in and the white families moved a few blocks further east.

The problem was that these white teens had no conception of the political and economic dynamics that had had such a dramatic impact on their lives. Their previous neighborhood had been targeted by the government and business interests for an antipoverty housing program. The banks offered federally-guaranteed, low-interest mortgages to low-income black home-buyers. Then when a few black families moved in, the real estate people came door-to-door encouraging whites to sell quickly before the blacks moved in and sent the value of their homes plummeting. Whites sold at a loss and their racist fears deepened. Poor black families moved into the old houses, but when the houses needed repairs, they discovered their area had been redlined, so no loans were available. Homes were foreclosed and abandoned, then often torched. The new black community was left devastated and disorganized. The real estate interests and banks made a financial killing, and the taxpayers paid the bill. Now the white teens feared the cycle was beginning yet again, without understanding the deeper causes of their earlier displacement.

Through the long process of that meeting and subsequent gatherings, the concerns and fears of the teens and their families were heard. A clear statement was made by other community members that no violence would be tolerated, but that they would all work together to strengthen and improve the neighborhood so all could live in peace. When unemployment was identified by the teens as a major problem, a community group hired three of them to work in renovating abandoned houses. Some other adults assisted some drop-outs in getting their Graduate Equivalency Diplomas. Other adults became sympathetic listeners for teens who had become alienated from their parents, to help them work through the traumas of adolescence. The community relations police officer showed a deep commitment to work with the relational issues and keep police action in line with the cooperative direction of the community's peace effort. Neighborhood patrols were set up, not only to put a damper on criminal activity, but to bring adults and youth into more regular contact. Police officers on patrol often chatted with the kids in the park and got to know them by name. They also walked beats around the park, which strengthened their relationship to the community while increasing security. The city resumed a park restoration project that had been halted after many of the play areas had been torn up. With neighborhood input a hockey area (which white kids wanted) and a basketball court (which black kids wanted) were constructed. When the park renovation was completed, an inaugural basketball game was held. The mayor (who was once an All-American basketball player), Dave Cowens of the Celtics, and police officers played against an integrated neighborhood all-star team.

In a two-year period of such community building efforts with intentional communication, Wainwright Park changed from being the main racial turf battleground in the area to a center for community life. Black and white children, teens, parents, and older people could be seen in the park. Racial tensions continued throughout Dorchester and erupted again near Wainwright Park when Vietnamese families moved into the same house that had been firebombed before. But the community had developed a network to handle its crises constructively, bringing a measure of hope for those who lived there. The process involved a local church acting as community mediator, people willing to listen to each other, a systemic analysis of the dynamics that had impacted the community, nonviolent protective action, cooperative relationships with governmental agencies such as the police and the city's parks department, and a determination to find a win/win solution rather than let the conflict spiral into destructive patterns of revenge.

In many urban communities gangs and gang violence have become dominant and dangerous elements of neighborhood life. Hundreds of youths and innocent bystanders have been killed each year in Los Angeles alone through gang warfare. In early 1992, a truce was developed between many of the factions of the two largest Los Angeles gangs, the Bloods and the Crips, and similar truces had been developed among gangs in Chicago and Minneapolis. Though the truces are not universally observed among the loose network of gangs, a significant core of gang leaders are trying to find ways to break out of the cycles of violence through which the gang members have helped to destroy their own communities and limit their own futures.

In June 1992, leaders in the truce between the Bloods and Crips invited Carl Upchurch to visit them and assist in making contact with community organizations that could support their efforts for neighborhood peace. Upchurch had been raised amidst urban violence in Philadelphia and had spent ten years in prison. After his conversion to Christianity, he had become an active proponent of nonviolence and had founded the Progressive Prisoners Movement. After Upchurch made numerous contacts with gang leaders, the idea of a national gang summit for peace and justice began to germinate. Additional contacts were made with gangs and community organizations engaged in gang programs in cities across the United States. With the organizational and financial support of the religious community, the idea of the summit gathered momentum.

From April 29 to May 2, 1993, over one hundred sixty gang members from twenty-six cities met in churches in Kansas City. They told their stories, analyzed the dynamics and roots of urban violence, and worked on ways to establish and extend truces. They talked with leaders from the churches and peace groups about how they could work together to address the issues of despair, racism, joblessness, and poverty underlying the violence. The gang leaders and participants from the religious community returned to their cities with new vision, inspiration, and partnerships to build justice and peace at the neighborhood level. Local summits were then held in Cleveland, San Francisco, St. Paul, and Chicago. Churches became the safe places, or "sanctuaries," for all the gangs to meet to discuss ending the violence on the streets.[4]

A key part of conflict resolution at the community level is relationship building, especially in a society where diversity is so extensive. The war in the Persian Gulf was reflected in tensions in U.S. communities where hate crimes against Arab-Americans and Muslims dramatically escalated. Many churches took advantage of that crisis to develop and deepen ties with their Jewish and Muslim neighbors. Forums were held for people to listen to one another and gain a better understanding of other cultures and perspectives. Outbreaks of ethnic conflict can prompt people who have been isolated in their own enclaves to reach beyond their group to build common cause and community with another. As conflict escalated between many black and Korean communities, for example, one African-American church in New York City hosted the ordination service of a Korean pastor as a relationship-building event and witness to the larger community.

Relationship-building can be fostered in all kinds of settings. Workplaces can be used as a place for developing respect for others as people engage in a shared task. Arty de Silva, a Baptist pastor in Sri Lanka, uses employment as a means of forging reconciliation. Sri Lanka has been torn by civil war between the majority Sinhalese and the Tamils. De Silva has developed a program to aid refugees from both groups and to rebuild communities where Sinhalese and Tamils work side by side. A printing business was set up at which Christian workers from both groups train displaced persons from both groups in the occupation. An intentional effort is made to break down stereotypes and replace the "enemy" with a "colleague" or even "friend." This same philosophy undergirds other ministries de Silva organizes to aid victims of the violence: "What we do is to use Tamil relief workers in Sinhalese areas, and we see Sinhalese and Tamil people together, building their own homes." With the youth, programs are held with all the ethnic groups mixed together: "They are open to each other, to each other's culture, to each other's language, to each other's hopes and aspirations. Here we find, although we are different in many ways, still underneath we are the same, we are one."[5] Eroding the ethnic hostility at the base of many conflicts through relationship-building can be a ministry embraced by local churches and by Christians in their communities and workplaces.

Christians are also participating in conflict resolution through community organizations. Many are involved as mediators in court-sponsored alternative dispute resolution programs. Others work in neighborhood schools to train children in conflict resolution. St. Louis Park Junior High School in St. Louis Park, Minnesota, is one of many schools across the United States with conflict resolution programs. Teams of students are selected by their peers to be conflict managers. At the beginning of the school year the conflict managers are given two days of training in communication skills, attentive listening, and role-playing. Once a week the team goes to a room where students with disputes can come for a hearing and assistance in working out a solution. Students must come to the conflict managers in pairs since the goal is mutually designed conflict resolution. The conflict managers explain the rules (no name-calling or interrupting, be as honest as you can, speak directly to the conflict managers when telling your story), define the facts, reflect the feelings, search for solutions, and create a peace plan, which is put in writing. The conflict managers then monitor the situation to see how the solution is working. Conflicts that cannot be resolved with the student conflict manager are referred to the guidance counselor.[6]

If Christian churches recognize that ministry includes activities of their members on the job, in the community, and at school, as well as within the organized structures of the church, then these involvements can be affirmed and supported as part of the Christian peacemaking mission.

Bringing Nonviolence Home

American society is one of the most violent in the world. The prevalence of handguns and their frequent use has given this country one of the highest murder rates in the world. Every year approximately thirty thousand people in the United States are killed by firearms, either through homicide, suicide, or accident, half the total number of U.S. soldiers killed during the decade-long involvement in the war in Vietnam. When violence erupts in a community, the automatic response is more violence. Following the Los Angeles riots, there was a 50 percent increase in handgun sales in the state of California.[7] When any legislative attempts are made to restrict or control firearms, even semi-automatic weapons, the lobbying efforts of the National Rifle Association and the arms manufacturers usually intimidate enough legislators to ensure that the control bills go nowhere. The front lines of the issue of gun control are the neighborhood streets and private homes, where in some communities gunfire is a daily occurrence and children speak in a matter-of-fact voice about violence. Gunfire is the eleventh most frequent cause of death in the United States, the sixth leading cause for people under sixty-five. For young black men in the inner city, homicide—usually by bullets from a handgun—is the number one cause of death.

Many communities have responded with candlelight vigils and marches. Some neighborhoods have developed neighborhood patrols. During the recent uprising in Los Angeles some local churches organized members to patrol their neighborhood, sometimes putting themselves between police and youths as a nonviolent buffer. The Guardian Angels is a group which stirred controversy in the cities where they were organized. Though they have a paramilitary style, complete with identifiable uniforms and organizational structure, they have used nonviolent tactics to deter and oppose crime. Some of the same sociological dynamics operate in urban gangs and the Guardian Angels, but in the latter group these dynamics have been channeled into a productive purpose.

Addressing such pervasive violence will require a broad, multifaceted strategy ranging from neighborhood organizing to national legislative coalitions, and from education in the local schools to reshaping the cultural heroes glorified in the entertainment industry. Our culture of violence needs to be overturned by a counterculture, a new culture of nonviolence. A partnership must develop between grassroots organizations, community groups, churches, and responsive national political, media, and religious leaders. The plethora of individuals and organizations seeking to live in a nonviolent way are a sign of hope, but they have not been welded together or given the focus sufficient to become a movement able to reshape the culture.

Violence has often clustered around the drug trade. A nonviolent response to drug trafficking was a group called "Yes, We Can," which was organized in Boston by religious and community leaders. The group would identify a particular neighborhood where drug dealing was occurring. They would then move into a house near the dealing site or crack house. Sometimes the building would be abandoned, and the group members would occupy the unheated structure with no plumbing or electricity. They would camp there and observe all that was going on. Conversations would be initiated with the dealers, seeking not to attack them as persons but firmly to oppose their activities. "Yes, We Can" members would organize the people on the street so that the local residents could advocate for better police protection and break out of their own prisons of fear to help bring their neighborhood under control. By the end of the campaign, the dealers were forced out, probably moving to another site to continue business as usual. But the neighborhood had gained pride and strength in the knowledge that they could stand up to the gun-wielding drug dealers.

Most of the violence, however, is not on the streets but in the homes.

Domestic violence is a national plague. The National Woman Abuse Prevention Project estimates three to four million women are battered each year by their husbands and partners. Abused women comprise approximately 20 percent of women presenting with injury to hospital emergency services.[8] Many of these women feel powerless, with few options for freeing themselves from the abuse. Often their victimization is reinforced by religious teaching about the wife being submissive to the husband. Child abuse, physical and sexual, is a parallel horror which has also been covered up in many churches and families by blithely quoting Bible verses such as "Do not withhold discipline from your children; if you beat them with a rod, they will not die" (Proverbs 23:13). When victims of abuse feel God is on the abuser's side, their sense of helplessness can be overwhelming.

A nonviolent response is not passively to accept abuse through a distorted use of "turning the other cheek" (Matthew 5:39). As our earlier study on transforming initiatives in the Bible showed, Jesus called for action that affirmed the humanity of the oppressed one and exposed the evil of the oppressive situation, though not at the cost of denying the humanity of the oppressor. In cases of domestic violence, the humanity of the abused woman or child must be affirmed. A key step in dealing with the conflict of abuse is providing education about the abuse through confidential conversations with a friend, a hotline or guidance counselor, or a pastor so abused persons can come to see the dynamics that have ensnared them. Then they can take the next step of empowerment, in which options can be developed, such as escape to a shelter, getting a restraining order, accompaniment for a person in danger, or divorce. Empowerment can also be aided through support groups, where people can share their struggles and help each other take the courageous steps needed to reclaim their freedom and dignity. Within churches reconciliation is such a high priority that in cases of domestic violence reconciliation can be promoted prematurely, but this would merely play into the cycles of abuse rather than changing the reality of the abusive relationship. The conflict must be brought into the open and dealt with at the basic level of either respecting or denying the humanity of the people involved. Reconciliation may be possible down the road, but to be genuine that would require transformation of the abuser and free choice of the one who had been abused. Appropriate resolution to the conflict is more likely to be providing the person who is being abused a way out of the situation, while restraining the abuser.

Besides the neighborhood and the home, the workplace is often a place of conflict. Nonviolence and conflict resolution have been highly

developed in the area of labor/management relations. Contract negotiations, arbitration, and grievance procedures have become an accepted part of much of the business world. Strikes and picketing have
been frequently employed in labor disputes. Usually churches do not
get involved in labor disputes, though when a business is central to
the life of a community the churches may enter a conflict.

The strike against the Pittston Coal Company in southwest Virginia by the United Mine Workers of America (UMWA) was an
inspiring departure from the often violent strikes common in the coal
fields.[9] Miners have one of the most dangerous jobs in the country,
tend to be poorly paid, and frequently succumb to "black lung," a
deadly respiratory disease brought on by breathing coal dust. In 1988,
the UMWA contract with the Pittston Company expired, and the
company decided to try to break the union. Fifteen hundred widows,
pensioners, and disabled miners had their health benefits termi-
nated. After over a year of negotiation and no contract, the miners
went on strike. From a blending of UMWA history, the civil rights
movement, and deeply held Christian faith, the strikers developed a
powerful and inspiring nonviolence strategy. Clad in combat fatigues
and singing hymns and civil rights and labor struggle songs, the
miners set up Camp Solidarity in Lebanon, Virginia. The camp
became the gathering point for the struggle, with weekly rallies
drawing people in expressions of solidarity from around the country,
as well as miners from Poland, Sweden, and the Soviet Union.

The miners engaged in massive sit-ins to block mine entrances.
Virginia troopers were sent in to escort the coal trucks. Thousands
were arrested, filling the county jails. Some miners and family members were hospitalized because of injuries from police violence. But
the resistance spread among the community. Students who went on
strike in three counties were "punished" by principals, who made
them write papers on the history of the UMWA. Tow truck operators
refused to remove strikers' vehicles blocking roads, and some gas
stations refused to sell to state troopers. When a strikebreaker
deliberately ran his truck into a crowd of strikers, injuring four, two
critically, the immediate response was to assault the driver. But even
as the anger spread, strike leaders were able to maintain nonviolent
discipline, one urging, "We don't have to fight violence with violence.... We can win it without violence.... We can win our way. We're
gonna win it right."[10] In one action thirty-nine women calling themselves "the daughters of Mother Jones," clad in camouflage scarves
and carrying carnations and flags, occupied the Pittston offices in
Lebanon.

After almost two years, the strike was settled through Department of Labor mediation, and the health and pension benefits that had been cut were restored and guaranteed. Local pastors, many of them miners themselves or retired miners, had played a significant role in providing leadership and preaching nonviolence. National religious groups helped mobilize support and put pressure on Pittston. With the help of clergy in Greenwich, Connecticut, where Pittston's headquarters are located, the strikers took their protests to the heart of the corporation. Though formal links between religious groups and labor were not developed, the Pittston strike opened up new lines of communication and shared concern between churches and unions.

The involvement of people in conflict resolution and nonviolence can begin in any area of life, and the changed perspectives and the skills which have been developed can then be applied to other areas. What begins at home with the training of our children continues through our close neighborhood relationships, our relationships in the schools and on the job, and international relationships. Peace comes not just through the negotiations of diplomats, but through the work to deal justly and nonviolently with those with whom we live and share this planet most intimately.

Chapter 8

Peacemaking into the
Next Century

I first heard of Miguel Tomás Castro when I received a telephone call from our denominational offices. I was a pastor in Boston, connected to a Central American emergency network. Miguel Tomás Castro, pastor of the Emmanuel Baptist Church in San Salvador, El Salvador, had become one of the "disappeared." I joined scores of others in contacting the U.S. Embassy in San Salvador and various Salvadoran officials, requesting information about his whereabouts and pressing for his safety and release. Three days later he was "found" in police custody. He was promptly released and thrown out of the country. Miguel later told me about being in prison. He had been tortured as a matter of course. When he was being interrogated, he could see just a bit under the corner of his blindfold. The police interrogators had sheaves of paper in their hands and kept demanding, "Who knows you? How do they know you're here?" That gave him hope, for he knew people on the outside were raising a fuss.

Years later Miguel and I were together at an International Baptist Peace Conference in Nicaragua where he was a speaker. Six months earlier the Salvadoran peace accords had been signed, bringing an end to the civil war in El Salvador which had lasted over a decade and claimed more than seventy-five thousand lives. His eyes shone with joy and hope, though sorrow and suffering were still intimately woven into his heart. He had seen friends and church members killed, tortured, exiled, and torn by grief. He had ministered to the victims directly, especially the orphans whom his church raised. He had been in the marches, spoken out while in exile, been a part of the National Debate for Peace, and paid a personal toll for his witness for justice and peace. But now peace was dawning. The guns were silent.

Miguel knew well how far his country had to go for peace to truly blossom. He knew the resistance of the army officers to the accords; he knew the grinding poverty of the vast majority of Salvadorans; he knew the inequities that lay at the root of the civil war still cried out for justice. But he also knew the people of El Salvador had achieved

165

peace through their own strength developed in the fierce smelter of suffering. Perhaps now the suffering could be eased and the reconstruction of the people and the land could begin. The flower of hope had sprung up, and its promise shone in Miguel's eyes.

Christian peacemaking is about making that hope blossom and that promise come alive. Christians have played important roles in seeking justice and peace in many conflicts throughout history and in the explosion of events in the 1980s and the early 1990s. But will Christian people and churches continue to play a leading role for peace in the twenty-first century, or will we become reactionary or focused merely on our own institutional survival? God will continue to raise up people like Gustavo Parajón, Saboi Jum, Longri Ao, Sojourner Truth, Martin Luther King, Hildegard and Jean Goss-Mayr, Adolfo Pérez Esquivel, Desmond Tutu, and the many others, great and small, who have worked through nonviolent action or mediation to forge peace and establish justice. The question is whether the Christian community as a whole and its institutional expressions will join in these struggles as creative and supportive participants, or whether the peacemaking saints will merely be acknowledged at a distance—or, worse yet, resisted because of the challenges they bring to the status quo.

The record is a mixed one for the church. Sometimes Christians and church leaders have been in the forefront of struggle, waging nonviolent campaigns against injustice or taking the risks to mediate between warring factions. At other times the church has been timid and stayed on the sidelines even while its daughters and sons laid down their lives. At still other times the church has blessed war and served as chaplain to oppressive powers. For those who believe Christians should press on in the quest for justice and peace in the name of God, this chapter offers some reflections on the issues to be faced as we build upon the accomplishments of recent years.

Limits of Nonviolence and Conflict Resolution

Nonviolence and conflict resolution are not panaceas for dealing with all the ills of a conflicted world. Many of the heroic stories told in these pages have endings far from living "happily ever after." In the Philippines, for example, the People Power movement brought Corey Aquino to the presidency following the downfall of Ferdinand Marcos, but within a year it was evident that Aquino would not address fundamental inequities in the society and economy. Furthermore, the government responded to the guerrilla war of the New People's Army with a total war policy and the continued militarization of the Philippines. People Power could bring down a dictatorship and install a democratic system, but the hidden powers of economic and military elites remained firmly in control.

However, the struggle for justice in the Philippines continues, often through the very church groups that provided the core of the People Power movement. Grassroots organizations and networks continued to function. Bishop Francisco Claver, a leader of the nonviolence movement, speaks of the ongoing nature of the effort to bring a total peace:

> Active nonviolence is not just a tactic to be used to achieve an end, to be discarded if it does not achieve that end effectively. It is a way of life, an ethic, a spirituality, something that goes beyond the mere utilitarian and practical.[1]

In that spirit, and with the memory of the events on the Avenue of the Epiphany of the Saints, Christians press on in the long quest to overhaul the social structures and create a new value system for Filipino society, though this peacemaking work is hidden from the view of most of the world.

Even the great movements that shaped our understanding of nonviolence had critical failures. The civil rights movement succeeding in bringing about major changes in the legal system in the United States and in eradicating many of the visible expressions of racism. But the lines of class became the new Jim Crow which left the majority of blacks in a plight as bad if not worse than the early days of the movement. Thirty years after Martin Luther King's "I Have a Dream" speech, black rates of unemployment, infant mortality, imprisonment, life span, earnings and other indices of economic and quality of life standing are dramatically worse than for white America. Whereas progress was achieved by black Americans in the 1960s and 1970s in economic, political and social sectors, the momentum for social change stalled in the late 1970s. The Reagan-Bush era saw a reversal in which the absolute and relative position of African-Americans worsened in relation to whites in many significant areas. Equality receives lip service, and King's birthday is now a national holiday; but racism is as deeply as entrenched as ever in the United States.[2]

In India, Mahatma Gandhi's nonviolence movement drove the British colonizers out, but it could not hold Indian society together. While on the verge of independence, Hindus and Muslims slaughtered each other as India was partitioned into two nations by religious warfare. Further wars followed, and religious intolerance continues to threaten the fabric of Indian society today. The legacy of the apostles of nonviolence, the Hindu Mahatma Gandhi and the Muslim Badshah Khan, dramatic and powerful as it was, could not halt the national schism.

Clearly, nonviolent campaigns have their limits, for nonviolent action is more a form of struggle than a program for social development. Adherents to a thoroughgoing philosophy of nonviolence often have broader components of their vision than just direct action against oppressive structures; they also speak of the ways human beings should relate to one another, and even develop institutions to incorporate the values of nonviolence in their operating procedures. But building justice takes more than resistance against oppression or respect for the integrity of life of other human beings. Justice requires economic, political, administrative, and ecological skills. It requires a range of disciplines and enterprises to provide for human need and for the efficient coordination of society. Nonviolence can provide critical skills to handle the inevitable conflicts with as little destruction as possible, but both the potential and limitations of nonviolence must be understood if peacemakers are to make effective use of it.

The new structures that develop after a successful nonviolent campaign are critical to the long-term success of the campaign. If an oppressive system is overturned, what will take its place? Sometimes enough organizational strength has developed through the course of the struggle that a new ruling party is ready to step up or the peace agreements spell out the process of transition adequately. The Congress Party in India, which Gandhi and Nehru led, became the ruling party following independence, with Nehru as Prime Minister. In Poland, Solidarity grew from a union to an opposition party and then to the ruling party as the power of the Communists and the army eroded away. But sometimes nonviolent struggles can succeed before dissident organizations have had time to develop. In Eastern Europe and the Soviet Union, the revolutions that toppled communism caught most countries by surprise, with the exception of the Poles, who had been struggling for a decade and had a well-developed organization in Solidarity. In the political and philosophical vacuum left by the collapse of communism, nationalist and ethnocentric ideologies are flourishing. The horror of ethnic cleansing in Yugoslavia is also emerging in ethnic battles in former Soviet republics, in the rise of fascist nationalism in Russia, and in the rise of neo-Nazis in Germany.

Jesus told a parable which speaks to this danger:

When the unclean spirit has gone out of a person, it wanders through waterless regions looking for a resting place, but it finds none. Then it says, "I will return to my house from which I came." When it comes, it finds it empty, swept, and put in order. Then it goes and brings along seven other spirits more evil than itself, and they enter and live there; and the last state of that person is worse than the first. So will it be also with this evil generation (Matthew 12:43-45).

Demons of communism and Stalinism have been swept out, but old demons of nationalism, racism, and fascism are coming back, bringing suffering and horror in their wake. In nonviolent struggle it is vital to develop a clear sense of what the movement is for, not just what it is against. History is full of surprises, many of them unpleasant, so it is of critical importance that constructive social visions be put forward in the heart of struggle. The churches can play a vital role in that endeavor, as they have in El Salvador, South Africa, Germany, and the Philippines. They must nurture and proclaim a dream which reaches farther than the immediacy of the particular struggle for freedom and justice; in fact, that vision needs to be a driving hope to energize the struggle with positive passion instead of letting it be fueled by hatred and rage.

Like nonviolence, conflict resolution also has its limits and potential problems. Sometimes negotiations can bring a halt to a war of which both sides have grown weary, providing a temporary solution but not addressing the deeper issues. As a result, these issues may resurface again. Like a fire only partially smothered, the ashes may hide coals that can be blown back to flame with sufficient fuel. Cycles of wars in the Middle East, on the India/Pakistan border, and in the Sudan show peace agreements that brought temporary halts to conflicts but no long-lasting solutions. The partial solution negotiated between Israel and Egypt at Camp David brought peace between those two countries but failed to produce an adequate solution to the issue of the self-determination and national identity of the Palestinian people. That deliberate oversight severely limited the accords and left untouched the most volatile issue in the region. In Nicaragua and El Salvador savage wars were halted, but the gulf between the rich and the poor that led to revolution and rebellion remains as vast as ever. Still, the wars have been stopped, which is a step in the right direction since the destruction of war does nothing to aid the poor, who are always victimized.

Out of a desire to end the tensions and, in some cases, the violence of a conflict, a resolution can be achieved prematurely. Morton

Deutsch sees premature conflict resolution as a pathology of conflict, along with avoidance, excessive involvement in conflict, and position rigidification. Deutsch holds that in a premature resolution "the conflicting parties come to an agreement before they have adequately explored the issues involved in their conflict. The typical result is that the agreement will not last long. It will break down as soon as the realities reveal its superficial nature."[3] Premature efforts to resolve the revolution that brought the downfall of the Duvalier regime in Haiti short-circuited a desperately needed restructuring of Haitian society. Though some progress was made toward a new Haiti through the elections that brought Jean Baptiste Aristide to the presidency, the elites had by then utilized the time to consolidate their post-Duvalier positions. When Aristide threatened to press ahead with the agenda to remake Haiti, he was ousted in a coup supported by those elites. At the family level, efforts to mediate domestic conflict where there is spouse abuse would be premature and merely guarantee a return to the abusive situation if nothing is done to address the structure of domination in the home. Conflict resolution is premature if there is a gross imbalance between the two parties; it then becomes a tool for merely restoring order for the dominant one.

Conflict resolution may also involve moral compromise. In the wars following the dissolution of Yugoslavia, what kind of negotiated settlement is acceptable? Is it appropriate to create ethnic conclaves to end the fighting, which just formalizes the ethnic cleansing pursued in Serbian policies? The moral evil and crimes against humanity are then brushed aside in a pragmatic effort to end the killing and draw at least some boundary to separate the sides. Can that model be followed, given all the ethnic mixing that has taken place in so many countries? National lines and ethnic lines do not coincide, and in many cases could never be drawn even if one wanted to. A negotiated settlement that ratifies at least in part the fruits of ethnic cleansing provides a subtle but very real endorsement of that reprehensible policy. Conflict resolution then must be more than just a cease-fire, but must address fundamental issues of human rights. The processes must involve not only professional diplomats, but also other institutions, including religious institutions, that shape the culture and corporate mindset of groups in conflict. In Yugoslavia, religious leaders in the Catholic, Orthodox, and Muslim faiths have as much responsibility to develop a framework for peace as do diplomats from the European Community and the United Nations.

I have personally agonized over the question of the appropriateness of mediation in a morally difficult conflict. In Burma, the military government has been exposed by the United Nations and Amnesty International as one of the worst violators of human rights in the world. A strong case can be made that conflict resolution is premature at this point. Any effort to negotiate with the Burmese government would convey some sense of legitimacy to them and thus undercut movements for genuine freedom and justice. Many people in the opposition have been critical of peace initiatives on these grounds as well as the assumption that any concessions by the government are cynical ploys to split the opposition. In such situations are negotiations and mediation ill-advised? Would it be better to intensify struggle, hopefully through nonviolent means, and just use negotiations to develop terms for military surrender when victory is near? Can one morally make a deal with the enemy? On the other hand, many groups have suffered for over forty years from the war. Dreams of victory border on fantasy for some people, so how does one realistically seek a course which will ease the suffering of the people of Burma yet open up more political participation and uphold the respect for human rights? If those issues can be brought into the negotiation process, then a significant portion of the political goals of the opposition might be achieved peacefully.

The answers to such questions are never easy or clean. When a war drags on and on, leaving a society in ruin with tens of thousands dead and still more maimed physically or emotionally, at what point does one try to find the path of peace? People we do not like often have to be faced, and conflict resolution can be used to try to humanize the relationship. The brutalizing mindset of the group in power may be changed to some degree through the process of relationship-building that takes place in negotiation. The tears of the Sudanese general over the slaughter between "brothers" gave witness to the potential for hardened warriors to find the humanity of the enemy. Sometimes people on both sides can become ensnared in their own histories, hatreds, and policies; an effective conciliation process can help both sides find the way to their positive values and enable them to build from that basis an agreement that leads them out of the morass of bloodshed.

Sometimes even the worst possible enemy might be the one who negotiates peace. It was a president of the ARENA party in El Salvador and a prime minister of the Likud party in Israel who participated in the processes to negotiate the end to the Salvadoran civil war and the Israeli/Egyptian peace treaty. ARENA and Likud were the most reactionary governments their respective countries had elected, yet they were able to participate effectively in processes of conflict resolution. Those fighting for social change, for justice and freedom, must beware of so demonizing those in power that they cut off any avenue for change through negotiated means. Progressive forces can be willing to sacrifice their own followers for the cause of their political agendas through the continued use of violence when there is little chance for success, even though negotiations could change the political context to allow for the nonviolent pursuit of social and political change. In that case the resistance may have become as corrupted as the oppressive regime against which they struggle.

Building the Just Community

Nonviolent action and conflict resolution can be brought together under the comprehensive task of building the just community among human beings. Martin Luther King, Jr., spoke of building the "beloved community." Out of the profound diversity of people and cultures we must find common bonds in our shared humanness and on the one earth in which we must live and for which we must care. If we do not, we have the capability of destroying ourselves and the ecosystems that sustain our lives. However, if we are to find a measure of peace, we will also have to build justice. Injustice is an infection in the body politic that will fester and threaten the life of the whole unless it is truly healed. Ignoring it or simply covering it up will not bring healing. So if the human family is to achieve community, it will have to be found along the road of justice.

In the tool box for building justice and peace, then, two of the most important tools are nonviolent action and conflict resolution. They have different roles to play, even as a saw and a hammer serve different functions for the carpenter. Nonviolent action is the tool for tearing away what is rotten, for confronting evil, for restoring pride to the oppressed, for shifting power imbalances, and for creating and extending values that affirm life and human dignity. Conflict resolution is the tool for opening communication, for understanding the other side, for meeting as many interests of the conflicted parties as possible, for finding common purpose, for forgiveness and reconciliation.

Even as a carpenter cannot build a house with only one tool, the house of justice and peace will not be built by nonviolent action or conflict resolution alone. Historical tasks arise when each is needed, and the challenge of the peacemaker is to discern which tool is right at what time. Often both are necessary. Nonviolent actions by Salvadorans calling for peace talks and by Americans calling for a halt to funds for the Salvadoran military were essential to create the climate for a peace process. But they were not sufficient. The United Nations mediated the peace process with the National Debate for Peace, providing political pressure and concrete proposals to keep the negotiations on track. Nonviolent action was one of the strategies of the anti-apartheid movement in South Africa, as well as armed resistance, finally forcing the government to release Nelson Mandela and legalize the African National Congress. Nonviolent action in the United States and other countries through demonstrations for divestment and the shareholder resolutions in companies doing business in South Africa brought about international pressure and a consensus for change. But the transition to majority rule, bloody and convulsive as it has been, would have been far more difficult if negotiations had not been undertaken.

Within the community of Christians engaged in peacemaking, we can learn from the use the apostle Paul made of the human body as an illustration of the church:

> For as in one body we have many members, and not all the members have the same function, so we, who are many, are one body in Christ, and individually we are members one of another. We have gifts that differ according to the grace given to us (Romans 12:4-6).

Each person has different skills and abilities, different networks of relationships, different experiences upon which to draw, and different opportunities in which to act. We each must do what we can do where we can do it, and our work for justice and peace will be different from the work of others. Some will organize nonviolent direct actions; others will mediate in negotiations. Some will speak and write, commit civil disobedience, or lobby in government circles. Others will accompany those in danger, witnessing and reporting on the situation. A few will make friends with people on the other side. Some will enter the corporate world to seek economic justice, while others will cry from the slums to demand economic justice. Some will travel far; some will stay at home. Some will concentrate on "peace issues" and others will concentrate on "justice issues." It is easy to see one's particular peacemaking task as the most important and to downplay or even denigrate what another might do. Yet Paul warned, "The eye cannot say to the hand, 'I have no need of you,' nor again the head to the feet, 'I have no need of you'" (1 Corinthians 12:21). Those engaged in bringing justice and peace need to recognize one another as allies and affirm the various works in which we are all engaged. When possible, we need to stand in solidarity with one another. If we can see the big picture, the overarching vision of the just community for which we strive, then perhaps we can coordinate our functioning better.

A part of that efficient functioning is to heed the advice of the preacher in Ecclesiastes, "For everything there is a season, and a time for every matter under heaven" (Ecclesiastes 3:1). The timing of conflict resolution is critical to its success. The danger of premature conflict resolution can be lessened with an appropriate understanding of the need for adequate awareness of the root issues of the conflict and a balance, though not usually symmetrical, of power between the conflicted parties if mediation is to be effective. Maire A. Dugan holds that efforts to bring the conflict to the surface, to make all parties aware of the conflict, and to create a degree of empowerment for the weaker party are essential in the earlier stages of a conflict as preparation for successful mediation. She believes that "the more appropriate roles for a conflict intervener to play at these early stages are those of activist and advocate rather than mediator or conciliator."[4] To help raise awareness, education is required. Then, as people recognize the conflict, confrontation is necessary in order to achieve a more balanced situation. At this stage the use of nonviolence is especially potent as it brings the conflict to a head, strengthens the nonviolent actionists in ways that are harder for a dominating power to counter than violent attempts to shift the balance, and does the least amount of damage to the relationship in the confrontation so that the conflict can move toward mediation and resolution. As there are times when the work of the eye is most vital and other times when the ear provides the critical data, so, too, nonviolence and conflict resolution each have their best moments in the unfolding of a conflict to be creative elements in the struggle for a just peace. At other times, or even simultaneously, other forms of peacemaking action may be most appropriate, such as grassroots organizing, government intervention, electoral campaigns, litigation, or education. A wise peacemaker is able to welcome and participate in a variety of these activities.

Building the just community requires working on concrete solutions to often very mundane problems. Sometimes the solutions grow out of demands in a nonviolence movement or an agreement negotiated through a conflict resolution process. At other times the justice building is preemptive, striving to find a solution to a problem before it explodes into a destructive conflict. For example, working out distribution of water in the Middle East is a critical piece to the peace puzzle. Any lasting peace settlement will have to address successfully the issues of control, use, and access to water, for water is absolutely essential in determining where people live and the economic enterprises which can take place. Water is an interest that all parties bring to the table, whenever they get that far. It is not as dynamic a news story as terrorist attacks or military incursions, but it is one major component of the problem underlying those violent forms of conflict. Every conflict has its specific issues or cluster of concerns that require practical solutions if resolution is to be achieved over the long haul. Technical issues about environmental control, environmental cleanup, immigration, prison reform, police training, community relations, administrative efficiency, public input, cross-cultural understanding, arms agreement verification, air traffic control, and a host of others may arise in the effort to find or sustain peace from a local or international level. Christians, indeed any and all people of good will, acting competently in these areas need to be recognized and affirmed in their role in establishing justice and creating peace.

Community means relationship, and building relationships across the fault lines of conflict is a vital piece of peacemaking work. Nonviolence assumes a human connection between the resister and the one in power. Nonviolent protesters in the Philippines, in the Soviet Union during the August 1991 coup attempt, and in China sought to establish common bonds with the soldiers sent to repress them, sometime providing them food or giving them flowers. When the relationships were strong enough, the soldiers sometimes refused to follow orders or even joined in the opposition. In conflict resolution, relationship-building is essential in establishing enough trust to enter into negotiations. That relationship may be too strained to stand on its own; a mediator may be required as the bonding agent. In the peace talks in Nicaragua between the Sandinistas and the Indian resistance, in the Sudan, and at Camp David, relationships played an important role in helping the parties find the way to agreement.

Relationship-building can be encouraged at many levels. Creating a climate for peace requires efforts to overcome enemy stereotypes and build enough conflict-transcending linkages that a joint stake is developed in the conciliation process. Prior to the ending of the Cold War, thousands of American and Soviet citizens had traveled to the other's country, meeting "the enemy" face-to-face and hearing the desire for peace. Many peace organizations and professional groups have sponsored friendship tours or exchanges with countries on the "other side." Cities and towns have developed partnerships with cities and towns in other nations. All these ties help to humanize the other in our minds. In the mental formation of "the enemy," truth is the first

casualty. We dehumanize and even demonize the other. One prominent magazine during the build-up to the Gulf War put a touched-up
photo of Saddam Hussein on their cover; his mustache was drawn to
look exactly like Adolf Hitler's. Enemies can become nonpersons in
our eyes. I heard a U.S. diplomat at the U.N. publicly refer to how
few lives were lost in the Gulf War, effectively discounting the one
hundred thousand Iraqis who were killed in those few short months.
Intentional distortion of the other is a part of our way of waging
conflict, so any way the true face of the enemy can be encountered
helps to erode the barriers of lies and stereotypes built up between
the sides.[5]

Today, relationship-building is going on throughout the world. In
Israel and the occupied territories, Elias Chacour, a Palestinian
Melkite priest, has established a peace center in Galilee where Israeli
Jews and Palestinians listen to each other's stories of persecution,
displacement, death, and sorrow. Palestinian students live on *kibbut-
zim,* and Jewish students live in Palestinian villages for short periods
of time.[6] Relationships are made that may help provide a common
bond to support a joint search for peace. Relationship-building is also
going on in South Africa. Koinonia Southern Africa is an ecumenical
organization that brings blacks and white together. The main program is a four-family grouping, two black and two white, who meet
at each family's home for meals and discussion about their nation's
future. At the end of the rotation, the group makes some sort of public
witness, such as going together to a park to play and eat.

In American cities with school systems reflecting the diversity of
the United Nations, relationship-building is occurring through community organizations and churches. Public education in appreciating
various cultures in our society is attempting to shape a new generation of citizens who can deal more constructively with the pluralism
of modern America. In Northern Ireland, the YMCA provides cross-
community seminars and trains volunteers to facilitate group discussions between Catholics and Protestants. They have an official
position of Reconciliation Coordinator to carry on peacemaking efforts through relationship-building at the local level.

The task of building the just community on a global scale has seen
major strides taken in the past decades. For all its limitations and
failings, the United Nations has continued to develop as a system for
the nations of the world to work on common problems, to resolve
conflicts, and to hammer out shared values. Though compliance is far
from universal, statements such as the Universal Declaration on the
Rights of the Child and the Universal Declaration on Human Rights

and other conventions have given expression to a growing consensus about basic values that transcend cultures and political systems. Agencies such as the World Health Organization have been the means for international cooperation to tackle challenges facing many parts of the human community.

The International Court of Justice at The Hague has provided a place for conflicts to be peacefully adjudicated. The Conference on Disarmament, an ongoing negotiating body, has established numerous arms treaties, including the recent global ban on chemical weapons. Though many conflicts and areas of disarmament have not been adequately addressed through the United Nations system due to political differences among the nation-states or because of funding shortages, the attempt to build a system for international global coordination is moving the world to a political stage of development as profound as that of the development of the nation-state.

But governments who are the members of the United Nations are not the exclusive participants in the process of building the global community. Even the U.N. recognizes the importance of nongovernmental organizations (NGOs) in this endeavor. NGOs often connect people across national divides far more intimately and positively than governments and inter-governmental agencies can. Organizations along professional lines, such as parliamentarians or educators, bring people together to exchange ideas and solve problems on issues that affect many countries. Human rights organizations promote international values and standards of conduct, as well as monitor adherence or lack of adherence to those basic standards. Relief agencies mobilize resources from around the world to assist in areas of greatest need. Religious organizations link people of common faith together across national, linguistic, and cultural boundaries and bring people of different faiths together in a quest for common foundations and values. The growing web of relationships is vital for developing an understanding of each other, our cultures, and our needs, so we can work together to resolve crises and solve problems which threaten us all. These ties also help us to have a common stake in peace, so that our energies will be directed to protecting that global fabric rather than tearing it apart out of the myopic focus on my own or my group's own little thread. Every step in building that community is a step toward peace.

Education

In light of the expansion and increased sophistication of both nonviolence and conflict resolution in the last decade, what can churches do to participate more effectively in the ministry of peace-making? What adjustments need to be made to become leaders in the quest for justice and peace rather than remaining ponderous institutions reacting to challenges from other sectors of society?

I see three central areas where the work of churches could be instrumental in advancing the cause of peace, if the commitment exists to follow through on this historic opportunity: education, relationship-building, and infrastructure. Education has always been a major sphere of ministry for churches. Education needs to be more thoroughly developed in both the biblical basis for peacemaking and practical application in contemporary contexts. Some sectors of the global Christian community have done extensive teaching on peace and justice. Liberation theology, for example, has developed in many cultural settings to provide critical reflection on the intersecting of the gospel and human struggles for justice and freedom. The World Council of Churches has lifted up the theme of "Justice, Peace and the Integrity of Creation" to give direction and focus to their corporate mission. There are some serious theological problems with liberation theologies, but matters of justice, poverty, and peace are explicitly brought to the forefront of teaching and ethics. Other segments of the Christian community, however, are functionally illiterate when it comes to understanding or even recognizing the biblical teachings on justice and peace. There is more in the Bible on the poor than on the Holy Spirit, yet many Christians who know almost every verse related to the Holy Spirit know little, if anything, about the biblical perspective on poverty. There are more verses on peace than about the Second Coming of Christ, yet Christian bookstores have many shelves with titles ranging from the responsible to the ridiculous about eschatology, and most of the books related to war and peace spout militaristic ideology. There are significant parts of the Christian community where creative working out of evangelism and social ethics is taking place, but there is still much to be done to bring such holistic teaching across the Christian theological spectrum.

The lack of biblical knowledge on justice and peace might not seem a serious issue, but because the more conservative wings of Christianity are active in evangelistic outreach, they are expanding in membership, while more socially involved mainline denominations in the United States and Europe are in severe decline. The media has become a vehicle for the expansion of a chauvinistic and right-wing version of the gospel that is often intimately linked with capitalist expansion and American national interests. Biblical teaching on peace and justice is spiritualized, and liberation theology, which seeks to apply those teachings in the context of contemporary struggle, is roundly denounced. The result is that the gospel being offered in many mission settings is inadequate to face the traumas of conflict. I received a letter from one church leader in a country torn by war. He wrote about how the churches had never learned about the Bible's teaching on peace; they never were taught about the ministry of peacemaking. So when the war broke out, most of the churches were at a loss as to how to minister in the rapid changes sweeping through their country.

A solid and cogent grounding in the biblical teachings about justice and peace is necessary to strengthen and build our peacemaking work. As the early church tried to grapple with the implications of Jesus' life and teaching, they focused on two primarily ethical keys. They knew they were on the right track if their faith was working out in the areas of ethnic relations and poverty. The Jew/Gentile struggle in the church definitely had theological dimensions, but it also was clearly expressed in the social patterns among Christians who had supposedly worked the theology out. In Paul's writings the issue gets down to the mundane matter of who you eat with (Galatians 2:11-21) because of the very nature of Christ's death. Christ overcomes the social labels we bear, making us all one (Colossians 3:11, Galatians 3:28). When the Jerusalem Council met on the issue of inclusion of Gentiles into what had until then been viewed as an ethnically homogeneous church, the other defining ethical issue was concern for the poor (Galatians 2:10), not the dietary rules that faded away as the church became more culturally inclusive. Jesus called the rich young ruler to do the one thing he lacked: sell what he owned and give the money to the poor (Mark 10:21). John discerned if love was genuinely of God by how one cared for the poor (1 John 3:17). James declared that faith that does not care for the poor is dead (James 2:15-17), and that care for the poor is the central mark of a religion that is "pure and undefiled" (James 1:27).

The conflicts in the post-Cold War era are primarily rooted in ethnic hatred and economic injustice. The gospel of the early church directly addressed these root issues of conflict, yet how much of Western Christianity presents a gospel that says little if anything on these topics? Far too many Christian communities are wrapped up in homogeneous groups, segregated in the worship services that are the center of our corporate lives. We thank God for our prosperity and perhaps undertake small missions of mercy to the unfortunate, but we dare not challenge economic structures that are increasing the gap between the rich and the poor because our own livelihood and institutional maintenance are wedded to those structures. The church, particularly in the West but also in the "Two-Thirds World" where our missions have often carried these distortions of the gospel, needs a renewal of teaching and application of the gospel message regarding justice and peace. We need to hear the centrality of ethnic reconciliation through Christ who is our Peace in a land where hate crimes are on the rise and in a world where ethnic cleansing is becoming a policy of choice for some people. We need to hear the vision of justice and peace embracing (Psalm 85:10) in a world where the haves and have-nots move further apart and where wars are waged to maintain the economic interests of those who have control of the resources.

Ephesians 4:11-12 speaks of the gifts given to people in the church, particularly pastors and teachers, "to equip the saints for the work of ministry." If Christians are to engage effectively in nonviolent actions or conflict resolution processes, whether in their communities or in national and international struggles, they should be equipped for those ministries through the work of the church. Training in the principles and practice of nonviolence can be a part of Christian education curriculums. Our church in Boston once hosted a nonviolence training session since many of us were involved in the Pledge of Resistance to try to change U.S. policy in Central America. Some of our Sunday school teachers who were also meeting in the church that day were surprised to witness us dragging each other across the floor as we learned how to be disciplined and nonviolent in the face of potential police violence. During the civil rights movement, training sessions were held in churches to prepare people for the brutalities they would face as they marched for freedom. In the Philippines, nonviolence training in the churches was the foundation for the historic uprising of the People Power movement. No one can tell when a historic challenge will be issued to a neighborhood or a nation. No one can tell when the random violence in society will tear into their personal lives. If people are prepared by their training in nonviolence, they will be ready to rise to the occasion.

Christians need equipping in conflict resolution as well. Since everyone experiences some form of conflict almost on a daily basis, these are practical life skills that can immediately be put to use. Schools are offering conflict resolution training, but churches can also be centers for conflict resolution training out of the value system we have in the gospel of reconciliation. Some churches are developing Christian conflict resolution curriculums for use in their afterschool programs or youth groups. Adult classes can study books that have been published on the topic. Sermons and Bible studies on the case studies in this book can help people interpret their own conflicts and learn how to be more creatively involved in them.[7]

A church's education program can also include direct experience, breaking people out of the socially isolated setting of many middle- and upper-class American Christians. Contact needs to be made with the poor, the marginal, the despised, and the weak in the world, for they have much to teach those who are in positions of privilege. Listening to those who suffer under policies of exploitation and militarization, whether in the poor countries of the southern hemisphere or in impoverished urban neighborhoods, can open up our eyes to the nature and cost of such policies. Direct encounters of this sort can stimulate us to reexamine our theological assumptions, open our eyes to overlooked portions of Scripture, and change our lifestyles to be more just.

The educational process can be supported and invigorated by a congregation's worship experiences. In worship God's values and vision for humanity can be lifted up, celebrated, and brought into creative tension with our present. Readings and sermons can draw from the wealth in the Bible on God's passion for justice and peace; prayers, songs, and liturgies can give form to the response coming from the wellsprings of our spirituality. In addition to experiencing encouragement for our spiritual journey, we can be convicted about our complicity in the present order and its injustices. A holy dissatisfaction can be fed, prompting us to engage more deeply in projects for renewing the world and alleviating the suffering caused by injustice and war.

I experienced the conjunction of worship, divine values, and the world's conflict at a vigil outside the United Nations. We had gathered in support of the U.N.'s Third Special Session of Disarmament in 1988. As we stood beneath the "Isaiah Wall" that speaks of nations beating their swords into plowshares, we sang an old revivalist hymn:

What have I to dread, what have I to fear,
Leaning on the everlasting arms.
I have blessed peace with my Lord so near,
Leaning on the everlasting arms.
Leaning on Jesus, leaning on Jesus,
Safe and secure from all alarms,
Leaning on Jesus, leaning on Jesus,
Leaning on the everlasting arms.

In that moment of history and at that place, with delegates gathered from the nations of the world to try to slow the arms race, that old hymn took on a new prophetic power. Our trust was not in nuclear arms, but God's everlasting arms. Our faith was a critique to our world, our nations, and ourselves for the idolatry of military might which had created such obscene levels of armaments. That hymn could no longer be only about personal piety, but was a challenge to the powers that be in the world which seduce us to lean on nuclear arms in order to be safe and secure.

Placing our Christian education, our worship, and our spirituality in the context of the conflicted world can transform and energize congregational life. We are building upon our strengths as churches as we seek to expand our creative impact in the world. If our Christian education is biblically based, tuned to the hurts of the world, connected directly to people's needs and experiences, and woven into the worshiping life of the church, then it will be truly transformative. Our education will not only affect the world around us by what it enables us to do, but also energize our faith as we see how the gospel does have something to give us in the midst of our struggles and pains.

Relationship-Building

Churches need to strengthen their peacemaking ministry in relationship-building. Because of mission partnerships built over the years and the basic Christian ethic of love, relationships that cross cultural and national lines have been a major component of Christian community. Though there has been much cultural chauvinism on the part of Western Christians, the growing cross-cultural sensitivity in missions has seen more partnership models develop. These ties between Christians from different nations have deeper roots than the political alignments of the current period and will probably outlast them. Thus, the relationships between Christians in different national churches can provide a conciliating link upon which peacemaking efforts can build.

In Nicaragua, the link in partnerships between the Nicaraguan Baptist Convention and the American Baptist Churches had a definite impact upon the quest for peace. The Nicaraguan Baptists sent a series of pastoral letters to the churches in the United States, relating the situation in their country in a way which was very different from that presented by the U.S. administration. Through the testimony of Baptist missionaries to Nicaragua returning on home assignments, an alternative viewpoint critical of U.S. policy was presented in the churches, adding fuel to the resistance through advocacy and demonstrations in the United States. Gustavo Parajón, a native Nicaraguan, is supported by the ABC International Ministries, and his mediation effort was sustained in large part from that mission partnership. These partnerships also inspired American Baptists to participate in Witness for Peace and the Pledge of Resistance. The group in our church made a huge banner with a quotation from one of the Nicaraguan Baptist Convention's pastoral letters; we displayed the banner during protests at the Federal Building in Boston. Some of our members who committed civil disobedience said that they never would have considered such action if it were not for the sense of Christian family linking them to the Nicaraguan Baptists.

The same kind of relational history has been important in Burma. Adoniram and Ann Judson were the first missionaries in Burma, and through their efforts and many other colleagues, Baptists are the largest religious group among some of the hill tribes. One hundred and seventy-five years of mission history have given Baptists credibility there, which becomes an asset in trying to find the way to peace. My own involvement in mediation efforts was based mostly on my identity as a Baptist from the United States, which led to a partnership with a Kachin Baptist leader who was working as the mediator from within the conflict. The insurgent leader, Brang Seng, was a Baptist, and our religious ties were important in establishing the trust necessary to take the risks for opening up the peace process. Support for peace, human rights, and democracy in Burma has been generated in the United States in part through Christians who have emotional ties to the mission work there. Burma is insignificant to U.S. policy, but to Americans who are bonded to people in Burma by love through decades of Christian mission, Burma is very important. Besides the Burmese exile community, church-related groups are probably the most motivated to bring international pressure upon the Burmese government to overturn their repressive policies.

Mission partnerships have become the basis for peacemaking ministry in many denominations. The Lutherans have had a special role in Namibia and El Salvador because of the leadership of indigenous Lutherans, including Bishop Medardo Gomez of El Salvador. Presbyterians have extensive ties in the Middle East and so can assist others in understanding and action. Roman Catholics have done cutting-edge mission work for justice and peace, especially through the work of orders such as the Maryknolls and Jesuits. The martyred priests and religious women in El Salvador both testified to their peacework amidst that country's war and inspired the ongoing commitment to advocacy and solidarity actions in the United States and Europe. The web of mission partnerships has been intentionally used to strengthen ministry for justice and peace, including the transnational solidarity linkages. These long-standing relationships can be utilized more intentionally in assisting national church bodies to become more effective agents for building just community and in mobilizing North American churches for partnership in the mission for peace.

Relationships of love provide a motivation for sustained and risky action. They give the inner strength to stand against the social pressures to join the bandwagons of hatred when war policies are being developed. They provide an avenue for truth to be communicated when the media is dominated by the messages shaped by the programmatic goals of "government sources." Direct contacts between people in North America with people in other countries can take place through mission work tours or peacemaking "friendship tours." The Baptist Peace Fellowship of North America, a grassroots organization with members from thirteen Baptist conventions, has sponsored tours to many regions of conflict and to countries labeled as "the enemy." The emotional impact for relationship-building through such encounters can be far more energizing for peacemaking than the most cogent rational discourse. As a long-time peace activist, I have always been against nuclear weapons and the Cold War relationship of the United States and the Soviet Union; but it was only after visiting the Soviet Union and spending hours in conversation with people there that I felt the full horror of the evil in the nuclear threat posed by each side. While worshiping in Baptist churches in various cities in the Soviet Union, I knew that Christ was at ground zero where our missiles were targeted, and that God's image resided in atheists who spoke with me of their own hopes, fears, and frustrations. We have also hosted people from various countries in our home. In many cultures eating together is a sign of acceptance and commitment. I know all our guests continue to be carried in my heart and cannot be enemy to me no matter what our governments say or do to each other. Jesus said, "No one has greater love than this, to lay down one's life for one's friends" (John 15:13). Friends are made through building relationships, and as those friendships are forged, the motivation swells for taking loving risks for peace.

International friendships are not the only relationships that need to be established. Ethnic diversity, which could be a rich resource for us all to draw upon, far too often becomes a basis for polarization in American society. Relationships need to be established close at home. It can seem easy for Americans to love Russians, Nicaraguans, Palestinians, and black South Africans, and yet be alienated from the neighbors in our own communities. The uprising in Los Angeles in

1992 revealed the fractured nature of much of our society. Efforts to build bridges of understanding between blacks and whites and Hispanics and Asians and Native Americans have been going on for years, but often they do not get further than trite sentimentalities that make some people feel they have accomplished something, but which only add to the cynical frustration of others.

One of the best ways to build relationships is not to begin with the relationship itself but with a task. Ending the arms race and halting aid to the Contras gave American and Soviet citizens and American and Nicaraguan citizens a common purpose around which the relationships could grow. To make progress in peacemaking within the United States, common tasks need to be addressed with multicultural alliances. For example, improving housing or the economic development of poor communities or improving public education can become specific tasks in which a wide range of ethnic groups can join for common cause. "If you want peace, work for justice" is a refrain heard from many sectors of our society, especially from the minority communities. The flip side was chanted during the burning of Los Angeles: "No justice, no peace." Justice is built: it is a task, something one does. Adopting common mission tasks in the pursuit of justice will provide a context of commitment for the relationships to be built. Then, with a common ground and common stake in the project, the relationship itself can stand the strain of examination as the more insidious and deeply rooted issues of racism, sexism, and other relational injustices are intentionally examined. This is not to preclude the prophetic exposure and denunciation of such evils or their confrontation through nonviolence. Rather, building the relationship to bridge the divide created by human injustice will happen most effectively when the first step is a concrete task that both addresses a common need and that points toward a just future.

Infrastructure

When President Dwight Eisenhower gave his farewell address, he warned the nation of the rising power of the "military-industrial complex," that network of institutions, corporations, universities, and government entities who have a vested interest in sustaining a level of conflict high enough for profits to be made and careers enhanced. When conflict boils over to the point of war, this broad infrastructure can mobilize people, material, financial resources, and decision-making capabilities for the war. When the United States and its allies went to war against Iraq in the Persian Gulf, despite record budget deficits, tens of billions of dollars were rapidly raised for the use of all the mechanisms and forces in place for the goal of military victory. No comparable "peace-and-justice complex" exists in our nation or the world. Nations always find money to make war, while peace goes begging.

A conference at the Carter Center in Atlanta in January 1992 focused on exploring creative efforts to advance peace in eight specific conflicts: Angola, Sudan, Liberia, Cyprus, Korea, Burma, Afghanistan, and Cambodia. As the participants in each group reported on their challenges and opportunities in each conflict, a common theme emerged. In every case there were key elements of an infrastructure missing, and the most frequent missing element was money. In Liberia, elections had been agreed to by all the warring factions and monitors had been trained, but there was no money to hold the elections. In Cambodia, a U.N.-mediated agreement had been reached, but the U.N. was unable to get the thousands of administrative personnel and peacekeeping troops to Cambodia because funds were not available. The U.N. cannot levy taxes, so it is dependent upon the willingness of the member states to pay their assessments voluntarily. NGO mediating groups often have to limit their operations because of small budgets, which can lead to lost opportunities, stretched-out processes, increased losses of human life, and greater economic dislocation. Jimmy Carter is leading the way in developing the International Negotiation Network as one part of the solution to the need to develop an international infrastructure for peace, but the religious community needs to rise to the challenge and refine its peacemaking infrastructure as well.

Jesus told a parable that speaks to meeting changing situations:

> No one puts new wine into old wineskins; otherwise, the wine will burst the skins, and the wine is lost, and so are the skins; but one puts new wine into fresh wineskins (Mark 2:22).

The explosion of nonviolence movements and efforts in conflict resolution in the last decade is a new wine that is stretching the structural wineskins of our era, including the religious institutions. Some steps have been taken to provide fresh wineskins for this new wine. The historic peace churches have been in the best position to do this because of their long involvement in peacemaking endeavors. The American Friends Service Committee and the Mennonite Central Committee have engaged in many ventures to support peace, from mediating in conflicts to providing training and education in nonviolence. Some mainline denominations such as the Presbyterian Church (U.S.A.), the Evangelical Lutheran Church in America, the United Church of Christ, and the American Baptist Churches have established and staffed peace programs. The Anglican Church assigned Terry Waite as a special representative of the archbishop of Canterbury to engage in humanitarian negotiations in Libya, Iran, and Lebanon. Most of the peacemaking efforts, however, remain in the more traditional channels of advocacy and education. Nonviolence training or mediation are done on an *ad hoc* basis, if done at all. A challenge for the peacemaker involved in a mediation effort is to develop the financial basis for the project and to identify or create an administrative center to handle financial and logistical matters. In the terminology of Jesus, new wineskins must be made to properly hold the fermenting new wine.

One possible new wineskin is to develop a financial center, perhaps a foundation, in the wealthier countries that could be linked through the mission partnerships of churches to indigenous leaders involved in mediation or strategic peace initiatives in conflicted countries. The insider-partial mediators who might play a major role in peace processes in poorer countries often lack the resources to provide for their own travel between the warring parties, let alone host high-level talks. If a financial pool and a structure for accountability could be set up, these indigenous mediators could be teamed with mission partners with access to financial and technical assistance. The mediators would be able to focus their attention on the conflict itself rather than constantly worrying about scraping together the funds to take the next step.

Another new wineskin could be a religious version of Carter's International Negotiation Network. Carter has gathered notable persons from around the world to offer their services for mediation. Could not major religious leaders do the same? Many conflicts involve different religious groups, though often ethnicity or economics are the core issues in the conflict, not the religious differences. Yet once the conflict gets started, religion becomes a weapon. Each side claims divine blessing on its war-making. Iraq's Saddam Hussein, though his Baathist political party is secular, called upon Muslims to engage in a *jihad*, a holy war, against the Western coalition led by the United States. On the other side, George Bush defended his policies before the National Association of Religious Broadcasters in terms of the Christian just war position. An organized network of religious leaders from many faiths could withdraw religious blessing upon armed conflict in a particular setting and instead offer their services to work on conciliation. Imagine global figures in the Roman Catholic Church, the Orthodox Church, and Islam condemning the violence and offering to mediate in the conflict in former Yugoslavia. Imagine Christian,

Muslim, and Jewish leaders offering to help mediate in Lebanon, or between the Israelis and the Arab states and Palestinians. Imagine Buddhist and Hindu leaders offering to mediate in Sri Lanka. Imagine the pope, the archbishop of Canterbury, and high-level Protestant clerics offering their services in Northern Ireland. Such a dream would require those religious figures to begin peacemaking among themselves, but they have an ongoing interfaith dialogue to build upon, as well as "peace saints" in every religious tradition. A "heads of communions" group of Protestant leaders met with President Alfredo Christiani of El Salvador to call for an end to human rights abuses and to press for peace. That same group traveled to the Middle East, visiting Iraq, Jordan, and Israel prior to the outbreak of the Persian Gulf war, calling upon the opposing sides to pursue a nonviolent resolution to the crisis. These efforts are steps in the right direction, but the time may be ripe for a bolder, global network to be established.

Grassroots infrastructure is also vital for peacemaking, and this is where much of the driving force for change has been generated. Denominational peace fellowships and interfaith groups like the Fellowship of Reconciliation have mobilized ordinary people to do extraordinary peacemaking. These grassroots networks need to be affirmed as major expressions of the church's mission work for justice and peace. They have been new wineskins developed with the flexibility to respond quickly to the challenges of the day. Denominational bodies can see these grassroots organizations as partners, working together for common goals. Sometimes bureaucracies and grassroots organizations will come into conflict themselves, and here the personal practice of peacemaking is vital if the efficiency of both groups is to be maintained. The body image from the apostle Paul, in which each part has need of the others, can again be applied in the appreciation of the roles and strengths of both denominational religious structures and grassroots activist networks.

Taking the Risks for Peace

To follow the path of peace in the midst of conflict carries inherent risk, for peace has to be created out of contexts where life and death are at stake, along with a host of other interests. Some of the interests are resources, such as land or water, while others are political in nature, such as self-determination. But whatever the root issue of conflict may be, through the course of the strife a thick layer of bitterness, hurt, and anger builds up. Peacemakers insert themselves into that volatile context where there are no promises about the outcome or guarantees about safety. For the churches to participate fully as peacemakers into the next century, the risks must be acknowledged and accepted.

Like conflict resolution, nonviolence also carries risks. Although those taking nonviolent direct action may have the inner conviction and the discipline to maintain their nonviolence, they are engaged in conflict. The opposing side will choose its strategy for the conflict, which is often repressive and violent if such tactics have been habitual. In fact, if the nonviolence activists seriously challenge a power system, they can count on an initial reaction of repression. Gene Sharp sees repression as the natural step for a ruler to take:

> When a system largely characterized by political violence is actively, albeit non-violently, challenged, one can expect that the basic nature of that system will be more clearly revealed in the crisis than during less difficult times. The violence upon which the system depends is thus brought to the surface and revealed in unmistakable terms for all to see: it then becomes more possible to remove it.[8]

If church leaders in any way encourage or train people to participate in nonviolent action, they are risking the exposure of those people to violence. Just as people recruited to fight in the military risk becoming casualties, those who participate in nonviolent actions are putting their lives at risk. If the churches hold a prayer vigil and then march for democracy, as they did in Zaire, they should not be surprised when they are fired upon by the soldiers propping up the dictatorial regime. Those who confront oppressive powers, be they Jeremiah, John the Baptist, or Archbishop Romero, become targets of those powers who cannot stand moral challenges.

Of course, if one does not take the risk, evil is allowed to continue on its own course. Those gunned down as they prayed in Zaire could have quietly continued in their suffering, letting their children die of malnutrition while Mobutu grew rich off their poverty. A Christian gospel that speaks of life after death and of a Christ who modeled sacrificial love even to the point of death can inspire the courage to lay down one's life or to face the other terrors of repression. Adolfo Pérez Esquivel wrote his friends a letter on a piece of tissue paper smuggled out of an Argentine prison:

> Yet there's always a light shining, to clarify and explain all these trials—God's presence every moment in every move—the God of love who forgives from the cross, down across the ages: Father, forgive them; they do not know what they are doing. Here in prison I've lived Holy Week in the grace of a greater understanding of the commitment, sacrifice, and love of Christ who shed his blood for every-

*one, for all humanity. What Easter gladness—the gladness of Christ
as he triumphs by love, Christ risen and right here! Alleluia!*[9]

The risk to act nonviolently in resistance of oppression and for
justice and peace is a risk not taken alone. The testimony of Christians through the ages and even in so many of the recent struggles is
that Christ was present with them.

The risk of brutality is not as great in the United States, but anyone
who has been involved in an act of civil disobedience can bear witness
to the volatility of such events even when the demonstrators are
thoroughly committed to nonviolence in action and word. Police
officers can be unnecessarily and intentionally rough, sometimes
causing injury. The civil rights movement often saw police brutality
at its worst with fire hoses, attack dogs, and clubs used with abandon
against nonviolent marchers. In jail cells many people were severely
beaten when out of view of the cameras. When Vietnam veteran and
peace activist Brian Willson was run over by an arms train, he and
other demonstrators sitting on the tracks were scrambling to get off,
yet the train never applied the brakes. While recuperating in the
hospital from the loss of his legs, Willson said that he was joining the
thousands of Central Americans who had lost their legs in the war he
was protesting, many of whom he had met in his travels in the
region.[10] This bonding through relationships with those who suffer in
a conflict also gives one strength to face the risks of waging peace.

A number of peacemakers from around the world are experiment-
ing with nonviolent forms of intervention in conflicts, drawing upon
the experiences of Witness for Peace and other actions in conflict
zones. The Mennonites and Brethren churches have established
Christian Peacemaker Teams, volunteers trained extensively in nonviolence to engage in nonviolent actions, mediation, observation,
conflict transformation, and documentation of human rights abuses.
The Christian Peacemaker Teams are being deployed in areas of
conflict such as Haiti and the Gaza Strip. Peace Brigades International has been involved in similar activities, often accompanying
people who are at risk of assassination. Thousands of European and
North American Christians have been involved in nonviolent inter-
ventions in Bosnia and Croatia in 1993 and 1994. *Sjeme Mira* (Serbo-
Croatian for "Seeds of Peace") is working to establish a long-term
nonviolent witness in the midst of that war, promoting grassroots
reconciliation and working with the war victims. In 1993, many
activists from nongovernmental organizations and U.N. officials met
in New York to explore the possibilities of establishing a Global Peace
Service to deploy volunteers with peacemaking skills at crisis points,

providing a nonviolent and nongovernmental presence as a complementary alternative to the U.N. peacekeepers. All these efforts will put the volunteers at risk. Deaths are sure to come, for mortar shells in Sarajevo do not discriminate, to say nothing about actions of assassins, death squads, or military units who might view any outsiders as enemies. But even as military personnel recognize the risks of death or injury in war, peacemakers, too, recognize that such risks must be taken if they are to have any impact at the heart of the violence.

Whereas the nonviolence activist is engaging directly in the conflict, the mediator is seeking to assist everyone in solving it. The mediating position is hardly a safe one, however. Mediators are stepping between forces of often uncontrolled violence, and in such a setting they are often accused of being on the other side and sometimes treated accordingly. Proverbs from around the world attest the dangerous position of the mediators: "The hardest blow of the fight falls on the one who steps between." "The peacemaker gets two-thirds of the blows." "The mediator is struck from both sides."[11] A mediator will also have to be willing to face the risks.

The Chinese tell the story of Wu Fong, a mandarin assigned to pacify aboriginal tribes in Taiwan who had practiced headhunting. Wu Fong slowly won their trust and persuaded them to give up headhunting. The tribal people grew to love Wu Fong as they enjoyed the peace of their new lives. Then the land was struck by a severe drought, and religious leaders said their god was angry that heads were no longer being offered in sacrifice. Wu Fong tried to turn them aside from a return to their warring ways, and after failing to dissuade them offered an alternative. At a certain time and place a Chinese man dressed in red would ride by on horseback. He could be seized and sacrificed. As Wu Fong had prophesied, it happened. The people attacked the rider and beheaded him. When the head was erected on a stake at the village, they stared in shock; it was their friend Wu Fong. From then on headhunting was never practiced again.[12] Wu Fong's willingness to sacrifice himself for the sake of peace reflects the same mediator's love seen in Christ.

There can be a tremendous cost to forging peace as well as to providing encouragement for those who must face danger as they take on the role of mediator. Saboi Jum has received death threats and had property confiscated in the pursuit of peace in Burma. Terry Waite was held captive for five years in Lebanon after U.S. political intrigue over the Iran/Contra affair put him at risk while negotiating the release of other Western hostages in Lebanon. Leaders of the

National Debate for Peace in El Salvador were put on military death lists by people who wanted to prolong the war. A mediator is extremely vulnerable, yet that vulnerability is also an asset in trying to build the trust that may lead to negotiation. Carl Upchurch sees a significant part of his trustworthiness for urban gangs in that he has no "soldiers," no armed gang members to carry out his bidding. Vulnerability creates the safe place for peace to be nurtured.

John Paul Lederach endured threats to kidnap his daughter, threats of his own assassination, detainment, interrogation, and mob violence in the process of mediating in Nicaragua. In his reflections on his experiences in Nicaragua and the choices which he as a North American had to continue in the mediation effort, he wrote:

> The very essence of the gospel is most needed and vicariously experienced in those places where our safety, security and life may be most at risk. It is an intentional theology of choosing to take the risk of working on the ministry of reconciliation. It is choosing to make present the reconciling love of Christ in concrete ways in places where the most suspicion, animosity, and hatred exist.[13]

The mediator is following in the footsteps of Jesus, who went to the places of human pain and hatred to incarnate God's love. The same commitment that has propelled all Christian mission drives the work of these ministers of reconciliation.

There is an additional risk when Christian individuals or mission agencies enter as outsiders into a conflict. The kind of chauvinism that assumes that we know what is best for others can cloak itself in the most noble ideals, and what can be more noble than peace? Intrusion into the conflicts of others has been carried on through recent decades by intelligence agencies which act to advance the policy objectives of their own country. Though thinking themselves above such deception and manipulation, Christians may unconsciously impose cultural or religious norms upon others which are neither helpful nor valid. As outsiders, the mediators or nonviolence practitioners seeking to express solidarity may be manipulated themselves by participants in the conflict from one side or the other.

The risks of naive intrusion can be lessened if the peacemaker is humble enough to learn and remembers that the choices belong to the people who have to live with the conflict and whatever resolution is achieved. The peacemaker coming from outside can only provide some of the tools for building the house of justice and peace, adding to the toolbox by educating, training, and providing resources, opportunities, and a broader pool of experience upon which to draw. But the choice of which tools to use and when to use them will need to be made by the conflicted parties and by insiders who have assumed mediating roles. There is a risk here also in that people may choose to reject what we offer. Resistance movements may choose violence; our offers of mediation may not be accepted. Such choices may be painful and tragic to observe, but when they are made, they must be respected. That does not mean, however, the peacemaker gives up. The Latin American concept of *coyuntura* or "timing" needs to be remembered. The task of building peace may require perseverance, coming again and again with the offer of oneself to assist when the participants in a conflict are ready to make new efforts to find a way out of their destructive tangle.

The question of risk must ultimately be faced both by the individual peacemaker and by Christian churches and mission agencies in gospel terms. Jesus said repeatedly, "For those who want to save their life will lose it, and those who lose their life for my sake, and for the sake of the gospel, will save it" (Mark 8:35; Matthew 10:39; 16:25; Luke 9:24; 17:33; John 12:25). Transforming and reconciling power is unleashed amidst the world's conflicts when individuals and groups are willing to give of themselves in creative action rather than living merely to protect their personal or institutional lives. Life is found in laying it down. The world has been dramatically changed in the last decade because of the courage and commitment of people from every continent who have taken that risk. If Christians strengthen their resolve, deepen their spiritual roots, refine their practical understanding, and mobilize their institutional resources, the impact of their peacemaking ministry will bring even more hope into the dawning of the twenty-first century.

Appendix

The following list includes some of the organizations that are involved in peacemaking through nonviolent action or conflict resolution. To obtain further information or to participate in some of their projects, contact them at the addresses noted.

American Baptist
Peace Program
National Ministries
P.O. Box 851
Valley Forge, PA 19482

American Friends
Service Committee
1501 Cherry Street
Philadelphia, PA 19102

Baptist Peace Fellowship
of North America
499 South Patterson
Memphis, TN 38111

The Carter Center
1 Copenhill
Atlanta, GA 30307

Christian Peacemaker Teams
P. O. Box 6508
Chicago, IL 60608

The Fellowship
of Reconciliation
P. O. Box 271
Nyack, NY 10960

Mennonite Central Committee
21 South 12th Street, Box M
Akron, PA 17501

New Call to Peacemaking
P. O. Box 500
Akron, PA 17501

Pastors for Peace
331 17th Avenue, SE
Minneapolis, MN 55414

Peace Brigades International
347 Dolores Street #228
San Francisco, CA 94110

Sojourners
2401 15th Street, NW
Washington, D.C. 20078

Witness for Peace
2201 P Street, NW, Room 109
Washington, D.C. 20037

Notes

Notes to the Introduction

1. The military government changed the name of Burma to Myanmar following the democracy uprising in 1988. Though "Burma" is a name given to the country by the British and "Myanmar" is the name of the nation in the Burmese language, many of the opponents to the military regime retain the use of "Burma." Ethnic minorities view the name "Myanmar" as one more instance of the imposition of the Burmese majority cultural hegemony upon the diverse peoples of the country. Democracy advocates see the military as playing up Burmese nationalism to support the legitimacy of their regime. For these reasons I will retain the use of the name "Burma" in telling the story of peacemaking in that country.

2. See John Paul Lederach, "Understanding Conflict: The Experience, Structure and Dynamics of Conflict," *MCS Conciliation Quarterly* (Summer 1987), p. 2, and Charles R. McCollough, *Resolving Conflict with Justice and Peace* (New York: The Pilgrim Press, 1991), pp. 32-36.

3. Gene Sharp, *The Politics of Nonviolent Action*, Part One, *Power and Struggle* (Boston: Porter Sargent Publishers, 1973), p. 4.

4. Philip McManus, "Introduction: In Search of the Shalom Society," in *Relentless Persistence: Nonviolent Action in Latin America,* edited by Philip McManus and Gerald Schlabach (Philadelphia: New Society Publishers, 1991), p. 6.

Notes to Chapter 1

1. Beldon C. Lane, "Spirituality and Political Commitment: Notes on a Liberation Theology of Nonviolence," in *The Universe Bends Toward Justice,* edited by Angie O'Gorman (Philadelphia: New Society Publishers, 1990), p. 223.

2. Vidkun Quisling was the Norwegian fascist who was installed by the Nazis as "Minister-President" during the German occupation in World War II.

3. Glen Stassen, *Just Peacemaking: Transforming Initiatives for Justice on Peace* (Louisville, Ky.: Westminster/John Knox Press, 1992), pp. 37-38.

4. R. V. G. Tasker, *The Gospel According to St. Matthew* (Grand Rapids: Eerdmans, 1961), p. 70.

5. Walter Wink, *Violence and Nonviolence in South Africa* (Philadelphia: New Society Publishers, 1987), pp. 13ff.

6. Clarence Jordan, "The Lesson On the Mount—II" in *The Universe Bends Toward Justice*, p. 141. Italics are mine.

7. Wink, *Violence and Nonviolence in South Africa*, p. 15.

8. Robert Guelich, *The Sermon on the Mount* (Waco, Tex.: Word Books, 1982), p. 251.

9. The question of which garment is asked for and which is to be given up in addition is discussed in full by many commentators, but the answer does not change the impact of what Jesus is saying. In Matthew the plaintiff claims the *chiton*, a long, close-fitting undergarment. The outer garment, *himation*, is a cloak, which was viewed as an inalienable possession. The cloak was the garment referred to in the Old Testament legal codes as a pledge to be returned at night. Perhaps Matthew's Gospel envisions someone making a suit within the legal limits of the law but certainly contrary to the spirit of the law. The action of stripping completely shows the blatant hypocrisy behind such legalisms when the poor are being economically crushed by an oppressive system. Luke has this teaching in the context of a robbery, and the outer garment, the one most physically accessible, is the one demanded. Luke puts the teaching in the context of loving one's enemies rather than the legal context, which would have been alien to his non-Jewish readers. Wink uses the Lukan order with the Matthean context, but this is not necessary to understand the transforming initiative Jesus presents.

10. Wink, *Violence and Nonviolence in South Africa,* p. 19.

11. Ibid., p. 21.

12. Following Esther's successful appeal and the downfall of Haman, the Jews engaged in a slaughter of 75,000 followers of Haman who had been poised to carry out their own pogrom, showing that nonviolence was a mere tactic and not a philosophy in this case.

13. Commentators and translations disagree over whether the whip was used on people or on the livestock. The Greek text of John is ambiguous at this point. Raymond Brown (*The Gospel According to John, I-XII* [Garden City, N.Y.: Doubleday and Company, 1966], p. 115) holds that since no sticks or weapons were allowed in the Temple precincts, the whip was probably made from the rushes used as bedding for the animals. Such a whip would not be effective for violent acts but would be a helpful tool in driving animals.

Notes to Chapter 2

1. See my book *Bringing Your Church Back to Life: Beyond Survival Mentality* (Valley Forge, Pa.: Judson Press, 1988) for that story 2. Stassen, *Just Peacemaking,* pp. 77-81.

3. Martin Luther King, Jr., *Why We Can't Wait* (Harper and Row, 1964), p. 83.

4. See David W. Augsburger, *Conflict Mediation Across Cultures: Pathways and Patterns* (Louisville: Westminster/John Knox Press, 1992), pp. 200-205 for a comparison of modern Western and traditional styles of mediation.

5. See the end of Gideon's career in Judges 8:22-28 and the violence precipitated by his son Abimelech's grab for power in Judges 9:1-57.

6. Eating meat with blood still in it, a result of strangulation, was expressly forbidden in Jewish law because "its blood is its life" (Leviticus 17:10-14).

Notes to Chapter 3

1. Margaret Bacon, "Let Me Be the One: Mary Dyer, Witness to Religious Liberty," in *The Universe Bends Toward Justice,* p. 12.

2. Paul Deker's *For the Healing of the Nations: Baptist Peacemakers* (Macon, Ga.: Smyth & Helwys, 1993) is one inspiring collection of peace and justice "saint stories" from the Baptist traditions.

3. John Woolman, "Considerations on the Payment of a Tax Laid for

Carrying on the War Against the Indians," in *The Universe Bends Toward Justice*, p. 28.

4. Gene Sharp, *The Politics of Nonviolent Action*, Part Three, *The Dynamics of Nonviolent Action* (Boston: Porter Sargent Publishers, 1973), pp. 613-614.

5. Ibid., p. 794. Charles K. Whipple argued in the early 1800s that the violent phase of the American revolution both delayed independence and resulted in a staggering cost in lives, property, and morality, a case supported by some contemporary historians. See Charles K. Whipple, "Evils of the Revolutionary War," in *The Universe Bends Toward Justice*, p. 65. See also Walter H. Conser, Jr., et. al., ed., *Resistance, Politics and the American Struggle for Independence* (Boulder, Colo.: Lynne Rienner Publishers, 1987).

6. Maggie Fisher, "Harriet Tubman: Liberator," in *The Universe Bends Toward Justice*, p. 81.

7. Margaret Hope Bacon, "I Ask No Favor For My Sex: Lucretia Mott and Non-Resistance," in *The Universe Bends Toward Justice*, p. 85.

8. Jill Wallis, "The British FOR and the International Movement," *Fellowship* (October 1989), p. 5.

9. Dallas Lee, "Clarence Jordan: A Biographical Sketch," in *The Universe Bends Toward Justice*, p. 135.

10. Howard Zinn, *A People's History of the United States* (New York: HarperCollins, 1980), pp. 322ff.

11. Roger Velásquez, "Yes, It Can Be Done: In Remembrance of Cesar Chavez," *The Baptist Peacemaker* (Summer 1993), p. 11.

12. Quoted in Louis Fischer, ed., *The Essential Gandhi* (New York: Random House, 1962), p. 110.

13. See Eknath Easwaran, *A Man to Match His Mountains: Badshah Khan, Nonviolent Soldier of Islam* (Petaluma, Calif.: Nilgiri Press, 1984).

14. Ibid., p. 111.

15. Ibid., p. 122.

16. Ibid., p. 123, and Gene Sharp, *The Politics of Nonviolent Action*, Part Three, p. 675.

17. Easwaran, *A Man to Match His Mountains*, p. 125.

18. Quoted in Fischer, ed., *The Essential Gandhi*, p. 169.

19. Ibid., p. 201.

20. Ibid., p. 199.

21. Ibid., p. 342.

22. Ibid., p. 176.

23. Ibid., p. 205.

24. Ibid., p. 286.

25. Ibid., p. 154.

26. Sharp, *The Politics of Nonviolent Action*, Part One, p. 28.

27. Quoted in Peter R. Breggin, *Beyond Conflict: From Self-Help and Psychotherapy to Peacemaking* (New York: St. Martin's Press, 1992), p. 175.

28. Quoted in Fischer, ed., *The Essential Gandhi*, p. 190.

29. Ibid., pp. 155-156.

30. Ibid., p. 298.

31. Aldon Morris, *The Origins of the Civil Rights Movement: Black Communities Organizing for Change* (New York: The Free Press, 1984), pp. 141-157.

32. John Swomley, "F.O.R.'s Early Efforts for Racial Equality," *Fellowship* (July/August 1990), pp. 7-9.

33. Morris, *The Origins of the Civil Rights Movement*, p. 146.

34. Ibid., p. 51.

35. Martin Luther King, Jr., *Strength to Love* (Philadelphia: Fortress Press, 1963), pp. 54-55.

36. See Morris, *The Origins of the Civil Rights Movement*, p. 77.

37. Susan Kling, "Baptism by Fire: The Story of Fannie Lou Hamer," in *The Universe Bends Toward Justice*, p. 153.

38. Martin Luther King, Jr., "I Have a Dream," in *A Testament of Hope: The Essential Writings and Speeches of Martin Luther King, Jr.*, ed. James M. Washington (New York: HarperCollins Publishers, 1986), p. 219.

39. Martin Luther, King, Jr., *Why We Can't Wait*, pp. 79-80.

40. King, *Strength to Love*, p. 54.

41. Martin Luther King, Jr., *The Trumpet of Conscience* (New York: Harper and Row, 1968), pp. 24, 32.

42. Martin Luther King, Jr., "Beyond Vietnam," reprinted in *Sojourners* (January 1983), p. 15.

43. Ibid., p. 12.

44. King, *Why We Can't Wait*, p. 79.

45. Ibid., p. 39.

46. Zinn, *A People's History of the United States*, pp. 475-477.

47. Ibid., p. 477.

48. Ibid., p. 486.

49. Martin Luther King, Jr., "Declaration of Independence From the War in Vietnam," A. J. Muste Memorial Institute Essay Series, No. 1 (New York: A. J. Muste Memorial Institute), p. 44.

50. Initially CALC stood for "Clergy and Laymen Concerned," but the name was changed due to a growing awareness of sexist language.

Notes to Chapter 4

1. *Perestroika* means "restructuring" in Russian and was the term used to signify the political, economic, and social changes brought about in the Soviet Union under the leadership of Mikhail Gorbachev.

2. "Catholic Bishops: Medellin Declaration (1968)," in *The Central American Crisis Reader,* edited by Robert S. Leiken and Barry Rubin (New York: Summit Books, 1987), p. 126.

3. Quoted in Penny Lernoux, *Cry of the People* (New York: Penguin Books, 1980), p. 438.

4. Ibid., p. 74.

5. See "The Greatest Love: An Interview with Jon Sobrino," *Sojourners* (April 1990), p. 19.

6. Lernoux, *Cry of the People*, p. 76.

7. Joyce Hollyday, "A Martyr's Abiding Hope," *Sojourners* (May 1980), p. 3.

8. Archbishop Oscar Romero, "A Pastor's Last Homily," *Sojourners* (May 1980), p. 16.

9. Scott Wright, Minor Sinclair, Margaret Lyle, and David Scott, eds., *El Salvador: A Spring Whose Waters Never Run Dry* (Washington, D.C.: Ecumenical Program on Central America and the Caribbean [EPICA], 1990), p. 73.

10. McManus, "Introduction: In Search of the Shalom Society," in *Relentless Persistence*, p. 82.

11. Blanca Yáñez Berríos and Omor Williams Lopez, "Cultural Action for

Liberation in Chile," in *Relentless Persistence,* pp. 122-124.

12. The full story is told by Wilson T. Boots in "Miracle in Bolivia: Four Women Confront a Nation," in *Relentless Persistence,* pp. 48-61.

13. Edmond Mulet, "The Palace Coup that Failed," *Campesino* (Summer 1993), p. 3.

14. "Ecuadorean Indians Protest Rights Abuse," *Fellowship* (October/November 1992), p. 11.

15. Michael T. Kaufman, *Mad Dreams and Saving Graces* (New York: Random House, 1989), pp. 140-141, quoted in Niels Nielsen, *Revolutions in Eastern Europe* (Maryknoll, N.Y.: Orbis Books, 1991), p. 76.

16. Stassen, *Just Peacemaking,* p. 23.

17. Ibid., p. 25.

18. See Robert Goeckel, "The Evangelical-Lutheran Church and the East German Revolution," in *Occasional Papers on Religion in Eastern Europe* (November 1990).

19. Vincent and Jane Kavoloski, "Moral Power and the Czech Revolution, *Fellowship* (January/February 1992), p. 10.

20. Nielsen, *Revolutions in Eastern Europe,* p. 87.

21. Jo Becker, "Lithuania's Nonviolent Struggle," *Fellowship* (December 1990), p. 21.

22. Douglas J. Elwood, *Philippine Revolution 1986* (Quezon City, Philippines: New Day Publishers, 1986), p. 16.

23. Ibid., pp. 3-4.

24. Ibid., p. 30.

25. See Bertil Linter's *Outrage: Burma's Struggle for Democracy* (Hong Kong: Review Publishing Company, 1989) for a detailed account of the democracy uprising in Burma.

26. Aung San Suu Kyi, *Freedom From Fear and Other Writings,* edited by Michael Aris (London, England: Viking Press, 1991), p. 184.

27. Ma Than E, "A Flowering of the Spirit: Memories of Suu and Her Family," in *Freedom From Fear and Other Writings,* p. 256.

28. Shen Tong, one of the student leaders of the democracy movement, provides a compelling inside view of the events in Beijing in 1989 in *Almost a Revolution* (Boston: Houghton Mifflin Company, 1990).

29. See Gordon D. Aeschliman, *Apartheid: Tragedy in Black and White* (Ventura, Calif.: Regal Books, 1986), pp. 80-81 and 93-97, for a discussion of the church roots of apartheid.

30. From an interview with Frank Chikane in *Sojourners* (September 1988), p. 25.

31. Jane Perlez, "Zambia's Democratic Shock to Africa," *New York Times* (November 5, 1991), p. A14.

32. Jean Zaru, "The Intifada, Nonviolence, and the Bible," in *Faith and the Intifada: Palestinian Christian Voices,* edited by Naim S. Ateek, Marc Ellis, and Rosemary Radford Ruether (Maryknoll, N.Y.: Orbis Books, 1992), p. 127.

33. The Palestinian Center for the Study of Nonviolence has documented that 95 percent of the actions urged in leaflets from the United Command for the Intifada/PLO are nonviolent. Rock throwing and use of knives and molotov cocktails are urged in 5 percent of the leaflets.

34. Quoted in Terry Rogers, "Beit Sahour: A Model of Resistance," *Fellowship* (June 1990), p. 10.

35. Munir Fasheh, "Reclaiming Our Identity and Redefining Ourselves,"

in *Faith and the Intifada*, p. 65.

36. Zoughbi Elias Zoughbi, "Faith, Nonviolence and the Palestinian Struggle," in *Faith and the Intifada,* p. 102.

37. Ibid., p. 106.

38. Melanie Morrison, "Hollanditis Up Close," *Sojourners* (February 1982), p. 24.

39. See Chapter 5 in Glen Stassen's *Just Peacemaking* for a behind-the-scenes report on the development of the INF Treaty.

40. Ed Griffin-Nolan, *Witness for Peace* (Louisville: Westminster/John Knox, 1991), p. 25.

41. Vicki Kemper, "Guilty of the Gospel," *Sojourners* (June 1986), p. 8.

42. King, *Why We Can't Wait,* p. 39.

43. The story is told in more detail in Vera Kadaeva's article, "At the Barricades with the Gospel," in *The Baptist Peacemaker* (Winter 1991/Spring 1992), p. 25.

44. "There Comes a Time...," *Koinonia South Africa Newsletter* (April-June 1989), p. 4.

45. *Myanmar* (Amnesty International Publications, 1990), p. 24, and *Myanmar, Amnesty International Briefing* (Amnesty International Publications, 1990), pp. 5, 13.

46. Mark Elliott, "László Tökés, Timisoara and the Romanian Revolution," *Occasional Papers on Religion in Eastern Europe* (October 1990), p. 26.

Notes to Chapter 5

1. Barry Hart, "Conflict/Division/Reconciliation," in *Blueprint for Social Justice,* Volume XLI, No. 5 (New Orleans: Institute of Human Relations, Loyola University, January 1988), p. 3.

2. Dean G. Pruitt, "Trends in the Scientific Study of Negotiation and Mediation," *Negotiation Journal,* Vol. 2, No. 3 (July 1986), p. 237.

3. James Laue, "The Emergence and Institutionalization of Third Party Roles in Conflict," *Conflict Resolution: Track Two Diplomacy,* edited by John W. McDonald, Jr., and Diane B. Bondahmane (Washington, D.C.: Foreign Services Institute, U.S. Department of State, 1987), p. 23.

4. Hart, "Conflict/Division/Reconciliation," pp. 4-5.

5. See Landrum R. Bolling, "Quaker Work in the Middle East after the June 1967 War," and C. H. "Mike" Yarrow, "Quaker Efforts Toward Conciliation in the India-Pakistan War of 1965," in *Unofficial Diplomats,* edited by Maureen R. Berman and Joseph E. Johnson (New York: Columbia University Press, 1977).

6. See Peter S. Adler, "Is ADR a Social Movement?," *Negotiation Journal,* Vol. 3, No. 1 (January 1987), pp. 66-67 for a fuller discussion of these criticisms.

7. Roger Fisher and William Ury, *Getting to Yes: Negotiating Agreement Without Giving In* (New York: Penguin Books, 1981).

8. Ibid., pp. 17-39.

9. Ibid., pp. 40-55.

10. Ibid., pp. 58-80.

11. Ibid., 81-94.

12. John Paul Lederach, "The Mediator's Cultural Assumption," *MCS Conciliation Quarterly* (Summer 1986), p. 4.

13. See John Paul Lederach, "Transformation from Within: Peacemaking in the East Coast of Nicaragua: Or, The Conflict in Nicaragua's Atlantic

Coast: An Inside View of War and Peacemaking," draft text for inclusion in a book, *Approaches to Peacemaking in Chronic Conflicts*, for the U.S. Institute for Peace/George Fox College Center for Peace, pp. 35-57. Used by permission from author.

14. Augsburger, *Conflict Mediation Across Cultures*, p. 153.

15. Ibid., pp. 157-159.

16. Laue, "The Emergence and Institutionalization of Third Party Roles in Conflict," p. 26.

17. Paul Wehr and John Paul Lederach, "Mediating Conflict in Central America," *Journal of Peace Research*, Vol. 28, No. 1 (February 1991), pp. 88-90.

18. Hizkias Assefa, *Mediation of Civil Wars: Approaches and Strategies—The Sudan Conflict* (Boulder, Colo.: Westview Press, 1987), pp. 139-140, 146, 178.

19. See "Mideast Miracle Makes Headlines for a Diplomat from the North," *U.N. Observer and International Report* (September 1993), p. 15, and "Old Foes Met on a Secret Path," *The Philadelphia Inquirer* (September 5, 1993), pp. 1-2.

20. Wehr and Lederach, "Mediating Conflict in Central America," pp. 94, 97, and Lederach, "Transformation from Within," pp. 35-57.

21. See Hizkias Assefa's *Mediation of Civil Wars: Approaches and Strategies—The Sudan Conflict* for a detailed account and analysis of the mediation process that ended the civil war in Sudan.

22. Ibid., p. 175.

23. For a more complete version of the peace process and the role of Longri Ao, see *Longri Ao: A Biography* by O. M. Rao (Guwahati, Assam (India): Christian Literature Centre, 1986).

24. Ibid., p. 79.

25. Ibid., p. 80.

26. Ibid., p. 81.

27. Ibid., p. 151.

28. See Jimmy Carter's *Keeping Faith: Memoirs of a President* (New York: Bantam Books, 1982), pp. 269-429, for a detailed description of the Camp David negotiations and related developments.

29. Ibid., pp. 315-316.

30. Ibid., p. 359.

31. Ibid., p. 358.

32. Ibid., p. 392.

33. Ibid., p. 399.

Notes to Chapter 6

1. Wehr and Lederach, "Mediating Conflict in Central America," pp. 90-91.

2. Lederach, "Transformation from Within," p. 7.

3. John Paul Lederach, "Missionaries Facing Conflict and Violence: Problems and Prospects," *Missiology: An International Review*, Vol. XX, No. 1 (January 1992), pp. 11-12; and Andy Stone, "Our Man in Managua," *The Sunday Camera Magazine* (May 29, 1988), p. 10. During the Iran/Contra hearings other CIA efforts to undermine peace efforts were revealed in the testimony of Robert Owen of the National Security Council that MISURASATA, an Atlantic Coast resistance organization, had been bribed with $100,000 to break off negotiations in 1985 (Lederach, "Transformation from Within," p. 20).

4. Dave Brubaker, "International Mediation: An Unexpected Role," *MCS Conciliation Quarterly* (Spring 1988), p. 5.

5. *Condoning the Killing: Ten Years of Massacres in El Salvador,* edited by the Ecumenical Program on Central America and the Caribbean (Washington, D.C.: EPICA, 1990), p. 67.

6. Quoted in the unpublished paper "National Debate for Peace in El Salvador," from the National Debate for Peace in El Salvador.

7. H. Wayne Pipkin, ed., *Seek Peace and Pursue It* (Memphis: Baptist Peace Fellowship of North America, 1989), pp. 179-180.

8. Carter, *Keeping Faith,* p. 426.

9. "United Nations Peace-Keeping Operations: Information Notes," Department of Public Information, United Nations (September 1992), p. 2.

10. The United Nations Association, 485 Fifth Avenue, New York, New York 10017 can provide up-to-date information on the status of U.S. financial support of the U.N. as well as other information on the status of U.S. policies in relation to the U.N.

Notes to Chapter 7

1. This story is told in *The Universe Bends Toward Justice,* p. 15.

2. Interview with Larry Trapp and Michael Weisser by Daniel S. Levy, "The Cantor and the Klansman," *Time* (February 17, 1992), p. 14.

3. Kenneth W. Morgan, "A Fist and a Kiss in Old Damascus," Letters to the Editor, *New York Times* (January 30, 1991).

4. See the August 1993 issue of *Sojourners* for an extensive report on the gang summit.

5. Arty de Silva, "A 'Sign of the Kingdom' in Sri Lanka," *Seek Peace and Pursue It,* p. 195.

6. Jean Martensen, "Mediation in the Junior High School," *Peace Petitions: News for ELCA Peacemakers* (Spring 1993).

7. *New York Times* (May 14, 1992), p. 1.

8. "General Facts About Domestic Violence," National Woman Abuse Prevention Project. This resource is available in the *Family Violence Packet* from National Ministries, American Baptist Churches, U.S.A., P.O. Box 851, Valley Forge, PA 19482-0851.

9. See Joyce Hollyday, "Amazing Grace," *Sojourners* (July 1989), pp. 12-22; Kim Christman and Stan Dotson, "Beyond Jackrocks and Prayer," *The Baptist Peacemaker* (Spring 1990), pp. 6-7; and Denise Giardina, "No End in Sight," *Sojourners* (November 1989), pp. 8-10.

10. Hollyday, "Amazing Grace," p. 17.

Notes to Chapter 8

1. Francisco F. Claver, "What Happened to the Philippines?" *Fellowship* (July/August 1989), p. 6.

2. James Cone's masterful book, *Martin and Malcolm and America* (Maryknoll, N.Y.: Orbis Books, 1991), provides an insightful analysis of Martin Luther King's strengths and weaknesses, growth and accomplishments. The comparison with Malcolm X is not only historically valuable but helps to reveal the weakness in the civil rights movement and some of the challenges ahead in confronting racial injustice. See Billy J. Tidwell, ed., *The State of Black America 1993* (New York: The National Urban League, 1993) for a detailed analysis of the economic, political, and social status of African Americans today.

3. Morton Deutsch, "A Theoretical Perspective on Conflict and Conflict Resolution," *Conflict Management and Problem Solving: Interpersonal to International Applications,* edited by Dennis J. D. Sandole and Ingrid Sandole-Staroste (Washington Square, N.Y.: New York University Press, 1987), p. 39.

4. Maire A. Dugan, "Intervener Roles and Conflict Pathologies," *Conflict Management and Problem Solving,* p. 58.

5. Sam Keene has effectively documented and analyzed the way we distort the enemy so we can engage in war and organized slaughter in his book *Faces of the Enemy: Reflections of the Hostile Imagination* (New York: Harper and Row, 1986).

6. Elias Chacour, *Blood Brothers* (Old Tappan, N.J.: Chosen Books, 1984), p. 222.

7. Charles R. McCollough's *Resolving Conflict with Justice and Peace* (New York: The Pilgrim Press, 1991) would make an excellent text for group study. It contains fourteen sessions to provide a solid basis in the practice of conflict resolution. *A Bible Study Guide on Conflict Resolution* by Daniel Buttry is a six-session workbook for church groups to use; it is available through National Ministries Literature Resources, P. O. Box 851, Valley Forge, Pennsylvania 19482.

8. Sharp, *The Politics of Nonviolent Action,* Part Three p. 543.

9. Adolfo Pérez Esquivel, *Christ in a Poncho* (Maryknoll, N.Y.: Orbis Books, 1983), pp. 20-21.

10. John Dear, "The Road to Transformation: A Conversation with Brian Willson," *Fellowship* (March 1990), p. 4.

11. Scottish, Montenegrin, and Kurdish proverbs quoted in Augsburger's *Conflict Mediation Across Cultures,* p. 191.

12. Told in Augsburger's *Conflict Mediation Across Cultures,* pp. 188-189.

13. Lederach, "Missionaries Facing Conflict and Violence," p. 15.

Index